How to
Build a
Computer

Other Computer Titles

by

Robert Penfold

How to Build a Computer

Robert Penfold

Bernard Babani (publishing) Ltd
The Grampians
Shepherds Bush Road
London W6 7NF
England
www.babanibooks.com

Please note

Although every care has been taken with the production of this book to ensure that any projects, designs, modifications, and/or programs, etc., contained herewith, operate in a correct and safe manner and also that any components specified are normally available in Great Britain, the Publisher and Author do not accept responsibility in any way for the failure (including fault in design) of any projects, design, modification, or program to work correctly or to cause damage to any equipment that it may be connected to or used in conjunction with, or in respect of any other damage or injury that may be caused, nor do the Publishers accept responsibility in any way for the failure to obtain specified components.

Notice is also given that if any equipment that is still under warranty is modified in any way or used or connected with home-built equipment then that warranty may be void.

© 2008 BERNARD BABANI (publishing) LTD

First Published - February 2008
Reprinted - August 2008

British Library Cataloguing in Publication Data
A catalogue record for this book is available from the British Library

ISBN   978 0 85934 591 0

Cover Design by Gregor Arthur
Printed and bound in Great Britain by J. H. Haynes & Co. Ltd., Sparkford

Preface

Although assembling a PC might seem to be something that is only suitable for experts, it is really much easier than most people realise. All the parts required are available from computer shops, mail order warehouses, and computer fairs. Whether you wish to build the most budget of budget PCs, an up-market PC using the latest high-tech components, or anything in between, all the parts required are readily available. These days the majority of the components for a typical PC cost remarkably little, so you do not have to spend a fortune in order to get started in PC assembly. One might reasonably expect that some expensive tools and equipment are need in order to build a PC, but it is really a pretty straightforward assembly job. It is basically just a matter of bolting things in place and plugging in a few cables. A crosshead screwdriver might be the only tool required, and it is unlikely that anything else apart from a pair of pliers will be needed. No soldering iron is required, and neither is any experience of electronics construction methods.

All this does not mean that PC building can be undertaken by absolutely anyone. Some experience of using and dealing with PCs is essential, and you need to be reasonably practical. Obviously some technical knowledge is needed in order to buy the right components and get everything put together properly. This book, which is fully updated from its popular predecessor "Build Your Own PC" (BP534), explains in simple terms exactly what components are required and how to assemble them to produce a working PC.

Having built your first PC it then requires more technical knowledge to get everything set up correctly and the operating system installed. Again, this book explains in simple terms, how to get the BIOS set up correctly. The complexity of a modern BIOS Setup program can be a bit intimidating, but in most cases it will set suitable defaults. The user just has to do little more than some "fine tuning". Chapter 5 explains in detail how to install and set up Windows Vista. The finished PC is unlikely to give any problems, but the final chapter deals with simple troubleshooting techniques.

A home produced PC should have a comparable level of performance to a ready made equivalent. With wise buying it will probably cost somewhat less than a ready built PC of similar specification, although any savings are not likely to be large. However, by "rolling your own" it is possible to produce a computer that exactly meets your requirements, and you will learn a great deal in the process. It is also good fun and should impress your friends!

Robert Penfold

Trademarks

Microsoft, Windows, Windows XP, and Windows Vista are either registered trademarks or trademarks of Microsoft Corporation.

Pentium and Celeron are registered trademarks of Intel Corp. Athlon, Duron, Sempron, and Phenom are registered trademarks of Advanced Micro Devices Inc. (AMD)

All other brand and product names used in this book are recognised trademarks, or registered trademarks of their respective companies. There is no intent to use any trademarks generically and readers should investigate ownership of a trademark before using it for any purpose.

Contents

3

Assembly 83

4

The BIOS 173

5

The Operating System 209

6

Troubleshooting 263

Fundamentals

Ups and downs

In days of yore the most obvious change in the world of PCs was the steady, and often quite fast, improvement in performance and facilities. Computers were much faster than those of a year earlier, had bigger hard disc drives, more memory, and so on. While technology has continued to march on, I suspect that these days the most obvious change for most PC users is not the continuing improvement of the hardware. The most amazing change is the way prices have fallen, and continued to fall. In recent years the reductions in price have resulted in a complete PC with a very respectable specification costing less than just the cost of the microprocessor a few years ago.

It would seem reasonable to expect this to have a negative effect on do-it-yourself PC assembly, with there being little apparent point in taking time and effort to put together a PC that could be obtained ready-made at quite low cost. In fact the opposite seems to have occurred, with home PC construction now being more popular than ever. It is probable that most people who undertake PC building are not actually trying to save money by doing so. As explained later in this chapter, it might be possible to save money in this way, but there are other advantages that are of greater importance for most people.

The probable reason for the increasing interest in PC construction is that the prices of PC components have fallen in line with the cost of complete PCs. It now costs comparatively little to have some fun building your own, and it can cost "peanuts" if you already have some spare components that can be salvaged from an existing computer. In fact many home constructed PCs are actually old units that have been rebuilt to a modern specification for a minimal outlay. There is plenty to be gained by building your own PC or rebuilding an existing unit to a higher specification, but little risk involved.

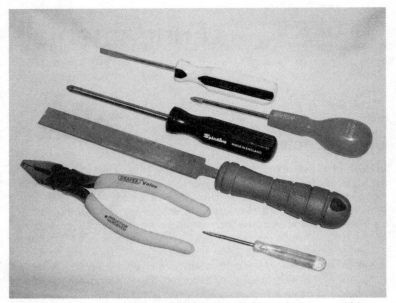

Fig.1.1 Some basic tools are all that is needed in order to assemble a PC

What's involved?

Constructing your own PC may seem a daunting prospect, but it is actually much easier than most people realise. It has to be emphasised that we are not talking here in terms of getting out a soldering iron and making your own motherboard, video card, etc., or even in terms of doing some metalwork to produce your own case. Due to the predominance of specialist electronic components in the PC world, most of which are not generally available, this approach is probably not viable even for those prepared to put in the massive time and effort involved. Also, by the time your completely home-made PC was finished it would probably be well and truly out of date!

What we are really talking about here is a home assembled PC based on a set of ready-made boards and housed in a commercially produced case. Everything you need to make a PC is readily available, and the tools needed to assemble one are minimal. In fact one medium size cross-point screwdriver is quite possibly the only tool you will require, but a few additional tools (Figure 1.1) might be needed. All the tools required are the type of thing that will already be present in most households.

Depending on your opinion of these things, building your own PC is as easy or as difficult as putting together your own self-assembly furniture. Inevitably there are some questions that anyone contemplating PC assembly will need answered. We will consider some of the more common questions before taking a look at the basic steps involved in making your own PC. Subsequent chapters consider each of these steps in detail.

The real thing?

Having put together your PC will it work as well as the ready-made "real thing", or will you end up with a low specification PC that is incapable of running high-end software? Provided you compare like with like there is no reason for any difference in performance and capabilities between a ready-made PC and a home-made machine. It pays to bear in mind that most PC manufacturers do not actually make their own motherboards, sound cards, etc., but instead put together PCs from "off the shelf" components.

In other words, most ready-made PCs are put together in the same way as a home-made PC, and apart from the nameplate a ready-made PC is no different to a home produced equivalent. The larger PC manufacturers often make PC components themselves or have them made to their own specification, but the underlying technology is much the same as that used in "off the shelf" components. Of course, if you put together a PC from all the cheapest parts you can lay your hands on it would be naive to expect it to equal the latest thing in commercially produced PC technology. It works the other way, and a homemade PC built using the latest upmarket components will cost more than a readymade budget PC, but it will easily outperform the budget PC. With PCs, as with most things in life, you tend to get what you pay for.

Will it work?

Whether you buy a PC ready-made or make it yourself it is impossible to guarantee that it will work first time and that it will continue to work flawlessly for many years. Neither is it possible to guarantee that there will not be the odd incompatibility problem with a certain piece of hardware refusing to peacefully coexist with a certain piece of software.

Provided the PC is built using good quality components and you are not tempted to cut corners it should work first time.

Once it is "up and running", with average luck it should be at least a few years before a major breakdown occurs. Obviously some constructors will have worse than average luck, and will have to deal with a fault or faults. Others will fare better than average, and will not have to fix any faults during the working life of the PC, even if it is used for many years.

Home-made and ready-made PCs should both be covered by manufacturers' warranties, but these operate in very different ways with the two types of PC. With a ready-made PC the manufacturer's guarantee should cover the PC as a whole. If anything goes wrong the manufacturer should locate the fault and fix it for you. There may be a return to base warranty, or some form of on-site maintenance agreement. The latter is clearly preferable to the former, but is likely to be reflected in a much higher price tag for the PC, or it will be an expensive optional extra. In either case, unless you buy a lemon the time taken getting things put right should be reasonably short, and no technical skills will be required on your part.

With a home assembled PC you should have individual guarantees for every component in the system, but there is no manufacturer to provide an overall guarantee for the complete PC. If something goes wrong it is up to you to find out just what has gone awry and get the faulty component exchanged under warranty. Locating the faulty component is not usually too difficult, but getting it replaced quickly is not always possible.

If the faulty component was ordered by mail order you will have to send it back, it is likely that it will then go through some sort of testing, and then the replacement will be sent. This could leave the PC out of action for several days. Of course, if you buy a ready-made PC by mail order and it has a return to base warranty, you have the same problem. In fact matters are worse because the whole PC often has to be returned, not just the faulty component.

This lack of speed in getting things fixed may or may not matter. Where it is important to get a PC working straight away, and to keep it working, a ready-made PC with an on-site maintenance agreement with a reputable company is the safest option. You have no absolute guarantee of quick fixes, but there is a good chance of keeping any downtimes to a minimum. You may find a company prepared to offer on-site maintenance on a home constructed PC, but this is by no means certain.

The odd incompatibility problem is likely to be difficult to solve whether you buy a ready-made PC or build one yourself. Whoever you complain to, it is always the other company's fault! Fortunately, this type of thing is much rarer than it used to be, and it is probably not a major issue any more. These incompatibility problems are usually the result of faults in one of the device drivers, rather than a problem with the hardware itself. Improved drivers usually appear on the manufacturer's web site before too long.

Will I save money?

Many people try their hand at DIY PC construction in an attempt to save money. Provided you purchase the individual components wisely it is likely that there will be a small cost saving. However, do not expect to get a half price PC by building it yourself. A saving of around 10 percent is certainly quite possible, and with careful buying of "special offers" you may even achieve a saving of as much as 20 percent or so. On the other hand, with imprudent buying you could easily end up paying 10 or 20 percent more for your PC. Assembling a PC takes no more than a very few hours work, and it would be unrealistic to expect the DIY approach to produce massive cost savings.

It is probably not the assembly costs that account for the majority of the savings anyway. When you buy a new PC it generally comes complete with some form of support package such as a one-year onsite maintenance contract and some sort of telephone support system. With a home produced PC you have to be more self-sufficient. There may well be telephone or Email support for some of the components, but in general it is up to you to sort things out when problems arise. If you are able to sort out these problems yourself it makes sense to do so rather than pay for support that you do not really need, and will probably never use.

Can I do it?

As pointed out previously, actually putting the computer together does not require a great deal of skill. Someone who is completely impractical would be well advised not to attempt building a PC, or anything else for that matter. Provided you are not a DIY disaster waiting to happen, you should be able to physically put the PC together. This is not to say that anyone who can use a screwdriver is properly qualified to build a PC. When dealing with computers odd little problems tend to develop, particularly when dealing with device drivers and software installation.

Someone with a few years experience of using PCs should be able to sort out these problems without too much difficulty. For "old hands" at computing this sort of thing is just part of the fun. For a newcomer to PCs it could be difficult and time consuming to get the finished product set up and really working well. In fact it could be difficult to get the PC set up and working at all. Consequently, I would only recommend PC assembly if you have had a few years experience with PCs and are not going to panic if minor problems occur.

Why bother?

If constructing your own PC is not going to save large amounts of money, and you will have to sort out any minor problems yourself, why bother? Although any savings in cost are not likely to be huge, a worthwhile saving can still be made. Alternatively, for the same money it should be possible to produce a PC with a higher specification by doing it yourself. As, already pointed out, for most constructors the main motivation is not saving money. Many people find that making their own PC is a fun and interesting experience. If you like making things, having built one PC it is unlikely that you will return to the world of ready-made PCs. I suppose that for many people the kudos of building your own PC is another plus point. It is a good way to impress your friends.

For most PC builders the main advantage is that you can build a PC having the exact specification you require. Many PC companies will to some extent customise one of their standard PCs to suit your requirements, but few will build one to your exact specification. By doing it yourself you can have the video and soundcards you deem the best, the most suitable monitor for your requirements, and so on. If you only need a small hard disc drive but need an advanced 3D-video card and large monitor, then that is what you buy. The time you save in searching for a PC with the right specification at the right price should be more than enough to build the PC yourself. Financial constraints may force a few compromises, but you should end up with the best possible PC for your requirements, or something as near to it as the available money permits.

Another potential advantage of building your own is that it may be possible to use parts from your previous PC. Being realistic about it, there will probably be few (if any) original parts from a really old PC that will be suitable for use in a new one. A few items such as the mouse, keyboard, and floppy disc drive will probably be usable if they are in good condition, but little else is likely to be of much use. However, most PCs get a certain amount of upgrading over the years, and any recent additions to the old PC will probably be usable in the new one. For example, a recently added DVD or CD-RW drive, sound card, or loudspeaker system is usually suitable for transplanting into a new PC. Again, the saving in cost is not likely to be huge, but the cost of the new PC can be significantly reduced without severely compromising its performance.

The situation is rosier if you tend to switch to a new computer relatively often. In an extreme case it could just be a matter of replacing the existing motherboard, processor, and memory, with the rest of the computer being left untouched. I suppose that this type of thing should really be classified as rebuilding or upgrading rather than building a PC. Where you have an existing PC that is proving to be a bit slow, this type of rebuild or upgrade will often provide the cheapest way of moving up to a PC having an adequate specification for your purposes. However, do not overlook the possibility of building a new PC "from scratch" and keeping the existing PC as a standby, giving it to the children, or otherwise continuing to use it. It is wasteful if you discard PC components that still have years of life left in them.

One final point that is worth making is that you will learn a great deal about PCs by building your own. Constructing a PC will not turn you into a computer expert overnight, but you will certainly learn a great deal about the way everything functions. If any problems arise in the future or you wish to upgrade a PC it should be much easier to sort things out once you have some experience of PC construction.

Getting started

Having decided to "take the plunge" and build your own PC the first task is to make a list of all the components required, complete with brief notes detailing any special requirements. You may already have a fair idea of what you require, but otherwise it is a matter of studying reviews in computer magazines and looking through magazine advertisements in order to find the best components at a price you can afford.

If your aim is merely to produce a PC at a "rock bottom" price it becomes more a matter of scanning the advertisements for "special offers" and touring the local computer fairs for the best deals you can obtain. Before buying any "bargain" components make sure that they are compatible with the other items in the system, and are not totally out of date. Be particularly wary of very cheap motherboards, as these often require obsolete processors and memory modules that can cost a great deal and give relatively poor performance. If components are offered at very low prices there is usually a catch somewhere.

This list represents the minimum you will require in order to produce a working PC.

Case with PSU, set of fixing screws, etc.

Motherboard with cables, etc.

Memory modules to suit the motherboard

Microprocessor with matching heatsink and fan

Keyboard and mouse

Video card

Monitor

3.5-inch floppy disc drive

Hard disc drive

CD-ROM drive

A CD-ROM drive used to be considered something of a luxury, but as most software is now supplied on CD-ROMs you will probably not get far without one. The storage capacity of a floppy disc is very low compared to the amount of data produced by most applications, so a CD-RW drive is well worth the additional cost. In fact many users currently opt for a CD-RW drive plus a DVD type. This enables the PC to produce and read most types of disc, with the obvious exception that DVD discs can not be produced. DVD writers have fallen in price, as have the discs they use. They can read and write the various types of CD media as well as the appropriate DVD types, and probably represent the best choice these days. With the aid of modern software, DVD writers are no more difficult to use the the CD variety. Where the computer will only be equipped with one cd;DVD drive, a DVD writer is definitely the best option and should not be expensive.

Integrated audio/video

For multimedia applications, voice recognition, etc., you will also require a sound card and speakers plus (possibly) a headset and microphone. For most purposes one of the budget audio cards will suffice. A fair proportion of current motherboards have built-in audio circuits that offer a reasonable range of features and performance. In fact some of these integral sound facilities are very sophisticated. Integrated audio is probably the best option unless a top-notch audio system is required for some reason. There seems to be little difference in the cost of a motherboard having built-in audio and one having similar features but no integral audio. Integrated audio is therefore very cost-effective.

These days a fair proportion of motherboards have integrated video circuits. Whether integrated video is worthwhile depends on the way in which the PC will be used. It is unlikely that the performance of integrated video will satisfy dedicated computer gamers. In order to get the best results from the latest games it is necessary to have a high quality 3D video card that has all the latest tricks. For those not primarily interested in games it is quite possible that the integrated approach will be perfectly adequate. The built-in video circuits have some 3D capability, incidentally, but obviously they do not rival expensive video cards costing a few hundred pounds. Integrated video is generally regarded as more than adequate for a PC that will only be used to run business applications and the like.

Integrated video, like integrated audio, is very cost effective. It is therefore a good choice when building a budget PC. Bear in mind that most built-in video circuits share the main system memory. If (say) 128 megabytes of memory are used for the video generator, there are 128 megabytes less for everything else. This can slow down the PC slightly unless extra memory is fitted. As memory is now relatively cheap and most new PCs are equipped with large amounts of it, this is perhaps less of a problem than it was a few years ago. However, it is something to bear in mind if you will use an integrated video system in its most advanced modes together with an operating system that requires large amounts of memory in order to work well.

The list given previously omits some items that most PC users will require, such as a printer and a modem, but here we will only consider the main constituent parts of the PC itself. It is advisable to put together a basic PC and get it working, and then add peripherals such as scanners, printers, and broadband modems. Most people who build their own PC already have many of these peripherals anyway.

Right price?

Having selected the components for your new PC it is time to add up the cost. This tends to be higher than you would expect, so it may be

Fig.1.2 The case has bays for two sizes of drive

necessary to come up with some extra money or compromise slightly and choose some cheaper components. It is also worth looking through some catalogues and magazine adverts to see if you can find better deals on some of the components. It is essential to make sure that the components will actually fit together to produce a working PC. There are more options available than in days gone by, which means that there are also more opportunities for hardware incompatibility to creep in.

Chapter 2 covers each component in detail, and should help you to avoid buying parts that do not properly match up. Many of the motherboard manufacturers have downloadable versions of the instruction manuals on their sites. It is a good idea to look through the manual for your selected motherboard before buying any components. This should avoid any misunderstandings about the type or types of memory it can use, the processors it can accommodate, and so on. Checking the manual should avoid any costly mistakes.

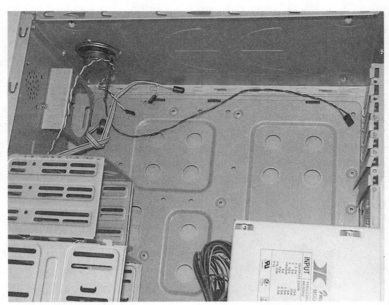

Fig.1.3 The empty area in the case is for the motherboard

Assembly

Having obtained a complete set of parts it is then time to assemble the PC. Before starting to build the PC, look at the various components, including minor items such as cables and small pieces of hardware, and try to get a mental picture of how everything fits together. If you have a ready-made PC it is a good idea to open it up and look inside so that you can see how it fits together. It is best for those with limited experience of computer hardware to adopt a "look but you mustn't touch" approach, so that there is no risk of accidentally damaging anything.

The case you have bought should have two sizes of drive bays (Figure 1.2). The smaller bays take 3.5-inch drives such as a 3.5-inch floppy disc drive and most hard drives. The larger bays are the 5.25-inch variety and take CD-ROM drives, CD-ROM writers, etc. Usually one or two of the 3.5-inch drive bays do not have cutouts in the front panel. These are used for hard disc drives, which do not have to be externally accessible. Since floppy disc drives are now often omitted from PCs, not every PC case actually has any 3.5-inch drive bays that are externally accessible. However, there are other accessories that require 3.5-inch bays that are

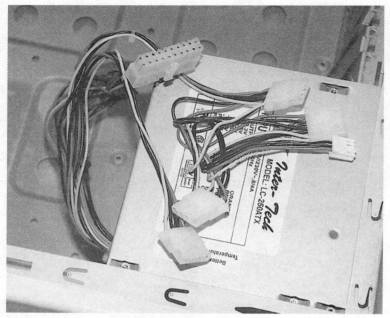

Fig.1.4 The power supply has upwards of six output cables

accessible, such as some sound systems and Flash card readers. Consequently, a case that has externally accessible 3.5-inch bays is more versatile and is perhaps a better choice.

There should be a large empty compartment in the case, and this is where the motherboard is mounted (Figure 1.3). The large box mounted on the rear panel of the case, usually in the top right-hand corner (as viewed from the front), is the power supply unit. This has mains input and (possibly) output connectors on the rear, and a selection of power leads for the motherboard and the drives (Figure 1.4). The original PC power supplies had a mains outlet that was intended for use with the monitor. Switching the PC on or off also resulted in the monitor being turned on or off.

In later power supplies the mains outlet was still included (Figure 1.5), but it was not switched. However, the monitor still switched on and off in sympathy with the PC. This automatic switching was provided by the energy saving facility of the monitor causing it to go into standby mode

Fig.1.5 This power supply has a mains output for a monitor

Fig.1.6 A modern power supply usually has an on/off switch

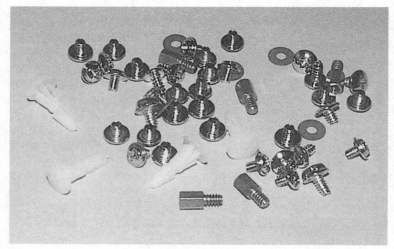

Fig.1.7 Small items of hardware should be included with the case

when the video signal from the PC ceased and power-up again when the signal started again. This is the method that is still used today.

In the past it was common for a PC power supply to have a voltage selector switch on the rear panel, but this is usually absent on modern supply units. Instead, there is a conventional on/off switch (Figure 1.6) that will always switch off the PC, even in situations where the switch on the front panels will not. Of course, make sure that voltage selector switch is set to the right voltage (230/240 volts for the UK) if the supply unit you obtain does have this feature. Do not worry about the absence of this switch. Most modern PC supply units automatically adjust to suit any mains supply voltage from about 90 to 250 volts. Others are designed specifically for operation with the 240 volt UK mains supply.

Small hardware

The case should be supplied complete with various small items of hardware (Figure 1.7), and it is bordering on the useless without them, so make sure it has the all-important polythene bag of odds and ends. These small items of hardware include the screws that are used to fix the various drives into their cages, although suitable screws may be included with some of the drives as well. In days gone by it was often quite awkward fitting the drives into the case, with plastic guide rails being

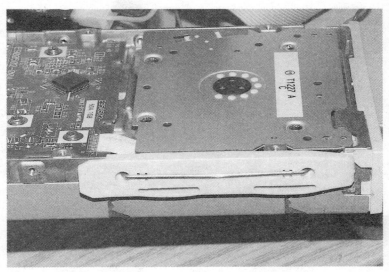

Fig.1.8 A plastic guide-rail clipped to a 3.5-inch drive

fitted to the drives before they were slid into place. The rails were then bolted to the case.

This system now seems to be totally obsolete, and with most cases the drives are bolted direct to the inner structure of the case. However, some recent PC cases use an updated version of the guide rail idea. The general scheme of things is to have a guide rail fitted to one side of the drive (Figure 1.8), and it is usually held in place via a wire clip. This side of the drive is not bolted into place and is only supported by the guide rail. The other side is held in place by two screws in the normal fashion.

As viewed from the front of the PC, it is the right-hand side of the drive that is fitted with the guide rail. I assume that the idea is to avoid using fixing screws on the right-hand side of the drive, which is usually less accessible than the left-hand side. In fact I have encountered PCs where it is only possible to access these screws by removing the motherboard. Anyway, any case that uses this system should be supplied with one guide rail per drive bay. Where this method of fixing is used it is not possible to fit a drive properly without a suitable guide rail. Note that the guide rails are normally used only for the 3.5-inch bays, with the 5.25-inch types having mounting screws both sides, but there could be some exceptions.

Fig.1.9 This motherboard has two memory sockets

Fig.1.10 A heatsink and fan for a Socket 775 processor

The motherboard has a socket for the processor, and two or more for the memory modules (Figure 1.9). In this example there are two memory sockets near the bottom edge of the board on the right-hand side. The socket for the processor is above and to the right of these. Modern processors require a heatsink (a piece of finned metal) and a fan to prevent overheating. The heatsink and fan are normally sold as a single unit (Figure 1.10). Most processors are sold complete with a matching heatsink and fan in a boxed retail version. The OEM (original equipment manufacturer) versions are cheaper but do not include the heatsink, fan, or any fitting instructions.

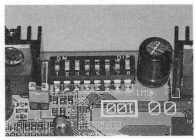

Fig.1.11 A bank of eight DIP-switches

Where possible it is better to fit the processor, heatsink and fan, and the memory modules to the motherboard before it is mounted inside the case. Even with the largest and best designed cases there is relatively poor access to the motherboard once it is inside the case, so it makes sense to do as much work as possible while the motherboard is still freely accessible. Unfortunately, with some cases it might be difficult or impossible to slide the motherboard into the case with everything preinstalled, but where possible you should certainly do so.

There may be some DIP-switches (Figure 1.11) or jumpers (Figure 1.12) on the motherboard that have to be given the correct settings for the particular microprocessor you are using. These set the clock frequencies, processor operating voltage and possibly one or two other things as well. These should be set before the board is installed in the case because it is then much easier to see exactly what you are doing, and mistakes are much less likely to occur. It can be very fiddly indeed to set the miniature switches or jumpers once the board is fitted in the case.

Not all motherboards are configured using switches or jumpers, and there is a strong trend towards so-called "jumperless" motherboards. These probe the processor to determine its type, and then set themselves up correctly without any guidance from the user. It is usually possible to override all or some of the settings manually if you do not agree with the default settings. This is done via the BIOS Setup program though, and not using switches or jumpers. Few

Fig.1.12 Some configuration jumpers

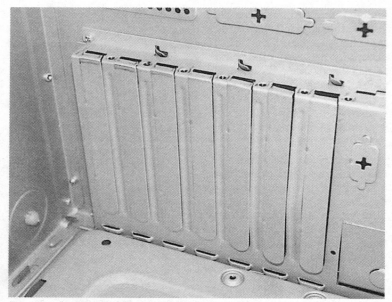

Fig.1.13 The blanking plates at the rear of the case

motherboards are genuinely "jumperless", so always check to see if there are one or two jumpers or switches that might need adjustment.

When the motherboard is finally installed in the case it must be held clear of the metal casing by mounting it on some form of stand-off. Without the stand-offs the connections on the underside of the board would simply short-circuit through the metal casing. The stand-offs might be moulded into the case or already installed, but they are usually in the bag of bits and pieces supplied with the case.

Cables

With the drives and motherboard in place it is time to start adding the cables. There are cables that connect the motherboard to the disc drives, and there will also be some leads sprouting from the front section of the case that connect to the motherboard. These provide functions such as the hard disc activity light and on/off switching. Depending on the type of power supply in use there will be one, two, or three power leads to

Fig.1.14 The black slot on the left is an AGP type, and the five to its right are ordinary PCI slots

connect to the motherboard. AT cases, motherboards, and power supplies are now obsolete, so the power supply will certainly be an ATX type. These have one power lead for motherboards that use AMD processors and three for those that use Intel chips, although only two of these are normally required. The power lead on the processor's fan is connected to the motherboard, as is the fan for the case if there is one. The disc drives are not powered via the cable that connects to the motherboard, and each one must be connected to one of the power supply's power leads.

With an ATX motherboard and case there is often no need to bother with wiring up the standard ports. The motherboard is fitted with standard connectors that can be accessed via cutouts in the rear of the case. This system worked fine at first, but some motherboards now support so many

*Fig.1.15 A 16X PCI Express slot to the right of the two ordinary PCI
types, and a 1X PCI Express slot to their left*

ports that they can not all be accommodated in the usual cluster on the
motherboard. Consequently, the connectors for some ports are mounted
elsewhere on the rear of the case. They are occasionally mounted on
the main casing, but these days it is more normal for the extra connectors
to be fitted on plates that are installed behind an unused PCI expansion
slot. The connectors are fitted with flying leads are connected to the
motherboard.

The ports that are most likely to be mounted away from the motherboard
are the so-called legacy types. This means the game, serial, and parallel

ports, that are little used in modern computing. Any additional hardware needed to implement these ports will not necessarily be included as standard with the motherboard. There is little point in paying extra to implement ports that will not be needed, so do not bother with these ports unless you have to. Most modern cases and motherboards have provision for sockets fitted on the front panel. Typically, the case will have sockets and leads for at least a couple of USB ports, a microphone, and headphones. The USB ports are in addition to those available at the rear of the case, and provide a useful boost to the PC's capabilities.

Next the expansion cards are slotted into place on the motherboard and their mounting brackets are bolted to the rear section of the case. The appropriate blanking plates at the rear of the case (Figure 1.13) must first be removed to clear the way for the expansion cards. With more and more features being handled by the motherboard the number of expansion cards is often quite low on a modern computer. With the sound and graphics integrated with the motherboard it is not essential to have any at all, but most PCs utilize two or three cards.

There are three types of expansion card, and therefore three types of expansion slots to accommodate them. There used to be a fourth type, but the old ISA expansion slots and cards are now completely obsolete and will not be considered further here. Most modern expansion cards are for PCI expansion slots. At one time PCI slots were used for graphics cards, but the need for greater speed resulted in the development of AGP expansion slots and cards. Until recently, the vast majority of modern motherboards had an AGP slot, but this type of interface is now being replaced by the PCI Express variety. Matters are complicated slightly by the development of two forms of PCI Express slot. The high speed (16X) type is used for graphics cards, and the slower (1X) type is used for everything else.

The AGP slot in Figure 1.14 is the one on the left, set well into the board. This board has five PCI expansion slots, which are to the right of the AGP type. Conventionally the PCI slots are white, and the AGP type is brown. However, there are some multicoloured motherboards that do not adhere to this convention. The small slot to the right of these is for a special modem card that has a minimal amount of hardware and makes use of hardware on the motherboard. It used to be common for motherboards to have a slot of this type, but it is a facility that has been little used in practice. Consequently, it is a feature that is not usually found on modern motherboards. Figure 1.15 shows a board that has two PCI expansion slots, with a 16X PCI Express to the right of these.

The small expansion slot to the left of the PCI slots is a 1x PCI Express type.

Cable confusion

To complete the PC any final cabling is added. In most cases this just means adding the cable which connects the audio output of the CD-ROM drive to the appropriate input connector on the sound card.

People contemplating building a PC for the first time are often worried about getting the cables connected incorrectly. In most cases this is simply not possible, because the cables are fitted with connectors that will only fit in the correct sockets the right way round. There are some cables where it is possible to make mistakes, but the instruction manual provided with the motherboard together with markings on the cables and connectors make it easy to get everything connected correctly.

Provided due care and attention is used when fitting the cables there should be no problems. Do not simply connect things together more in hope that expectation. Take the time and make the effort so that, as far as possible, things are right the first time. It is not a good idea to make a mistake, but if the worst should happen there is little risk of any damage occurring.

Static

Another common worry is that of damaging some of the components by "zapping" them with static electricity. It is true that most of the components in a PC are vulnerable to static voltages, and that these voltages are quite common in normal environments. It is also true that there are numerous items of anti-static equipment available, which can virtually eliminate the possibility of components being damaged by static charges. Some of these anti-static devices are quite cheap, but many are quite costly.

For professional PC builders and service engineers it is probably worthwhile spending a fair amount of money on static precautions, as over a period they will be handling computer equipment worth many thousands of pounds. For the do-it-yourself PC builder it is not worth spending much money on this type of thing because the safety equipment could easily cost more than the components it is protecting. On the other hand, few amateur PC builders can afford to take no precautions and simply replace anything that is accidentally "zapped".

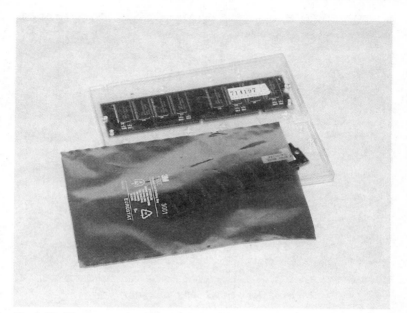

Fig.1.16 Two types of anti-static packaging

Fortunately, it is not necessary to spend large amounts of money in order to protect the components. Some low cost equipment and (or) some improvised safety devices are adequate to ensure that your PC components will not be damaged while the PC is being built. Computer components that are vulnerable to static damage are normally supplied in some form of anti-static packing. A couple of examples are shown in Figure 1.16. These either insulate the components from the outside world or encapsulate them in a conductive material. This leaves the components safe from damage by static charges, but only if you leave them inside the packing until it is time for installation. Avoid the temptation to remove components from the packing to have a look at them.

Setting up

On the face of it, having built your PC it is just a matter of connecting the peripherals such as the monitor and mouse, and then switching on to see if it works. Unfortunately, it is not quite as simple as that. When you buy a new computer it is normally supplied fully configured with the

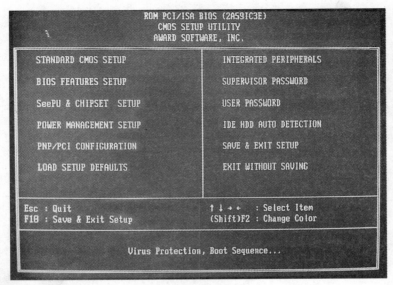

Fig.1.17 A typical menu for a BIOS Setup program

operating system installed, and possibly even with some applications software already installed. It is then just a matter of connecting everything together, switching on, going through some simple setting up procedures, and computing away merrily. When you build a PC it is necessary to configure it and install all the software yourself. This includes installing the operating system such as Windows Vista or a version of Linux.

The configuration is done using the Setup program built into the PC as part of its BIOS (Figure 1.17). The BIOS is the basic input/output system, and it is a program contained in a chip on the motherboard. It is sometimes referred to as the "ROM BIOS", because the chip that contains the program is a ROM (read only memory). A computer must always be running a valid program or it will crash, and the BIOS is the program that runs when you first switch on the computer. Its function is to do some basic checks on the hardware to ensure that the memory and processor are functioning properly, and to then run the operating system. The BIOS can be used by the operating system as an aid to handling the hardware.

A PC has some memory that does not lose its contents when the computer is switched off. This is normally in the form of CMOS RAM, which has a very low current consumption. As a result, a back-up battery is adequate to power this memory when the PC is switched off. In days gone by this battery was in the form of an ordinary battery pack that had to be changed periodically, or rechargeable cells that were charged up when the PC was switched on.

Fig.1.18 A lithium backup battery

These days the battery is usually a long-life lithium type that will last about 10 years and does not need to be replaced. It generally outlives the rest of the PC! It is usually easy to locate on the motherboard (Figure 1.18), and is a sort of giant size version of a "button" cell, as used in watches and older cameras. The battery can actually be replaced in the unlikely event of it running flat or leaking. Incidentally, this battery also runs a clock/calendar circuit that enables the operating system to determine the time and date.

Originally the BIOS used the CMOS RAM to store some basic information about the hardware, such as the amount of memory available, the main parameters for the hard disc drive, and the types of floppy drives installed. It still stores this information in the CMOS RAM, but it also uses it to hold numerous other facts and figures about the hardware. When your new PC is first switched on it is necessary to go into the BIOS Setup program to provide information about the drive types, to set the time and date, etc.

There are also numerous other facts and figures that need to be set. A modern BIOS requires a large amount of information, and there is no denying that much of this information is highly technical. On the other hand, a modern BIOS is semi-intelligent, and it will set sensible defaults for most of the settings. It can also use probing techniques to obtain facts and figures about the amount of memory, the hard drive parameters, etc. In order to get the PC working it does not require a great deal of input from the user, and neither is a vast technical knowledge required.

Disc formatting

In days gone by it was necessary to do low-level formatting of the hard disc drive, and then do high level formatting to suit the selected operating system. These days hard discs are supplied with the low level formatting already done, so it is only necessary to do the high level formatting. Whatever operating system you intend to use, it should have a formatting program that can handle hard disc drives.

Actually there is a step needed ahead of formatting the hard drive, and this is to set up the partitions. By partitioning the disc it can be used as if it was two or more smaller discs. Even if you wish to allocate all the capacity to one partition, the drive still has to be processed using the partitioning software to produce this single partition. Again, the operating system should be supplied with a utility program for partitioning the hard disc. With Windows XP, Windows Vista, and modern versions of Linux the partitioning and formatting is done as part of the installation process, so there is no need to do either prior to commencing the installation process.

Operating system

Just how difficult or easy it is to install the operating system depends on the particular operating system you select, and to some extent on the hardware in the PC. Getting a simple operating system like MS/DOS installed is quite quick and easy, but with a more modern operating system like Windows Vista or Linux it will take longer and is a little more difficult. Modern operating systems have quite sophisticated installer programs though, and to a large extent the installation is automatic. Installing an operating system on a PC is not quite as simple as loading a word processor or accounts program onto the hard drive, but it is not that much more difficult either.

With most operating systems and a modern PC you can boot from the installation CD-ROM. The programs on the CD-ROM may even handle things like partitioning and formatting the hard disc, leaving the user little to do apart from sitting back and watching what happens. With older operating systems, notably Windows 98 and ME, it is necessary to make a boot disc and boot from the floppy drive. The boot disc must include support for the CD-ROM drive so that you can run the Setup program on the installation disc once the computer has booted. It is then largely a matter of sitting back while the operating system installs itself on the hard drive.

Being realistic about things, if you are building a modern PC it makes sense to utilise a modern operating system that can fully exploit its potential, rather than trying to carry on using an obsolete operating system that may not work properly with modern hardware. If you are building a new PC it is definitely advisable to install a modern version of your selected

Fig.1.19 The finished article. This home constructed PC has an Athlon XP2000+ processor

operating system. In the case of Windows, this means Windows Vista. Like Microsoft, most of the hardware manufacturers have now ceased to support Windows ME and 98, which means that there is little chance of getting the correct driver software to use these operating systems on a modern PC. Another point to bear in mind is that a fair percentage of modern Windows application software will not work with anything other than Windows XP or Vista. Windows XP is still a current operating system at the time of writing this piece, and it has potential advantages when used with a PC having a relatively modest specification. Windows Vista is better future-proofed though, and in most cases is the better option.

Driver installation

There is usually a certain amount of work to do once the operating system has completed the automatic installation process. Some of the driver software for the hardware will not have been installed at all, and in other cases there will only be generic drivers. The motherboard, video card, etc., should all be supplied with driver software for the popular operating systems, and with this installed the computer should be fully working. The required screen resolution can then be set, and hardware such as the sound generator can be checked.

Once the operating system is fully "up and running" it is time to install the applications programs and start using the new computer. Installing all this software and getting it set up correctly can be very time consuming. Where you have an old PC with the operating system and applications installed there are possible shortcuts to getting the new computer set up correctly. One of these is to simply use the old hard disc in the new computer, but it is likely that you will wish to use a modern disc that is faster and has a much higher capacity than the old drive.

One way around this is to use the old drive as the boot drive, with a new drive being used as well to provide the extra storage capacity. This might not be as straightforward as you might think, because the new PC will have different hardware to the old one, and the operating system will require a substantial amount of reconfiguration before it will run in the new computer. It is possible to copy everything from the old drive to the new drive, but again, the operating system will have to be reconfigured before it will boot and run properly. This is not necessarily too difficult to achieve, and it is quite a popular option.

My preference would be to install everything "from scratch" even if it is very time consuming. When a PC has been in use for some time it tends to get cluttered up with all sorts of files that are no longer used, and the boot-up process often seems to slow down quite noticeably as a computer ages. Having built a new PC it is good practice to make a fresh start and only install those programs and files that you still need. This removes unwanted clutter from the hard disc drive and ensures that your new PC runs as quickly and smoothly as possible.

Points to remember

If you build your own PC to save money you can probably do so with careful buying, but do not expect to get a half price PC. If you do not shop around for the best buys it could actually cost substantially more to build your own PC.

The manual skills involved in building a PC are not great, and no special tools are required. A medium size crosshead screwdriver and pair of pliers are all you should need, and no soldering is involved. Even so, PC construction is not for those who are completely impractical.

Provided you go about things slowly and meticulously the finished PC should work, and work well. There should be no significant difference in performance between a home constructed PC and a ready built PC of equivalent specification.

By building your own PC, funds permitting, you can have a PC that exactly meets your perfect specification. You should also learn a great deal about PCs and have plenty of fun as well.

The completed PC will require a certain amount of setting up before it is ready for the operating system to be installed. There is a trend towards having the PC automatically detect the processor type and adjust itself accordingly, so the amount of manual setting-up may be minimal. Otherwise it is just a matter of setting a few switches or placing jumpers on the correct sets of terminals.

Some adjustments will be required to the BIOS, and these are performed via the built-in Setup program. The BIOS is admittedly highly technical, but to a large extent you can just leave the default settings. The user normally has to do little more than set the time and date, and provide some drive information.

Installing the operating system is not quite as easy as installing applications programs. On the other hand, modern operating systems have Setup programs that do most of the installation for you. It is necessary to provide some information when prompted, but little else is required.

With some operating systems it is necessary for the user to set up partitions on the hard disc and perform the high level formatting. This is not too difficult, and the operating system should be supplied with the necessary software to perform both the partitioning and the formatting.

No low level formatting is required with modern disc drives. The low level formatting is performed at the factory, and conventional low level formatting programs do not work properly will modern drives anyway.

There is no overall guarantee for the system if you build your own PC. If a component is faulty it is up to you to locate it and get it exchanged under the guarantee for that individual component. Locating faulty components is not usually too difficult, and in many cases the location of the fault is self-evident.

2

Components

Processor

All modern PCs are based on an Intel Pentium processor, or a compatible processor from another manufacturer. These days the only real competition to Intel is provided by AMD with their very popular Sempron, Athlon, and Phenom processor ranges. Pentium processors have additional instructions, but are basically just faster and more efficient versions of the 80486DX and earlier Intel processors in this series. The original Pentium chips ran at 60MHz and 66MHz, and in most speed tests did not perform significantly better than the faster 80486 chips. Later versions used higher clock rates, fitted into a different socket, and had improved motherboards. This provided a boost in performance that gave much better results than any 80486DX PCs could achieve. The clock frequencies for these "classic" Pentium processors are 75, 90, 100, 120, 133, 150, 166, and 200MHz.

These early Pentium processors are now obsolete and have not been used in new PCs for many years. Pentium processors with MMX (multimedia extension) technology replaced them. The MMX technology is actually an additional 57 processor instructions that are designed to speed up multimedia applications, but can also be used to good effect in other applications such as voice recognition. There were also some general improvements that produced an increase in performance by around 10 or 15 percent when using non-MMX specific software. These MMX Pentium processors were produced in 166MHz, 200MHz, and 233MHz versions.

These are now long obsolete as well, and were replaced by Pentium II, Pentium III, and Pentium 4 processors. The original Pentium II processors had a clock frequency of 233MHz, but much faster chips were soon produced. The original Pentium processors were fitted onto the motherboard via a conventional integrated circuit holder known as Socket 4. Those operating at 75MHz and above used an improved version called Socket 7. Pentium II processors look nothing like conventional

Fig.2.1 A Pentium II processor complete with heatsink and fan

processors, and in physical appearance they are like a cross between a videocassette and a memory module (Figure 2.1). They fit into a holder that is more like a PC expansion slot or holder for a memory module than an integrated circuit holder.

One reason for the change in style was that it potentially enabled higher clock speeds to be utilized. Another reason for the change in style was that Pentium II chips were so complex that with the technology of the time it was not possible to put the processor and cache memory on the same chip. Cache memory is high-speed memory that is used to store recently processed data. It is likely that this data will need to be accessed again, and having it available in high-speed memory ensures that it can be processed very efficiently when it is needed. In virtually all practical applications this substantially speeds up the rate at which data can be processed.

Extra cache

Previous Pentium processors had some cache memory (typically 32k) on the chip, with a much larger cache of about 256 to 512k on the motherboard. These are known as level 1 and level 2 cache respectively. Level 1 cache is faster, but there are practical limits on the amount of cache memory that can be included in the processor. With the Pentium II chips it had to be omitted altogether, but a "piggy-back" memory chip included in the processor module provides a 512k cache. This memory runs at half the speed of the processor clock and not at the bus speed of the motherboard, which gives a substantial boost in performance. Due to the relatively large size of the level 1 cache no level 2 cache was deemed to be necessary. Hence there is no cache memory on a Pentium II motherboard.

The Pentium II is really a development of the Pentium Pro processor. This relatively unsuccessful processor was an improved version of the "classic" Pentium design, but when running Windows 95 software it often failed to provide much improvement over an ordinary Pentium chip. The Pentium Pro became overshadowed by the MMX Pentium processors, which proved to be an immediate hit with PC buyers. The Pentium Pro is another one that is now long gone.

The Pentium II has the additional MMX instructions, and slightly improved performance compared to an ordinary MMX Pentium processor. The 350, 400, and 450MHz versions are designed to operate on motherboards that operate at a 100MHz clock frequency and use fast memory modules. The earlier Pentium and Pentium II processors operate with 66MHz motherboards and relatively slow RAM. This gives the 350, 400, and 450MHz chips a greater speed advantage over the slower versions than a comparison of the clock frequencies would suggest.

As one might expect, the Pentium II was replaced by the Pentium III, which has SIMD (single-instruction multiple data) technology. This is 70 new instructions designed to speed up certain types of software. These instructions are mainly aimed at high-speed 3D graphics and applications that include voice recognition. They are only of use with software that is written to take advantage of them.

Like the Pentium II processors, the Pentium III has 512k of cache memory running at half the clock speed. However, on the later chips this became 256k of on-chip memory running at the full clock speed. Also, these chips marked a return to socket technology, using a minor variation on the Socket 370 used for the Celeron chips of the period. The original

Fig.2.2 A Socket 478 Pentium 4

Pentium III processors used clock frequencies of 450 and 500MHz, but later chips took processor speeds beyond the 1GHz (1000MHz) mark. The Pentium III was phased out in favour of the Pentium 4, and it has entered the list of PC processors that are now obsolete.

Pentium 4/Dual-Core/Core 2

The Pentium 4 (Figure 2.2) was sold as an up-market alternative to the Pentium III for some time. The original Pentium 4 processors used Socket 423 motherboards, but later versions required boards of the Socket 478 variety. No doubt there are a few Socket 478 Pentium processors and motherboards still on sale, but they were manufactured some time ago. Newer versions of the Pentium 4 use Socket 775 motherboards, this represents a departure from the normal scheme of things. Normally the processor has hundreds of pins that fit into the socket on the motherboard. Things are reversed with Socket 775 processors, which effectively have the socket. The "socket" on the motherboard has hundreds of pins that fit into the underside of the processor (Figure 2.3)

The Pentium 4 processor is basically a faster version of the Pentium III, but extra instructions have been introduced over the years, and the

Fig.2.3 Socket 775 is actually more like a Plug 775, with the socket in the processor

amount of on-chip cache has been raised to 512k, then 1 megabyte, and so on up to 8 megabytes at the time of writing this. There have been improvements such as Hyper-Threading technology, which are designed to reduce the number of clock cycles per instruction, and speed up the internal handling of data.

The latest Pentium processors have dual core technology, which means that there are two processor cores within one chip, but often with some resources shared between the two cores. There are also quad core processors, but at the moment these are primarily intended for use in servers rather than acting as the basis of desktop PCs. Dual core technologies are relatively new, but are really just an extension of the old idea of having two entirely separate processors on one motherboard. Both methods are basic versions of parallel processing, where increased speed is obtained by having the computer work on two or more tasks simultaneously.

Although it may seem as though things have not progressed very far from the days of the first 1 gigahertz processors, with the current processors operating at around 3 gigahertz, modern processors are actually many times faster than those of a few years ago. The increased speed is obtained by greater efficiency rather than using ever high clock frequencies.

Celeron

The Intel processor for entry-level PCs was the Celeron. Its demise has been predicted for some time, but it is still in production. However, it is not currently used in desktop PCs to a significant degree. The Celeron is still used in laptop PCs, and is very popular in this role. It is possible that the Celeron, in some form or other, will be used in future desktop PCs, but at present it falls outside the scope of this book and it will not be considered further here.

Athlon 64/64 X2/Phenom

Over the years various manufacturers have offered Intel compatible processors that can be used in PCs. The only company currently offering real alternatives to the Intel Pentium and Celeron chips is AMD. The AMD chips have their origins back in the days of Socket 7 motherboards, and later on there was even a chip that used slot technology (Figure 2.4). This was the original Athlon processor, and it used AMD's own Slot A rather than Intel's Slot 1 technology.

Fig.2.4 The Slot A version of the AMD Athlon processor

Like the recent

Pentiums, modern AMD processors use conventional sockets, and they remain physically and electrically incompatible with the Pentium processors. A modern PC motherboard is designed to take one type of processor or the other, and although in some cases the two types of socket may look similar, they are totally incompatible. Fortunately, although the chips and the motherboards are different, they all run the same software and are fully compatible in that respect.

The Athlon chips have been produced in various versions with a wide range of clock frequencies. The Athlon 64 was the first widely available 64-bit processor for PCs. Modern AMD processors use dual core (Athlon 64 X2) or quad core (Phenom) technology, and are designed for use with Socket AM2 or Socket AM2 + motherboards respectively. Like their Intel equivalents, they provide a basic form of parallel processing with the cores simultaneously performing separate tasks, thus providing a large increase in processing speed. AMD processors for Socket, A, Socket 754 and Socket 939/940 motherboards are now largely obsolete. Fig.2.5 shows a Socket AM2 motherboard manufactured by Gigabyte.

Speed Ratings

The clock speeds and speed ratings of microprocessors has been a controversial subject for virtually the entire history of the PC. On the face of it, doubling the clock frequency of a microprocessor doubles the speed of the computer in which it is used. Unfortunately, it is not that simple in practice, since doubling the speed of the processor does not necessarily mean that the other parts of the computer will have their speed boosted by the same amount. In fact it is very unlikely that everything else in the computer would receive a similar boost in speed. The memory for example, has tended to lag behind the speed increases associated with processors. Matters are complicated by the fact that there are now several totally different processor designs, with some doing far more per clock cycle than others can manage. It is quite possible for an up-market process to have several times the processing power than an older or more basic design that operates at the same clock frequency.

There have been attempts to produce meaningful speed ratings that would provide a realistic comparison of processor speeds. For example, the speed ratings of some Athlon processors refer to their equivalent Pentium speed and not their actual clock frequencies. Being realstic about things though, the range of processors is now so broad that there is no easy way of precisely gauging the relative speeds of various chips. Also, the real-world speed is also dependent on the motherboard and

Fig.2.5 A Socket AM2 motherboard for modern AMD processors

other components in the system, and the type of software in use. You
can get a good idea of the relative speeds by looking at the test results
published in computer magazines and on the Internet. These should be
regarded as nothing more than a general guide, and bear in mind that
putting the latest super-fast processor into an otherwise mediocre PC is
unlikely to result in a really fast PC.

Duron and Sempron

The Duron processor is AMD's original equivalent to the Celeron, and it
is essentially a simplified Athlon with less cache. Although the Duron is
less potent that the Athlon, like the Celeron it achieved good popularity.
At one time a PC with a Duron operating at about 800 megahertz was the
standard choice for a business PC, and many years on, these computers
are still quite capable of running most standard business applications.
In fact speed is no longer the paramount issue that it was in the past,
and PCs that use budget processors but have plenty of memory are
good workhorse PCs that can run most applications.

The Sempron is the chip that replaced the Duron. The Sempron chips have been produced in Socket 754, Socket 939, and AM2 versions, and at the time of writing this they are still readily available. A Sempron based system has been a popular choice where a fast budget PC is required, but AMD seems to be concentrating its efforts on its more upmarket chips. The Sempron might not be an option for much longer.

Processor advice

The range of processors currently available is a bit bewildering, and seems to get ever more diverse. It can be difficult to decide which one is the most suitable for a given set of circumstances. Unless money is not an issue it is probably best not to opt for the last word in PC microprocessors. When 66MHz 80486DX microprocessors became available they were only 33MHz faster than the existing 33MHz chips, but that 33MHz represented a doubling in speed. A 3GHz chip is 200MHz faster than a 2.8GHz version, but offers an increase in performance of just a few percent. Even going from a 2.4GHz processor to a 3GHz type only represents a 25 percent increase.

Even with the more demanding applications software an increase in speed of a few percent will be barely noticeable. Programs that run slowly on a 2.8GHz PC will still run slowly on a 3GHz PC. Where there is a minimal difference in cost it might be worthwhile going for the slightly faster version of a processor, particularly if you are running processor intensive applications, but otherwise it does not make economic sense to do so. As pointed out previously, the situation is complicated by the fact that some achieve far more per clock cycle than do others.

Price is usually a good indication of relative processing power. At the budget end of the market there are modern but relatively simple processors, and older designs that are now being sold at a fraction of their original price. Older processors can offer excellent performance at low cost, but only if the motherboard and memory can be obtained at equally attractive prices. Bear in mind that a new PC of this type uses relatively old technology and is unlikely to be particularly futureproof. You are effectively building a PC that is a few year old. Going up in price, you then have a choice of mid-range modern processors and upmarket processors that are beginning to become a bit dated. In general, mid-priced processors are safe choices that offer good performance for the money, and do not require the latest mega-powerful (and expensive) motherboards and memory. In contrast, top end processors tend to be very expensive, require expensive motherboards and other components in order to work really well, and do not represent good value for money. Obtaining the last word in PC computing power is an expensive business, and the additional cost is often out of proportion to the increase in performance over mid-range options.

Intel or AMD?

Once a price range has been selected, a choice of Intel or AMD has to be made, and it pays to bear in mind that these use different motherboards. At one time the motherboards for Intel chips tended to be significantly more expensive than those for AMD processors. These days there is little difference in the prices of the two types, and the facilities offered by the motherboard is the main factor governing the price. When operating on a tight budget it is still a good idea to consider various processor and motherboard options, and to take into account the cost of different types of memory. Provided the rest of the system is up to the task, any AMD or Intel processor should provide excellent results together with good reliability.

Buying a fast processor and then economising on the rest of the system does not usually produce the best system for the money. Many applications programs will run better with a slightly slower processor plus more memory and a better video card. Overall results are likely to be best with a well balanced system that has no major weaknesses.

Even the cheapest of the current budget processors are adequate for most business and general applications. Many of these applications require large amounts of memory though, as does multitasking (running several programs simultaneously). Windows Vista tends to require more memory than Windows XP, and it is important to bear this in mind when building a PC that will run Windows Vista. A gigabyte of memory is the minimum for good results, and 2 gigabytes is preferable. Skimping on the memory to pay for an expensive processor is usually a mistake. Skimping slightly on the processor to fit more memory is often the better strategy.

Future-proof

Many people, quite understandably, would like their new PC to be as future-proof as possible. In other words, they would like the PC to be easy to upgrade in the future so that it remains reasonably up-to-date at low cost. Unfortunately, the fact that your PC has the right kind of socket does not necessarily mean that it will be able to use all the processors that use that type of socket. Newer and faster processors often need newer and faster motherboards and faster memory as well. New types of socket are likely to be used in the future. Even if future processors use the same type of socket, it is unlikely that most of the current motherboards will be able to operate at high enough clock speeds or have all the facilities needed to accommodate them.

You can try to choose a set-up that can be easily upgraded, but do not be surprised if a future processor upgrade requires the motherboard and memory modules to be upgraded as well. The best future-proofing is obtained by using a motherboard that uses a recent chip set. The current processors are unlikely to push the motherboard to anything approaching its limit, and with luck it will be usable with faster processors released a year or two later. Budget motherboards using old chip sets are unlikely to be compatible with future processors. In fact many of these boards can not accommodate the fastest of the current processors. A 64-bit processor is not necessary if you will be using a 32-bit operating system, which includes most versions of Windows, but it does leave your options open and provide slightly better future-proofing.

At the time of writing this piece, something like an AMD Athlon 64 X2 3800+ or 4800+ represents a popular choice for a mid-priced PC. However, as Harold Wilson almost said, "a week is a long time in computing", and things change rapidly. It has almost become a matter of looking to see how many processor prices have been cut today, and checking to see how many new processors have been announced this week! It is really a matter of deciding on the processing power you require, and then looking for the best bargain at that power level at the time.

Heatsink and fan

The original PC processors managed quite happily without any cooling system, but all modern PC processors are short lived unless they are kept cool by a heatsink and fan. A heatsink is simply a piece of metal having fins that enable it to efficiently transfer excess heat from the processor to the air inside the case. The cooling fan improves the efficiency of the heatsink by ensuring that there is a flow of cool air over it.

These days the heatsink and fan are invariably in the form of a single unit, and you do not buy them as separate entities. In fact processors are sometimes supplied as a sort of boxed set, complete with heatsink, fan, and fitting instructions, so you may not need to buy the heatsink and

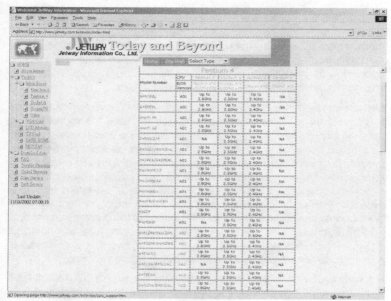

Fig.2.6 The processor compatibility chart on the Jetway web site

fan separately. This is the safe way to obtain the heatsink and fan, as they are guaranteed to be a correct match for the processor. Processors offered at "rock bottom" prices are usually the OEM (original equipment manufacturer) versions, which are "bare" processors.

When buying the heatsink and fan it is important to realise that there are different sizes and types. The Socket AM2 uses a totally different method of fixing to the Socket 775 types, and consequently needs a totally different heatsink and fan. Some processors generate more heat than others, and therefore need a larger heatsink. Other than buying them as a boxed set, the safest way to buy the heatsink and fan is to obtain them from the same source as the processor and at the same time, preferably getting an assurance that the cooling system is suitable for use with the processor. Any company selling processors should be able to supply a matching heatsink and fan. If anything should go wrong any reputable company should be prepared to make amends for their mistake.

Fig.2.7 This ATX motherboard has a very different layout to the one shown in Fig.2.5

Motherboard

Having selected the processor it is then a matter of finalising the choice of motherboard. As explained previously, AMD and Intel processors use different motherboards, so do not waste time looking at boards that are totally incompatible with your chosen processor. When you find some likely looking motherboards it is essential to carefully check their specifications to ascertain whether or not they will accept the processor you intend to use.

It is worthwhile investigating the web sites of some motherboard manufacturers where you will find a lot of technical information on their motherboards. There are often charts to show the processors that are

Fig.2.8 This ATX board is smaller than the one of Figure 2.7, and far from completely fills its compartment in the case

compatible with each board (Figure 2.6), and there may even be the full instruction manuals for the boards in downloadable form. Apart from helping you to select a suitable motherboard, reading through a few of these manuals can teach you a great deal about PC building and setting up the finished unit.

The vast majority of modern motherboards are of the ATX variety, and the earlier AT boards are now long gone. There are some variations within the ATX scheme of things, and if you look at a few ATX boards it will soon become apparent that they are produced in various shapes and sizes. They all fit into the same cases though, and are used in much the same way. The differences are due to the fact that technology has enabled modern motherboards to be made much smaller than those of a few years ago, despite the fact that the current boards are much more complex. Rather than produce full-size boards that are largely blank, the manufacturers have opted to make boards that are half size, or whatever. A wide variety of layouts are currently in use, and the ATX board of Figure 2.7 is clearly very different to the one used in the board shown previously in Figure 2.5. The motherboard in Figure 2.8 is much

Fig.2.9 The standard set of ATX ports

smaller and squarer than the other two. Consequently, there is a fair amount of excess space when the board is fitted in the case. In general, small boards are easier to use, but the small size is often reflected in a more limited range of facilities and expansion potential.

There are other styles of board available, but they are relatively difficult to obtain and can be awkward to use. Most are designed for use in tiny media PCs and require special cases and (possibly) other components. When building a system of this type it is usually a matter of buying a so-called "barebones" system, which usually means a motherboard, case, power supply, with perhaps one or two other components included in the system. You then add a processor, hard disc, etc., to produce a complete system of the required specification. Building a system of this type is not necessarily very difficult, but it is probably not an ideal starting point. It is not an aspect of PC construction that will be considered further in this book.

An ATX power supply is switched on and off by way of a simple pushbutton switch on the case, which connects to the power supply via the motherboard. The point of this system is that it permits automatic control of the on/off switching. With any modern version of Windows for example, when the system is closed down the power supply switches off automatically. The monitor, assuming it is a reasonably modern type, then goes into its power saving standby mode. This effectively results in the entire computer switching itself off when Windows is shut down.

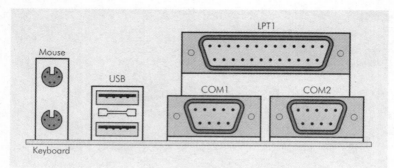

Fig.2.10 The basic set of ports for an ATX motherboard

ATX boards have many of the port connectors fitted on the board and accessible via cut-outs in the rear of the case. The original ATX boards had a standard cluster of ports. This has serial and parallel ports, two USB ports, a mouse port, and a PS/2 style keyboard port. Figure 2.9 shows a standard set of connectors, and Figure 2.10 identifies each port in the cluster. Modern motherboards often have far more ports than this original setup, with typical complement consisting of something like four USB ports, an array of audio connectors, and a LAN (local area network) port. Figure 2.11 shows a typical cluster of ports, which includes no less than 17 sockets.

Integrated functions

In recent years there has been a definite trend towards motherboards having integrated functions such as sound and video. Since motherboards that have these features do not cost a great deal more than those that do not, they are an attractive proposition for those requiring a low cost PC. On the other hand, by using a motherboard of this type you might be "painting yourself into a corner". Sometimes any integrated functions can be switched off, but with some motherboards there is no way of disabling them. This could make it difficult or impossible to upgrade to superior sound or graphics should you wish to do so at some later time.

Sometimes the motherboard has no AGP or 16X PCI Express expansion slot, so there is no way of installing the latest AGP wonder video card even if the on-board graphics can be disabled. Also bear in mind that with many of these boards the main system memory is used by the on-board video and (or) sound circuits, so some extra memory has to be

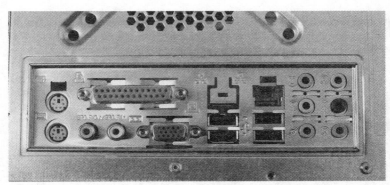

Fig.2.11 The range of ports provided by many ATX motherboards is substantial, with no less than 17 connectors in this example

fitted in order to compensate for this. This is perhaps less of an issue than it used to be, as some extra memory costs very little these days.

Of course, if you simply require a good low cost PC, and will never need highly sophisticated sound facilities or the latest high speed 3D graphics, one of these integrated motherboards probably represents the best choice. They certainly seem to be gaining in popularity, and even some of the more upmarket motherboards now have integrated sound and (or) graphics, albeit with the option of switching them off and using a sound or graphics card instead.

Case and PSU

Computer cases are mostly supplied complete with a power supply unit (PSU). There are four

Fig.2.12 Mini tower cases are small, but often have few drive bays

normal styles of case to choose from, and the most suitable style depends on the number of drive bays required and the space available for the finished PC. A mini tower case is usually the easiest to accommodate in your home or office (Figure 2.12), but there is often provision for just two 5.25-inch drives and three 3.5-inch drives. The one shown in Figure 2.12 does actually have three 5.25-inch drive bays. Two 5.25-inch bays

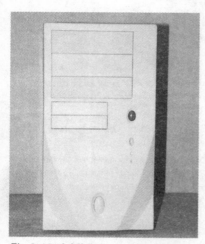

are sufficient for most purposes, since the majority of PCs have one 5.25-inch drive bay occupied by a DVD or CD-ROM drive, and two 3.5-inch drive bays taken up by the hard disc drive and a floppy disc drive. Even if a CD-ROM writer and a second hard disc drive are added, a mini tower will still have sufficient drive bays to accommodate them.

The main problem with mini tower cases for the do-it-yourself PC builder is that they can be difficult to deal with. With a great deal crammed into their limited dimensions it can be difficult to physically get everything reliably fitted into place and connected together. Some mini tower cases are actually quite easy to work on,

Fig.2.13 A Midi tower case is usually a good choice

while others are a constant pain to deal with. Also, some mini tower cases are easy to use with some motherboards, but with others it is difficult to gain access to the memory sockets, the connectors for the disc drive cables, and this type of thing.

Some of the larger motherboards are incompatible with very small cases such as mini tower types. They can accommodate the 5.25-inch drives or the memory modules, but not both. Another potential problem with small cases is that the power supply is often positioned over the processor. This can leave too little space for a tall heatsink and fan assembly. Especially when using a full-size motherboard, a larger case is a safer option.

A midi tower case (Figure 2.13) is slightly higher than the mini type, but a well designed case of this type has plenty of space for the components. A case of this type should have a minimum of three 5.25-inch and three

3.5-inch drive bays, and still has what is usually a less crowded interior than a mini tower case. The same is true of most desktop cases, but be slightly wary of some of the more compact desktop designs. These sometimes use unusual interior layouts that are not well suited to all motherboards. When building your own PC it is safest to opt for a conventional case

Fig.2.14 The 3.5-inch drive bays are often removable

that should take any standard PC components without difficulty.

The top of the range cases are the full-size towers, and one of these is the best choice if you will be installing a range of drives, or may wish to upgrade the PC by adding more drives in the future. Apart from having more drive bays, full-size tower cases are normally fitted with a slightly larger power supply that is well able to deal with extra drives. With a rating of around 300 watts an ordinary PC power supply should not be found wanting in this respect. However, with a PC that has more drives than usual it is as well to play safe and have a supply with a rating of around 450 watts. Physically the ATX supplies are a standard size and have standard mounting arrangements. There should be no difficulty in upgrading to a more powerful supply if the PC is eventually upgraded to the point where the original can no longer cope.

Most cases have some or all of the drive bays removable, which can make life much easier. The 3.5-inch bays are often well within the area of the case occupied by the motherboard, and to some extent the rear sections of the 3.5-inch drives will intrude over the top of the motherboard. Particularly with the smaller cases, it can be much easier to fit the motherboard if the 3.5-inch drive bays are temporarily removed from the case (Figure 2.14). It can also be easier to fit the drives into the loose bays first, and then fit this whole subassembly into the case. The bays are much more accessible when they are removed from the case. Only choose a case that does not have removable bays if you are sure that it is well designed and enables the motherboard and drives to be fitted reasonably easily.

Virtually all PC cases have provision for a cooling fan on the front panel (Figure 2.15) or the rear panel, or both, and these days many seem to be sold with at least one fan already fitted. Modern PCs generate significant amounts of heat, due to the large amounts of RAM used, complex processors that get very hot in operation, complex support chips on the motherboard that get hot, and so on. This tends to produce quite high operating temperatures inside the case, and can result in the over-temperature protection circuits on the motherboard coming into operation. This is most likely to occur on warm summer days when the air temperature inside the case is quite high even before the PC is switched on.

I would certainly recommend using a case that is fitted with a cooling fan, or adding a fan if it is not supplied as standard with the case. If you are building a fairly high specification PC it will probably be necessary to have front and rear fans fitted. The vast majority of cases take a standard 80 millimetre cooling fan. Whenever possible, obtain the fan complete with a set of fixing screws, or you may have to improvise in order to fix it on the case. If no other method of fixing can be found, a good adhesive will do the job well enough. Some cases are supplied with a plastic housing for the fan, and this simply clips into place on the case. Unfortunately, this method of fixing often allows the fan to vibrate and produce a fair amount of noise, so fixing bolts are preferred by many PC users.

Fig.2.15 A fan for the case is often an optional extra

Chipsets

When looking at the specifications for motherboards you will inevitably come across references to chipsets. These are the integrated circuits that provide various essential functions that are not included in the processor itself. In the original PCs these functions were provided by dozens of ordinary logic integrated circuits. Even though a modern PC requires much more help from the supporting electronics, there are normally just two or three support chips. Some low-cost motherboards have used a single support chip.

Over the years Intel has manufactured various chipsets to support the Pentium processors. However, other manufacturers make Pentium support chips. Similarly, AMD has produced support chips for its processors, but so have other chip manufacturers. In fact motherboards that use the genuine AMD support chips are probably a minority.

I suppose that using a motherboard having support chips made by AMD or Intel is the safe option, but the chip sets from other manufacturers have also proved to be reliable. Whether you opt for a board that uses Intel/AMD support chips or chips from another producer, it is advisable to select one that uses a modern chipset. There are usually plenty of bargain motherboards available, but most of these will not take modern processors. Unless the aim is to produce a budget PC with the specification being of little importance, choose a motherboard that is reasonably up to date.

Memory

Probably the most frequently asked of frequently asked PC questions is "how much RAM do I need." This is very much a "how long is a piece of string" style question, and it is entirely dependent on the applications software that you will be running. The software manuals should give details of the minimum requirements, but the minimum is the bare minimum needed to run the software at all. Most programs can run in a relatively small amount of RAM by using the hard disc for temporary storage space.

This usually works quite well, but gives noticeably slower results than when using RAM as the temporary data store. With complex graphics oriented programs the operating speed can be painfully slow unless the PC is equipped with large amounts of RAM. There will probably be a recommended minimum system to run the software, a typical system, or something of this type. I tend to regard the amount of RAM recommended for a typical system as the minimum that will really be usable in practice.

In the days of Windows 95, 98, and ME, most software would run using 32 megabytes of RAM, but even with these operating systems it was preferable to use upwards of 64 megabytes. The story is very different with Windows XP, where 128 megabytes represents a realistic minimum. At least 256 megabytes of memory is preferable, and I would install at least 512 megabytes in a PC that will run XP. With Windows Vista it is preferable to use a minimum of 512 megabytes, and I would not settle for less than one gigabyte. Some applications require large amounts of memory, and programs that handle photographic images or other large bitmaps are particularly demanding in this respect. Programs that handle video also require large amounts of memory, and probably hard disc space as well.

As an example, when handling large bitmap images in PhotoShop it is recommended that the amount of RAM in the PC should be at least double the size of the bitmap. In order to handle scanned bitmaps of around 25 to 30 megabytes at least 60 megabytes of RAM would therefore be required. With (say) four images of this size loaded into the program, the amount of RAM required would be about four times this figure, or some 240 megabytes. Bear in mind that this is in addition to the RAM required by PhotoShop itself, the operating system, and any other software that is running.

Bear in mind that large amounts of RAM can be needed in order to run several programs at once. In theory you do not need (say) 290 megabytes of RAM to multitask with two programs that require 120 and 170 megabytes of RAM. Somewhat less than 290 megabytes should suffice, because you are only running one copy of the operating system, and the two programs will share some resources. Practical experience would suggest that 290 megabytes would actually represent a realistic minimum in this situation, and with Windows XP or Vista it would probably be necessary to have substantially more than this.

Although memory has been very expensive in the past, it is currently quite cheap and putting large amounts of RAM into a PC is likely to be well worth the modest cost involved. Memory is like money, you know what, and hard disc space: you can never have too much of it. You do not hear people claiming that they have wasted money putting too much memory in their computers, but you do hear people expressing regret for not having specified more RAM when buying their PC.

SIMMs and DIMMs

The original PCs had memory in the form of memory chips mounted directly on the motherboard. Later PCs had the memory in the form of modules that fitted into holders on the motherboard, which made adding or removing the memory much quicker and easier. The original memory modules are called SIMMs (single in-line memory modules). A memory module of this type is a small printed circuit board, which is fitted with miniature DRAM chips of the surface-mount variety. The socket on the motherboard is like a sort of miniature version of the standard expansion slot system. The original SIMMs have 30 so-called pins, but there are no actual pins, and the connections to the device are via copper pads. The 30-pin SIMMs were superseded by the 72-pin type, but both types are now largely obsolete.

SIMMs were replaced by DIMMs (dual in-line memory modules), which look like outsize SIMMs. The original type of DIMM has 168 terminals (Figure 2.16). These DIMMs were produced in versions offering three different speeds, and these are normally referred to as "PC66", "PC100" and "PC133" DIMMs. The PC66 DIMMs are suitable for use in motherboards that operate at 66MHz, whereas the PC100 and PC133 DIMMs are suitable for bus speeds of up to 100MHz and 133MHz respectively.

It should perhaps be explained here that processor technology has consistently moved some way ahead of memory technology, resulting in the necessity to run the main system memory and the processor at different clock rates. This operates on the basis of having the processor operate at so many times the clock frequency of the motherboard. Particularly when an up-to-date processor is matched with older memory technology, the difference between the two operating frequencies can be massive. An Athlon XP 2000+ processor actually operates at 1.67GHz, which is still some 12.5 times faster than 133MHz memory modules. More modern memory modules can operate at higher frequencies, but still lag the fastest processors by a considerable margin. This is clearly far from ideal, but it is the best solution that the current technology can provide.

DDR memory

Unless you buy an old "bargain basement" motherboard it will not use ordinary DIMMs. Even with an old motherboard it is likely to have this type of memory as an alternative to the more recent DDR (double data rate) memory rather than as the only option. Since older forms of memory tend to cost more than the current types, there is probably no point in using the older types of DIMM.

The "double" part of the DDR name refers to the fact that the memory operates at twice the clock frequency of the motherboard. Clock

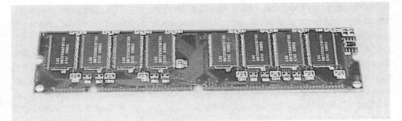

Fig.2.16 A 168-pin PC133 DIMM

frequencies of 200 megahertz and 266 megahertz are used with the original versions of DDR memory, and these respectively use motherboard bus frequencies of 100 and 133 megahertz. I think it is fair to say that DDR memory did not give the sort of speed increase that many had hoped for, but it did give a significant improvement. When the price of DDR memory became comparable to the PC100 and PC133 varieties it was inevitable that it would gradually take over.

DDR memory is sold in the form of 184-pin DIMMs (Figure 2.17). From the physical point of view a DDR DIMM is essentially just a slightly scaled-up version of the 168-pin components. The 200 and 233 megahertz DDR modules are sometimes sold as such, but they are more usually called PC1600 and PC2100 modules respectively. The number in each case refers to the bandwidth in megabits per second. The PC1600 modules seem to be relatively difficult to obtain these days, but the faster PC2100 type can be used instead.

Things moved on, with faster (PC2700, PC3200, and PC3500) DDR modules being produced. The PC2700 modules are for use at 333 megahertz, while the PC3200 and PC3500 modules are for operation at 400 megahertz and 433 megahertz respectively. Of course, these are the operating frequencies for the memory modules, and in standard DDR fashion the motherboards operate at half these frequencies.

With DDR memory, and possibly with other types, you may encounter a rating such as "CL3" or "CL2.5". This refers to a memory timing parameter in the BIOS Setup program, where it is usually called something like CAS Latency. A low figure here gives higher performance, but there is no guarantee that "bog standard" memory modules will work reliably with so-called "aggressive" memory timing. If you wish to push the system to its limits it is essential to obtain modules that are guaranteed to operate with a low CAS Latency setting.

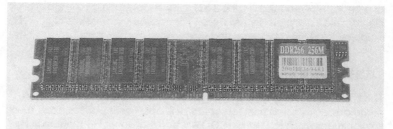

Fig.2.17 A 184-pin DIMM that has 266MHz DDR memory

While DDR memory is not yet obsolete, it is not the best that is currently available. Many motherboards are now designed to use an improved version called DDR2. DDR2 modules look very much like the ordinary DDR variety (Figure 2.18), but they are somewhat larger and have 240 terminals. This type of memory is available in various speeds up to about PC6400 (800 megahertz). Fitting DDR2 modules is much the same as fitting the DDR type. DDR2 memory modules are physically incompatible with ordinary DDR sockets, and there is no danger of fitting the wrong type of module to a motherboard. On the other hand, you obviously have to make sure that you order the right type for the particular motherboard you are using.

For the ultimate in performance you need DDR3 memory, but at the time of writing this it is not yet in widespread use. The DDR3 specification covers speeds from 800 to 1600 megahertz, so it carries on where DDR2 left off, and there are also improvements to the overall design. These two types of memory are totally incompatible. Although DDR3 memory

Fig.2.18 A DDR2 module has obvious similarities with a DDR type

is in the form of modules having 240 terminals, physically they are slightly different to DDR2 memory modules. This makes it impossible to fit DDR2 modules into DDR3 holders, and vice versa.

Other types

The types of memory detailed previously are the ones that have been in common use over the past few years. It is only fair to point out that there are variations such as 200-pin SODIMS and that some PC manufacturers have gone their own way with so-called proprietary memory. The memory chips on these modules are much the same as those on equivalent types of standard memory, but the modules are physically different to the standard types. Provided you build a PC using a standard motherboard from one of the large manufacturers it should only be necessary to use mainstream memory modules.

I would strongly recommend studying the manual for the motherboard before buying the memory. The manual should make clear which type or types of memory can be used, the maximum amount of memory that can be fitted, and anything else that you need to know. As pointed out previously, many motherboard manufacturers have the manuals freely available for download on their web sites, and it is well worthwhile downloading and reading the manual for any motherboard that you are thinking of buying. You can then see whether or not it is likely to suit your requirements before parting with any money. It is also worthwhile checking through the "fine print" to see if there are any shortcomings that the advertisements for the motherboards have conveniently forgotten to tell you!

Keyboard and mouse

The choice of keyboard and mouse is a personal one, but make sure that you obtain a keyboard that matches the motherboard. AT motherboards are equipped with a 5-way DIN keyboard connector, but the ATX boards have the smaller PS/2 style connector (Figure 2.19). There are still some keyboards on sale that are primarily intended for use as replacements for old PCs, and therefore have the AT style DIN connector. If you are using an ATX motherboard make sure that the keyboard you obtain has a PS/2 connector. Some keyboards have both types of connector, or an adaptor that enables them to operate with either type of motherboard. In either case the keyboard is obviously usable with AT or ATX motherboards. Keyboards that use a USB port are also

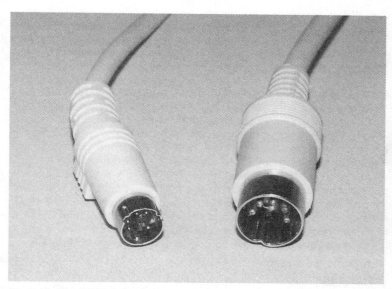

Fig.2.19 The PS/2 (left) and 5-way DIN (right) keyboard plugs

available. Depending on the number of USB ports available on the PC, there could be an advantage in using a PS/2 keyboard so that you are not blocking a USB port that might be needed for other purposes.

Modern computer rodents are for use with either a USB port or a PS/2 mouse port. Mice that use serial ports are now obsolete and should be avoided. If you have a serial mouse that you would like to use with your newly constructed PC, make sure that you obtain a motherboard that does actually have a serial port! It will not usually matter whether you use a USB or PS/2 type. As with a keyboard, I suppose that there is a potential advantage in using the PS/2 mouse port because this avoids occupying one of the USB ports and leaves the greatest possible scope for expansion.

At one time the mouse port variety had something of a reputation for causing hardware conflicts, but this mainly occurred where a mouse port mouse was used as a replacement for a serial mouse. This would sometimes cause problems with the mouse refusing to work properly. If the mouse was finally installed properly, sometimes another device such as a modem would refuse to work. Problems such as this are relatively rare these days, and do not normally occur anyway if a mouse port mouse is used from the outset.

Floppy disc

In these days of huge data files, software distribution via CD-ROMs, and mass storage devices such as DVD writers and CD writers, the humble floppy disc drive is rather less important than it once was. With Windows XP and Vista it is not normally necessary to have a floppy disc drive in order to install the operating system. Even so, many users still have numerous floppy discs packed with data, and therefore need a floppy disc drive in order to read these discs. The BIOS on most motherboards can handle any of the standard types of PC floppy disc drive. However, the chances of obtaining anything other than an ordinary 3.5-inch 1.44MB drive are slim. With other types of floppy disc drive it might be possible to obtain a working unit from an old PC. A motherboard only has one floppy drive interface, but this can be used with one or two drives.

CD-ROM

A CD-ROM drive used to be an optional extra, but these days it is an essential part of a PC. It is not possible to install Windows XP, or most other operating systems, without a drive that can read an ordinary CD-ROM. A DVD drive is needed in order to install Windows Vista. Most application software is supplied on a CD-ROM or DVD. Anyway, the cost of CD-ROM and DVD drives is now so low that there would be little point in not including one. The cheapest and easiest type to deal with are the drives which have a standard IDE interface, or ATAPI interface as it is often called in this context. These days there are few (if any) internal CD-ROM drives that use any other type of interface.

The IDE/ATAPI interface is the same type that is used for many hard disc drives, and most modern motherboards have at least two IDE interfaces. Each of these can handle up to two drives, making it possible to have a maximum of four drives. If you require something like two hard drives, a CD-ROM drive, and a CD-ROM writer, this set-up can be accommodated by the motherboard's built-in IDE interfaces. Note that internal CD-RW, DVD-ROM, and DVD writers also use an IDE/ATAPI interface. They are installed and set up in the same way as ordinary CD-ROM drives, but some additional software is then installed to enable the drive to burn CDs, play DVD movies, or whatever.

Hard drives

As pointed out previously, most hard disc drives have an IDE interface that enables them to be connected direct to the motherboard. Hard and floppy disc controller cards are not needed with modern PCs. As the disc capacities have increased over the years it has been necessary for the operating systems and BIOS programs to be altered in an attempt to keep up with things. How well or otherwise large discs are handled depends on the operating system you are using and the motherboard.

Assuming you are not building new PCs using very old surplus or second hand components there should be no major difficulty in using high capacity drives. Where necessary, very large drives are usually supplied complete with any utility software needed to fully exploit their capacity. In fact hard drives are often supplied complete with quite a range of software designed to make it easy to install them in a new system or as an upgrade in an existing computer.

Drive modes

The IDE interface has received various updates over the years, but it has full compatibility with older drives. Any IDE hard disc drive should therefore work perfectly well with any modern motherboard. When dealing with IDE interfaces and hard drives, etc., you will inevitably come across references to the various IDE operating modes. In most instances you do not have to bother too much about these modes, and you can simply let the system "do its own thing". The BIOS program should correctly determine and use the right mode for any device connected to it. However, it is worth taking a quick look at the various modes and the ways in which they differ.

PIO mode

A PIO (programmed input/output) mode is where the processor has direct control of the hard disc via one of the support chips on the motherboard. In order to place data on the disc or read it from the disc the processor must issue the appropriate commands to transfer the data between the disc and the computer's memory.

Master mode

In a master mode the microprocessor is not in direct control of the hard disc, but instead this task is handed over to one of the support chips. Obviously the processor still has to issue commands to the chipset so that it knows which data to access and where to place it, but the processor has little involvement beyond that. A Master mode is not inherently any quicker at transferring data than a PIO mode. However, it places less of a burden on the processor and can therefore provide a boost in performance in other respects.

DMA

This is direct memory access, and any mode where the chipset moves data between the disc and memory independently of the processor makes use of DMA.

There are five PIO modes numbered from 0 to 4 and the higher the number, the greater the maximum data transfer rate possible. There are three DMA modes numbered from 0 to 2, and again, the higher the mode number the faster the maximum transfer rate. These are the maximum rates for the four PIO modes and three DMA modes, but not all hard discs and PCs are necessarily capable of providing these rates. Also, not all drives can use the faster modes.

PIO Mode 0   3.3MB per second

PIO Mode 1   5.2MB per second

PIO Mode 2   8.3MB per second

PIO Mode 3   11.1MB per second

PIO Mode 4   16.6MB per second

DMA Mode 0   4.16MB per second

DMA Mode 1   13.3MB per second

DMA Mode 2   16.6MB per second

Any reasonably modern hard disc drive should be able to support the faster transfer modes, but other IDE devices such as CD-ROM drives and other interchangeable disc systems may not. Bear in mind that there is no point in using a fast transfer mode with a device that can only accept or supply data at relatively low rates.

UDMA33 to 133

All modern IDE hard disc drives support UDMA33 and some of the more advanced DMA modes (UDMA66/100/133). These are developments that can only be implemented if the IDE interface on the motherboard and the hard drive both support them. They also need support from the

Fig.2.20 These two IDE data cables look similar, but the one on the right has 80 wires and is suitable for UDMA66 and faster drives. The one on the left has 40 wires

operating system, and motherboards are usually supplied complete with drivers for various versions of Windows. As the names suggest, these modes provide transfer rates of up to 33, 66, 100, and 133 megabytes per second. UDMA33 uses the same connectors and cables as a standard IDE interface, but the UDMA66/100/133 interfaces require a different cable. The two types of cable actually look much the same (Figure 2.20), but the original type has 40 connecting wires whereas the new cables have 80.

It is possible to use one of the faster drives with a standard IDE cable, but it will only operate as a UDMA33 device. A UDMA33 or earlier device will work using an 80-way IDE cable, but obviously it will not work in one of the faster modes. The faster IDE interfaces adjust to suit the slowest device on the interface, which means that it is not a good idea to use a fast hard disc drive on the same IDE interface as a slower drive such as a CD-ROM or DVD type. This would result in the fast hard disc drive operating in one of the slower modes.

It is therefore advisable to have the hard disc as the sole drive on the primary IDE interface, and to use an 80-way data cable. This will enable

Fig.2.21 A group of four serial ATA ports on a motherboard. A serial ATA port can only be used with a single drive.

the drive to operate in the fastest mode that is supported by both the drive and the motherboard. The CD-ROM drive or drives should be used on the secondary IDE interface. CD-ROM drives do not usually have anything beyond a UDMA33 interface, so 40 and 80-way IDE cables are both suitable. If a second hard disc drive is fitted, this should be used as the slave device on the primary IDE interface. Note though, that this could result in the main hard drive operating below maximum speed if the second hard disc drive is an older type that has a slower version of the IDE interface.

SCSI

Some up-market hard disc drives and even some CD-ROM drives do not use any form of IDE interface, but instead use a SCSI type. SCSI stands for "small computer systems interface" and is generally pronounced something like "scuzzy". This is really a general-purpose

Fig.2.22 The serial ATA ports on the left are much smaller than the IDE and floppy ports on the right

computer interface that can be used with a wide range of internal and external peripherals such as scanners and scientific instruments. It is used with the more expensive drives to provide faster data transfers, but with improvements in the IDE interface over the years SCSI drives perhaps have rather less of an advantage than they once did. If the ultimate in performance is essential, such as for a network server, a SCSI drive might still be the best choice.

However, SCSI drives are not as straightforward to use as the IDE variety. Using a SCSI device has never been particularly easy, and matters have become more complicated over the years as new versions of this interface have evolved. Using a SCSI hard disc drive is certainly not something that could be recommended to first-time PC builders. Using a SCSI drive is not as difficult as it was in days gone by, where it was often necessary to use another drive to boot-up the system, and then use the SCSI drive as the main one once the operating system was set up successfully to recognise it.

Motherboard and operating system support for SCSI devices is now much improved, but this interface seems to be relatively little used these days. At one time there were a number of upmarket motherboards that had a built-in SCSI interface, but SCSI seems to have been dropped in favour of other interfaces such as Firewire. With the low cost of high performance drives that use other types of interface, there is probably no point in using SCSI drives any more. It would probably be an exaggeration to say that SCSI is completely obsolete, but it certainly seems to be heading in that direction.

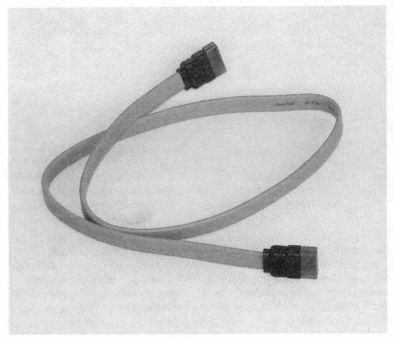

Fig.2.23 A serial ATA cable. It is much thinner and more flexible than an IDE cable

Serial ATA

Practically all new motherboard designs now include a relatively new type of disc interface called Serial ATA. This is essentially a serial version of the standard IDE disc interface, but with a maximum speed of 150 megabytes per second. It is sometimes referred to as an ATA 150 interface. Clearly a serial ATA interface is not much faster than a UDMA 133 IDE interface, and many real-world hard disc drives do not really utilize the speed available from either type of interface. There is also an improved serial ATA interface, which is called serial ATA 2. It can accommodate a maximum stransfer rate of 300 megabytes per second, and is backwards compatible with standard ATA devices.

The real advantage of a serial ATA interface is that the cabling is much easier to deal with. Far fewer connecting wires are needed with a serial interface, and this is reflected in the size of the connectors on the

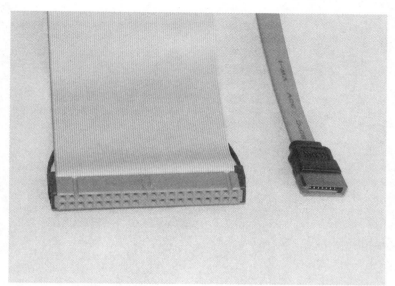

Fig.2.24 An IDE cable on the left and a serial ATA type on the right

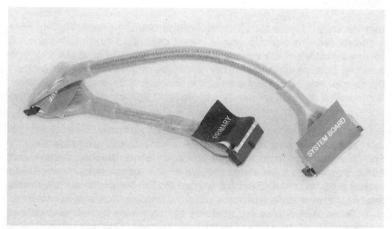

Fig.2.25 It is possible to obtain round IDE cables, but they are larger and less flexible than serial ATA cables

Fig.2.26 A 3.5-inch drive fitted in a 5.25-inch chassis

motherboard. Figure 2.21 shows a group of four serial ATA ports on a motherboard. In order to give a sense of scale, Figure 2.22 shows a zoomed-out view that includes a floppy disc port and a UDMA 133 type near the bottom left-hand corner. Perhaps of greater importance than the smaller size of the connectors, the serial cables can be much thinner. A serial ATA data cable is shown in Figure 2.23, and Figure 2.24 shows both types of cable.

A slight problem with the wide ribbon cables normally used for parallel disc interfaces is that they tend to hinder the flow of air inside the PC. This in turn tends to reduce the efficiency of the cooling system and raises the temperature inside the case. It is possible to obtain round versions of parallel IDE cables (Figure 2.25), but these are even less flexible than the type that uses ribbon cable, and can be awkward to use. Serial ATA cables are relatively flexible, easy to use, and do not significantly hinder the flow of air through the case. One relative weakness of the serial ATA approach is that each port can only be used with one drive, whereas each IDE port can be used with two drives.

Fig.2.27 An external Compact Flash card reader that connects to the
        PC via a USB 2.0 port

Other drives

At one time is was not uncommon for PCs to have some form of
interchangeable mass storage device such as a Zip drive or LS120 drive.
These were mainly IDE devices, but some used SCSI or USB ports. In
general, the IDE versions of these devices are handled much like a hard
disc or a CD-ROM drive, and for LS120 and Zip drives there is often
specific support available from the BIOS. In some cases it might even
be possible to boot from one of these drives. Where necessary any
driver software for operation with Windows should be included with the
drive. The popularity of CD and DVD drives has seen a steady decline in
these other types of mass storage drive. If you have data on Zip discs
(or whatever) it might be possible to obtain and install a matching drive.
However, in most cases finding a suitable drive could be difficult or
impossible. If no suitable IDE drive can be obtained, an external USB
version might be available. An external drive is likely to be the easiest
solution even if an IDE version is available.

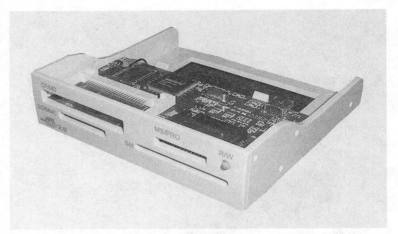

Fig.2.28 A reader for various types of memory card that fits into a 3.5-inch drive bay

There have been problems in the past with interchangeable disc drives that the operating system considered to be fixed drives. The practical consequence of this was that the only way to get the system to use a changed disc was to reboot! Provided you use an up-to-date operating system and motherboard this sort of problem should not occur.

There is a potential problem with drives that require 3.5-inch drive bays. This is simply that many cases have only one 3.5-inch bay with external access. With a 3.5-inch floppy disc drive already installed in this bay there is nowhere for a Zip, LS120, or similar drive to go. The usual solution is to mount the drive in an adaptor that enables it to fit into a 5.25-inch drive bay (Figure 2.26). Most cases have at least three 5.25-inch drive bays with external access, so there should be no problem in accommodating the drive once it is fitted in an adaptor.

Flash memory

CD and DVD drives provide mass storage, but they do not really provide the same sort of convenience associated with floppy discs. Although they have many good points, they are a bit cumbersome in some respects. Flash memory remains relatively expensive, but it does provide the sort of convenience associated with floppy discs, and high capacities

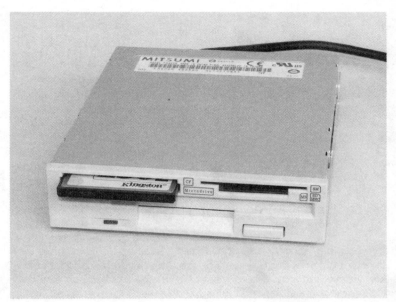

Fig.2.29 A combined card reader and 3.5-inch floppy disc drive

are now a practical proposition. You can rapidly copy data from a PC onto a flash card, and then take the memory card to a PC at another location and copy the data onto that PC. Flash cards are also used in cameras and various portable computing devices, and in many cases it is possible to read cards from these devices into a PC. The data on the card can be quickly and easily erased when it is no longer needed.

Of course, some form of card reader is needed in order to use Flash cards with a PC. It is not essential to have a built-in card reader, and there are plenty of good external readers that connect to the PC via a USB or Firewire port. The unit shown in Figure 2.27 is a high-speed reader for Compact Flash cards that connects to a USB port. The card reader shown in Figure 2.28 is for use with seven different types of media and also connects to a USB 2.0 port. However, it is designed to fit into an externally accessible 3.5-inch drive bay, and to connect to an internal USB 2.0 port.

The card reader shown in Figure 2.29 takes things a step further. It also takes a variety of Flash memory cards, fits into a 3.5-inch drive bay, and

Fig.2.30 AGP (top) and PCI (bottom) connectors are totally incompatible

connects to an internal USB port. It also contains a 3.5-inch floppy disc drive though, enabling a single 3.5-inch drive bay to be used for both a floppy drive and a multi-card reader. It has the usual floppy disc data and power connectors, and the floppy drive section is used just like an ordinary 3.5-inch floppy disc drive. Internal card readers are not particularly expensive and help to keep the number of external leads within reason. If you use Flash memory with your PC, it is definitely worth considering one of these gadgets.

Video cards

One of the great strengths of PCs has always been that the video circuits are not built onto the main circuit board. This gives manufacturers the freedom to produce ever bigger and better video cards and the consumer the freedom to choose the most suitable card. You do not have to spend a large amount of money on the latest super-fast 3D graphics card if all you require is a simple 2D type. Neither are you restricted to simple 2D graphics when you really need advanced 3D capabilities. The video card you choose will obviously depend on the money available and the type of software you will be running.

You may have the choice of a PCI, PCI Express, or AGP version of the selected video card. The original PC expansion slots used the ISA (industry standard architecture) interface. This was more or less the raw processor buses with some added wait states when an expansion card was accessed. These wait states were needed to slow things down so that the slower expansion cards could keep up. ISA expansion slots went through a certain amount of development, but are now obsolete and have largely been phased out. These days, new motherboards are not equipped with any ISA expansion slots.

As PC technology advanced, the ISA slots proved to be too slow. They also made it awkward to implement new ideas such as "plug-and-play", and made it difficult to accommodate large numbers of expansion cards without hardware conflicts occurring. Eventually the PCI standard was adopted, and this removes many of the restrictions associated with ISA expansion cards. PCI cards use a different connector, and the port itself is totally incompatible with ISA cards anyway. A PCI slot is really a form of input/output port, and it does not operate direct onto the processor's buses like an ISA slot.

AGP

While PCI slots are more than adequate for many purposes, they can limit performance when large amounts of data must be transferred. In practice this mainly means when a video card is producing rapidly changing graphics. Hence the development of AGP slots for video cards. With "run of the mill" 2D video cards there is probably little advantage in using an AGP interface, but for high performance 3D cards there is a substantial gain in performance. Note that PCI and AGP cards are physically incompatible (Figure 2.30), and electrically incompatible as well. An AGP video card is only usable with a modern motherboard that has an AGP expansion slot.

When building a new PC it makes sense to opt for the more up-to-date AGP version of a video card when both types of card are on offer. These days there are very few PCI video cards available, so there will probably be no choice anyway. The PCI video cards that are available are old designs that are intended to be used as upgrades or spares for ageing PCs. They are not really intended for use in new PCs.

There are now faster versions of the AGP interface, and these are the 2x, 4x, and 8x varieties. As the names suggest, these operate at two, four, and eight times faster rates than the original AGP bus. The original specification permits data to be transferred at up to 264 megabytes per second, which is twice the rate provided by the PCI bus. The faster versions offer correspondingly higher transfer rates, with the 4x AGP bus providing transfer rates of up to 1066 megabytes per second for example.

Do not assume that a motherboard having (say) an 8x AGP slot will accommodate slower video cards. For example, some motherboards lack support for 2x AGP cards, which operate at a higher voltage than the faster types. In fact some motherboards have a sticker on the AGP slot warning of dire consequences if it is used with some 2x AGP cards. It is advisable to read the relevant section of the motherboard's instruction manual to determine the AGP compatibility before buying the video card. Also check the modes supported by prospective AGP cards before parting with any money. Few suppliers will give full refunds on components that were bought by mistake.

Of course, some motherboards have integrated graphics adapters, and these are perfectly adequate where the ultimate in 3D graphics is not required. Integrated graphics probably offers the most cost effective method when only 2D graphics is required. Some of these motherboards have an AGP slot and permit the built-it video circuits to be switched off. Any compatible video card can then be used in the AGP slot in the usual way. In some cases there is no way of switching off the built-in graphics adapter, and no AGP slot for a video card. This gives some saving in cost, but clearly gives no upgrade path if a more advanced graphics adapter is needed at some future date.

PCI Express is designed to take video cards to a higher level of performance than can be achieved using AGP slots. 16X PCI Express slots have now largely ousted the AGP type. Motherboards that include an AGP slot are likely to be old designs, but should be suitable if the ultimate in graphics performance is not of great importance to you. However, integrated graphics could well provide a similar level of performance at lower cost. The latest PCI Express graphics wonder card will probably be required if super-fast video performance is of paramount importance.

Monitor

In the past there were various colour and monochrome display cards that required different types of monitor. These old standards such as the MDA and CGA varieties are now obsolete, and the majority of modern PC monitors are incompatible with some or all of these old standards. Modern PC monitors are multi-standard types that can be used in the standard 640 by 480 pixel VGA mode, plus various super-VGA modes. The number of additional modes available varies from monitor to monitor, but resolutions up to at least 1024 by 768 pixels should be available. Larger monitors should be able to accommodate higher resolutions.

The higher resolution modes such as 1280 by 1024 and 1600 x 1200 pixels are not usually available on 14-inch and 15-inch monitors, although few (if any) conventional monitors of these sizes are produced. Even if these modes were available, they would be unusable. With the Windows "big fonts" selected, menus, etc., would still be displayed too small to be really usable. In fact most PC monitors are barely usable in their highest resolution mode for this reason. As 17-inch and 19-inch monitors of reasonable quality are now available at low prices there is little point in opting for anything smaller.

For each of the supported resolutions a monitor has a maximum refresh rate. This is simply the maximum number of complete scans of the screen that can be produced in one second. This is an important factor with a conventional monitor, because a low scan rate will produce a display that flickers quite noticeably. A display of this type is not unusable, but most users find them unpleasant to use for long periods. The minimum acceptable scan rate is a matter of opinion, but anything from about 70Hz upwards should be perfectly usable. I am reasonably happy with a 65Hz refresh rate, but at anything much less than 65Hz the picture flicker becomes very noticeable indeed.

With CRT monitors the claimed size of the screen is something that is sometimes a bit over optimistic. Thankfully, some of the practices used in the past to inflate monitor sizes in specification sheets have now largely died out. If you buy a 17-inch monitor you should not find that the diagonal measurement of the picture is actually about 14 inches. On the other hand, it will not be 17 inches either. Because the picture tube has rounded corners the usable picture size is somewhat less than the notional size. Some monitors give a larger display than others of the same specified size, but in general the actual diagonal measurement is about an inch or so less than the stated screen size.

Flat-panel screens have become very popular in recent years, and they have the advantage of being relatively light and easy to accommodate on the average desktop. They also use less power and therefore have lower running costs. Unlike a conventional monitor based on a CRT, the geometry is perfect, with no curvature near the edges of the screen. They also have "square" corners, so a 17 inch flat-panel screen should have an actual diagonal measurement of 17 inches. The size of a 17 inch flat-panel screen is therefore about half-way between conventional 17 and 19 inch screens.

Despite the advantages of flat-panel screens, some users still prefer the colour accuracy and brightness of a conventional monitor. Conventional screens remain popular with those involved in photo-editing, but in the

Fig.2.31 *Many conventional monitors have the option of using five BNC connectors to make the connections to the PC. This method of connection is little used in practice*

end it is all just a matter of personal preference. Note that most flat-panel monitors can be used with a normal 15-pin video output, and some can only be used with this type of video output. Many now have a digital input, usually in addition to an analogue type. Where possible, a flat-panel monitor should be driven from a digital video output.

Screen adjustments

These days virtually all conventional monitors allow the horizontal and vertical sizes of the display to be adjusted so that it can be made to fill the screen. There should also be controls to enable the display to be accurately centred on the screen. Although you might expect two display cards operating in the same mode to position the display in more or less the same position on the screen, there can actually be quite large differences. Of more importance, the display can shift significantly when switching from one screen mode to another and it can also expand or shrink.

To avoid the need to readjust the controls each time the screen mode is altered, most monitors remember the control settings for each screen mode, and automatically switch to the appropriate settings when the mode is changed. Some video adaptors are supplied with a utility that enables the card to be adjusted to suit the monitor for each screen mode. Again, the appropriate settings are used when the screen mode is changed, making it unnecessary to make any manual adjustments. Conventional monitors normally have at least one or two controls that can be adjusted to minimise various forms of distortion, and in the case of larger monitors there are often several controls of this type. This type of thing is unnecessary with flat-panel monitors.

Connections

Most monitors have so-called captive video cables. In other words, the video cable is permanently connected to the monitor and does not unplug at the monitor end. One slight drawback of this system is that the whole monitor has to be returned for servicing if the video cable becomes damaged. The chances of this happening are probably quite low though. Actually connecting the monitor to the video card should present no problems if the monitor has the standard 15-way "D" style connector. Any video card should have a connector of this type. The original PC monitors used a nine-way connector, but this became obsolete many years ago.

The more upmarket CRT monitors often have five BNC connectors (Figure 2.31) that offer an alternative method of connection to the PC, but these days it is unlikely that your selected video card will have BNC outputs. The BNC sockets are probably included more as a means of showing that the monitor is an upmarket type and impressing potential buyers, than as a likely means of connecting the monitor to a PC. PC monitors are normally supplied with a suitable video cable, but if in doubt check this point before ordering.

If the monitor can use a digital input signal it will almost certainly have a DVI port or a captive lead fitted with a DVI connector. It is probably best to avoid digital monitors that can not connect to the PC via a DVI port. These days most video cards have a standard 15-pin video output and a DVI type (Figure 2.32). There is often an additional connector, such as an output socket for use with a television set. Motherboards with integrated video circuits usually lack a DVI output and only have the standard 15-pin video output socket. Therefore, it will probably be necessary to use a separate graphics card in order to use one of these with the digital input of a monitor. Note that a DVI connector can handle two types of digital signal and an analogue picture signal. Consequently, there are various types of DVI lead available. The monitor should be

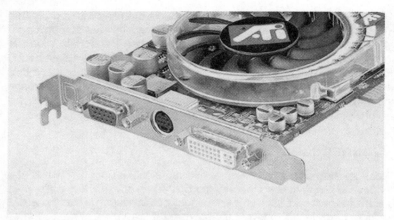

*Fig.2.32 This ATI graphics card has an ordinary 15-pin output (left) and
           a DVI output socket (right)*

supplied complete with a lead that is suitable for use with the digital DVI
output of a PC graphics card.

In the past there were two ways of powering the monitor. It could be
powered from the mains outlet on the PC's power supply unit or direct
from an ordinary mains socket. These days the power lead supplied
with the monitor will be a standard mains lead that enables the monitor
to be powered from an ordinary 13-amp mains socket. Even if the PC
has a mains outlet, which is unlikely, it is best to use the ordinary mains
lead and plug supplied with the monitor. The monitor will automatically
go into standby mode when the PC is switched off or the power
management facility comes into operation.

Soundcards

PCs have a built-in loudspeaker, but this is driven by some very basic
hardware that is really intended to do nothing more than produce a few
simple "beep" sounds. For anything more than this a proper soundcard
and a pair of active speakers is needed. In other words, speakers that
have built-in power amplifiers. Most soundcards do actually have built-
in amplifiers, but they only provide low output powers and generally
provide quite modest volume levels when used with passive speakers
(i.e. speakers that do not have built-in amplifiers).

The simplest soundcards only offer synthesised sounds, almost invariably produced using FM (frequency modulation) synthesis. FM synthesis gives adequate sound quality for many purposes, but more advanced methods such as wavetable synthesis are better for music making. Wavetable synthesis uses standard analogue synthesis techniques, but the basic sounds are short bursts of recorded instrument sounds rather than simple waveforms from oscillator circuits. Much more realistic results are produced using this method, although all wavetable soundcards seem to produce variable results. Another method of synthesis uses large amounts of processing power to mathematically model and mimic an acoustic instrument.

When dealing with soundcards you are likely to encounter frequent references to software and hardware wavetable synthesis. The hardware variety uses sound samples that are stored in a ROM on the soundcard, whereas software wavetable synthesis uses samples that are loaded from disc into the computer's main memory. Obviously the software type takes up some of the main memory, and less obviously it usually requires the processor to do more of the work.

With any type of synthesis there are usually a few hundred different sounds available, and I suppose it is inevitable that some will sound more convincing than others. Modern soundcards can typically produce 32 or 64 different sounds at once, or in some cases much more than this. They are capable of reproducing quite complex music sequences, and in most cases sound reasonably convincing. Even the cheapest cards have the ability to record and play back in high quality stereo, and to play back pre-recorded sound samples (WAV files).

Since modern PCs tend to have plenty of memory and processing power this is less important than was once the case. Software wavetable synthesis has the advantage that it is possible to add or change sounds quite easily. This is normally only possible with hardware wavetable soundcards if they have some added memory, effectively making them a form of software wavetable card. Some soundcards offer the best of both worlds by having a mixture of software and hardware wavetable sounds. These can usually provide a huge range of sounds operating on a large number of channels.

Some of the more upmarket soundcards, and particularly those aimed at music making using a PC, have too many connectors to fit onto the rear of the card. One way around this problem is to have the "orphan" connectors mounted on a bracket that fits in place behind an unused expansion slot. This bracket has leads that connect to sockets on the soundcard. With some cards this method is taken a stage further, and

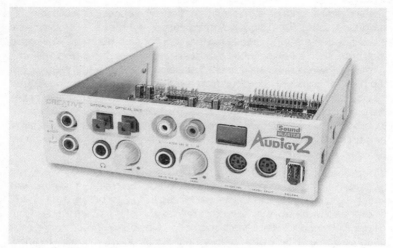

Fig.2.33 Many upmarket audio cards use controls and sockets mounted in a spare drive bay

the "orphan" sockets are mounted on a sort of dummy drive that fits into a spare drive bay (Figure 2.33). This system has the advantage of situating the sockets at the front of the computer where they are easily accessed. However, it is only practical if there is a spare drive bay of the appropriate size, and it is externally accessible. In addition to some extra sockets there will usually be duplicates of the sockets on the soundcard and probably some controls as well.

In theory the hardware wavetable and simple FM synthesiser cards should be the easiest to install and use. In practice the software wavetable cards have drivers that largely hide the differences between the two types of card. Soundcards in general have a reputation for being awkward to install, and likely to uninstall themselves given half a chance. Certainly in my experience the most likely troublesome component in a newly constructed PC is the soundcard. Fortunately, the current PCI soundcards seem rather better than the old ISA variety.

A substantial percentage of current motherboards have a built-in sound generator. This can usually be switched off so that a soundcard can be added into a PCI slot, but the built-in sound generators are adequate for most needs. Actually, some motherboards have quite advanced integral sound circuits having facilities that will satisfy all but the most demanding users.

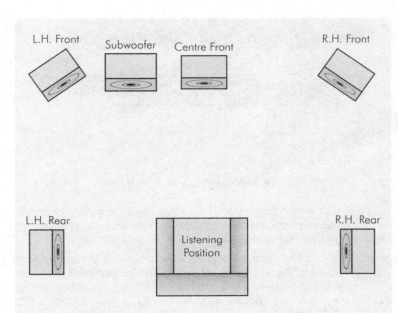

Fig.2.34 The normal arrangement used for the loudspeakers in a 5.1 surround sound system

It is increasingly common for integrated sound systems to offer some form of surround sound system. These are often referred to as something like a "5.1" system, and this means that the system uses five ordinary loudspeakers, and a subwoofer that is deigned to handle very low frequencies. A 5.1 surround sound system is designed to be used in a setup like the one shown in Figure 2.34. Note though, that you do not have to use all the speakers. The normal stereo setup with two speakers can be used if the surround sound effect is not required. Unless you genuinely need the facilities of a top-notch soundcard, integrated audio is the easiest and best option.

Joystick and MIDI

In addition to three or four audio input and output sockets, soundcards sometimes have a 15-way connector that is a combined MIDI port and game port (Figure 2.35). When used as a game port it takes standard PC joysticks and similar devices. Most new games controllers connect

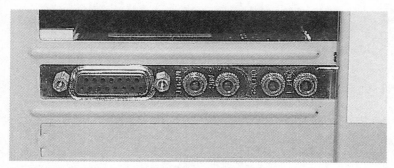

Fig.2.35 Soundcards normally have a joystick/MIDI port

to a USB port, so the game port is now little used in this role. For this reason the game port is not often included on modern sound cards, and it is unlikely to be found on the latest cards or upmarket cards.

When used as a MIDI port it enables music programs to operate with MIDI synthesisers, keyboards, sound modules, etc. However, note that standard MIDI cables have 5-way (180 degree) DIN plugs at both ends, and are therefore incompatible with the 15-way D connector of a PC soundcard. A special MIDI cable is needed to connect a PC soundcard to MIDI devices. Actually, it is rather more than a cable, and it includes a small amount of electronics. It is consequently more expensive than most other PC cables. Normal MIDI ports are normally included on expensive soundcards intended for musicians. These have 5-way DIN connectors and require no additional electronics in order to work properly with any MIDI equipped devices.

MIDI tends to cause a certain amount of confusion because most soundcards have two or three MIDI drivers. One of these is the MIDI port driver, and it will produce a Roland MPU-401 compatible port. This is the device you use in order to communicate with MIDI synthesisers, keyboards, etc., but it does not get the soundcard itself to produce any sound. There will be one or two other drivers that produce virtual MIDI synthesisers. These can be used with software that has the ability to drive a MIDI device, and they get the soundcard to operate as a MIDI synthesiser. If the card has wavetable and FM synthesis there will probably be a separate driver for each type of synthesis. Additionally, there will be a driver for the joystick port. It is probably this proliferation of drivers that makes soundcards relatively difficult to install.

Points to remember

You can not simply buy any motherboard and stick any processor on it. You must choose a processor and then look for a motherboard that supports the selected chip and has the features you require. Make sure the motherboard can handle a processor of the exact type and clock frequency you will be using.

Buy a matching heatsink and fan when you buy the processor. The retail boxed versions of processors are normally supplied complete with a suitable cooling system. The OEM versions are cheaper but are not normally supplied with a heatsink and fan. OEM and retail processor are the same, it is only the packing and supplied extras that are different.

There are differences in the performance of similar motherboards from different manufacturers, but with modern boards these differences seem to be too small to worry about. Choose a board on the basis of cost, quality, and features.

No-name generic motherboards are significantly cheaper than those from well-known manufacturers. On the other hand, there is generally little or no support from the manufacturer with these boards, and it might be impossible to obtain BIOS upgrades. For the beginner at PC construction a board from a well-known manufacturer is the safer option.

Make sure the case is supplied complete with small items of hardware. It is of little use without them. It is cheaper and easier if the case and power supply are bought as a single item rather than separately. Make sure the power supply is a modern type that has the correct power leads for the motherboard you are using.

A case that has removable drive bays is much easier to use than one where they are fixed. Small cases often give very restricted access to the interior, and medium or large cases are generally easier to deal with. In general they also have more drive bays.

Integrated video is fine for most software, but games devotees will require a PC having the latest 3D video card, or a good budget type anyway. It is preferable to use a motherboard that has a 16X PCI Express slot, and permits the built-in graphics adaptor to be switched off. This leaves the option of upgrading to an expensive 3D video card.

The old ISA expansion slots are now obsolete. If you have an old ISA card that you wish to use in the new PC, there is really no chance of finding a new motherboard that has an ISA expansion slot to accommodate it. The ISA card must be replaced with a modern alternative.

The motherboard should be supplied with a basic set of leads for the drives. It can be expensive to buy these leads separately, so a budget board sold without leads might not be such a good bargain after all.

CD-ROM drives, CD writers, DVD ROM drives, etc., normally have an ordinary IDE (ATAPI) interface. There are still plenty of hard disc drives that use this type of interface, and they provide excellent performance. However, with a new PC it makes sense to use the serial ATA interfaces for hard disc drives. Serial ATA cables are easier to deal with than the IDE variety.

Integrated audio is more than adequate for most purposes. Many integrated audio systems are now quite sophisticated, offering surround-sound and other advanced features.

Assembly

Protection racket

Those readers who are used to dealing with electronic components will no doubt be aware that most computer components are vulnerable to damage by static electricity. They will also be used to handling static-sensitive components and taking the necessary precautions to protect them from damage. Probably most readers are not familiar with these precautions, and I will therefore outline the basic steps necessary to ensure that no components are accidentally "zapped".

I think it is worth making the point that it does not take a large static charge complete with sparks and "cracking" sounds to damage sensitive electronic components. Large static discharges of that type are sufficient to damage most semiconductor components, and not just the more sensitive ones. Many of the components used in computing are so sensitive to static charges that they can be damaged by relatively small voltages.

In this context "small" still means a potential of a hundred volts or so, but by static standards this is not particularly large. Charges of this order will not generate noticeable sparks or make your hair stand on end, but they are nevertheless harmful to many electronic components. Hence you can "zap" these components simply by touching them, and in most cases would not be aware that anything had happened.

I think it is also worth making the point that it is not just the processor and memory modules that are vulnerable. Completed circuit boards such as video and soundcards are often vulnerable to static damage, as is the motherboard itself. In fact most modern expansion cards and all motherboards are vulnerable to damage from static charges. Even components such as the hard disc drive and CD-ROM drive can be damaged by static charges. The case and power supply assembly plus any heatsinks and cooling fans represent the only major components that you can assume to be zap-proof. Everything else should be regarded as potentially at risk and handled accordingly.

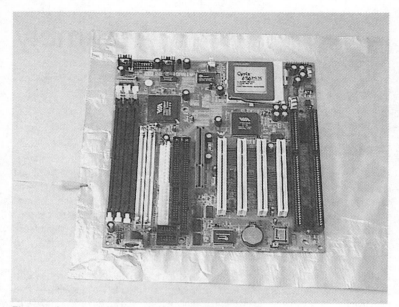

Fig.3.1 An improvised conductive work surface

When handling any vulnerable computer components you should always keep well away from any known or likely sources of static electricity. These includes such things as computer monitors, television sets, any carpets or furnishings that are known to be prone to static generation, and even any pets that are known to get charged-up fur coats. In general, objects that are wholly or partly made from metal are safer than those that are made entirely from plastic.

Avoid wearing any clothes that are known to give problems with static charges. This seems to be less of a problem than it once was, because few clothes these days are made from a cloth that consists entirely of man-made fibres. There is normally a significant content of natural fibres, and this seems to be sufficient to prevent any significant build-up of static charges. However, if you should have any garments that might give problems, make sure that you do not wear them when handling any computer equipment or components.

Anti-static equipment

Electronics and computing professionals often use quite expensive equipment to ensure that static charges are kept at bay. Most of these are not practical propositions for amateur computer enthusiasts or those who only deal with computers professionally on a very part-time basis. If you will only be working on computers from time to time, some very simple anti-static equipment is all that you need to ensure that there are no expensive accidents.

When working on a motherboard it is essential to have some form of conductive worktop that is earthed. These can be purchased from the larger electronic component suppliers, but something as basic as a large sheet of aluminium cooking foil laid out on the workbench will do the job very well (Figure 3.1). The only slight problem is that some way of earthing the foil must be devised.

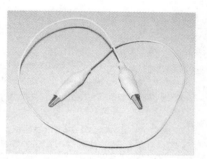

The method I generally adopt is to connect the foil to the metal chassis of a computer using a crocodile clip lead (Figure 3.2). Crocodile clips are available from electronic component suppliers, as are sets of made-up leads. The ready-made leads are often quite short, but several can be clipped together to make up a longer lead. The computer that acts as

Fig.3.2 A crocodile clip lead

the earth must be plugged into the mains supply so that it is earthed via the mains earth lead. The computer should be switched off, and the supply should also be switched off at the mains socket. The earth lead is never switched, and the case will remain earthed even when the computer is switched off.

If you wish to make quite sure that your body remains static-free, you can earth yourself to the computer by way of a proper earthing wristband. This is basically just a wristband made from electrically conductive material that connects to the earth via a lead and a high value resistor. The resistor does not prevent any static build-up in your body from leaking away to earth, but it will protect you from a significant shock if a fault should result in the earthing point becoming "live".

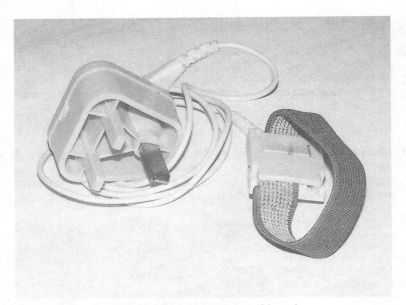

Fig.3.3 An anti-static wristband, lead, and earthing plug

There are two ways of earthing the wristband. One of these is to have a crocodile clip on the end of the earthing lead, and this can be connected to any piece of earthed metal that happens to be handy. In a PC context this usually means the chassis of a PC, but there might be other electrical gadgets having earthed chassis that could be used. The easier method is to have a sort of dummy mains plug on the earthing lead (Figure 3.3). This enables the wristband to be earthed via any mains socket.

Of course, only the earth pin of the plug connects to the wristband, and the rest of the plug is normally plastic so that there is no risk of a fault causing the wristband to be connected to a "live" pin. The resistor is included in the lead, so there is no danger of receiving a strong electric shock if, for instance, the mains socket's wiring is faulty.

Note that anti-static wrist-bands are sometimes sold as a complete kit with everything you need, but they are also sold as individual items (wristband, lead, and earthing plug or clip). Make sure that you know exactly what you are buying before parting with any money. If you are intending to do more than very occasional PC building, upgrading, or servicing, it is certainly worthwhile buying a good quality wristband kit.

It will ensure that you can handle computer components safely for many years.

Improvising

If you do not want to go to the expense of buying a wristband, a simple but effective alternative is to touch the conductive worktop or the metal chassis of the computer from time to time. This will leak away any gradual build-up of static electricity in your body before it has time to reach dangerous proportions. Again, the computer must be connected to the mains supply, but it should be switched off and the mains supply should be switched off at the mains outlet.

That is really all there is to it. Simply having a large chunk of earthed metal (in the form of the computer case) near the work area helps to discourage the build-up of any static charges in the first place. The few simple precautions outlined previously are then sufficient to ensure that there is no significant risk to the components.

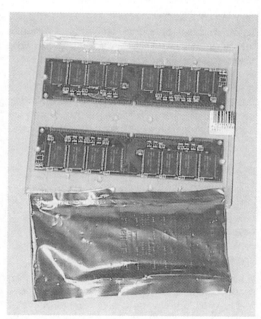

Do not be tempted to simply ignore the dangers of static electricity when

Fig.3.4 Two forms of anti-static packing that work in different ways but achieve the same thing

handling computer components. When building electronic gadgets I often ignore static precautions, but I am dealing with components that cost a matter of pence each. If one or two of the components should be zapped by a static charge, no great harm is done. The same is not true when dealing with computer components, some of which could cost in excess of a hundred pounds.

Anti-static packing

One final point is that any static sensitive components will be supplied in some form of anti-static packaging. This is usually nothing more than a plastic bag that is made from a special plastic that is slightly conductive. Processors and memory modules are often supplied in something more elaborate, such as conductive plastic clips and boxes. There is quite a range of anti-static packaging currently in use, and Figure 3.4 shows a couple of examples.

Although it is tempting to remove the components from the packing to have a good look at them, try to keep this type of thing to a minimum. When you do remove the components from the bags make sure that you and the bags are earthed first. Simply touching the earthed chassis of a computer while holding the component in its bag should ensure that everything is charge-free. Make sure that you always handle the components in an environment that is free from any likely sources of static charges. There will then be a minimal risk of any damage occurring.

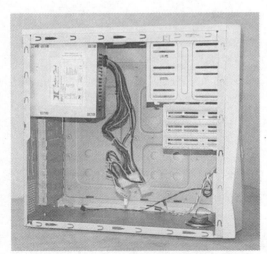

Fig.3.5 Removing one side panel gives good access to an ATX case

Case

Having set up any necessary anti-static precautions the next task is to get the case ready for assembly to begin. Unless you obtain one of the more exotic cases there should be no difficulty in opening the case. Removing four or six screws at the rear of the case should release the two side panels of a tower case, or the top and bottom panels of a desktop type. Look carefully to see which screws actually hold the outer casing in position, or you will probably find that you have removed the power supply instead! Figure 3.5 shows an ATX case with one side panel removed.

Some cases are now of the so-called "screwless" variety. These still have screws for such things are mounting the disc drives and holding the motherboard in place, but there are no screws to hold the side panels in position. Instead, there are usually a couple of plastic clips. In order to remove a side panel it is normally just a matter of pressing the clips with your thumbs and sliding the panel backwards until it comes free. However, there are a number of different types in common use, so it is a matter of taking a good look at the case and working out how to get it apart.

Note that many "screwless" cases still have the option of using four screws to secure the side panels. As supplied, it might be necessary to remove these screws before the panels can be unclipped. Thereafter you can use the four fixing screws or omit them. Some cases can tend to rattle slightly unless the side panels are fixed securely, so it is probably best to include them. It is increasingly common for cases to have the side panels secured using thumbscrews (Figure 3.6). These have the advantage of making it is easy to fit or remove the panels, but when fixed in place the panels are held very securely. Sets of thumbscrews are available from most companies that sell case modding equipment, so it is possible to use them with any normal PC case.

With some ATX cases you only need to remove the left-hand side panel (as viewed from the front) in order to assemble the PC. With most it is necessary to remove the other panel in order to get the drives properly fixed into the bays, and it might also be necessary in

Fig.3.6 Many cases have the panels secured by thumbscrews

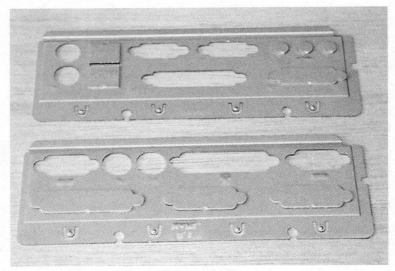

Fig.3.7 Alternative plates for the ATX port cluster

order to get the motherboard installed. It is a good idea to remove both panels anyway as this makes it easier to see what you are doing, and to see how the case fits together.

Inside the case there should be various accessories. It used to be normal for a mains lead to be included with a case that came complete with a power supply unit. However, this seems to be something of a rarity these days. Fortunately, the mains lead is a standard item that can be obtained cheaply from any computer or electrical store. The end that connects to the computer normally has a standard IEC plug, as used for most mains powered gadgets these days. There will also be various items of hardware such as screws, and there might also be two or three metal plates with various holes stamped in them (Figure 3.7). These fit on the rear of the case and accommodate various port configurations.

As pointed out in the previous chapters, an ATX motherboard has the standard ports actually fitted on the board, and the connectors for these ports are accessed via a cut-out in the case. However, as supplied most PC cases do not have the necessary cut-outs in the rear of the case. The upper plate in Figure 3.7 suits boards that have the standard port cluster. The lower square towards the left of the plate is pressed out if the motherboard has built-in USB ports, and the one above is removed if it has addition USB ports or LAN types. The removable plates on the right are pressed out to accommodate boards that have an integrated sound generator. The lower plate is for use with boards that have a built-in graphics adapter.

There are now so many different ATX port arrangements that many case manufacturers do not supply alternative plates. Instead, they leave it to the motherboard manufacturer to supply a plate having the appropriate layout. Any motherboard that has a non-standard layout, which these days means practically all of them, should be supplied complete with a matching plate that can be fitted to the rear of the case.

Knockout panels

If you look at the area of the case where the cutouts should be you will probably find that there is a metal panel instead. This panel will be largely cut from the case, and will only be held in place by two or three thin pieces of metal. This approach to things is used a great deal with modern computer cases, and it is a simple way of having optional cut-outs. It is

the same system that is used for the optional ports in the plates of Figure 3.7. Removing an unwanted panel is not difficult, and it is just a matter of pressing it with your finger to break one side free from the case (Figure 3.8). Then the panel is waggled backwards and forwards a few times until the fingers of metal securing it to the case fatigue and break.

There may be some rough edges produced where the metal fatigues and breaks. It is tempting to use a miniature file to rectify this, but filing or cutting a PC case using a saw is not something to be recommended. The problem is simply that the small metal fragments produced are difficult to thoroughly clean

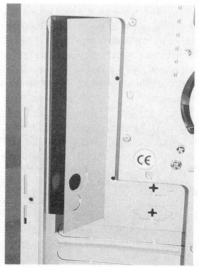

Fig.3.8 Removing a port cover plate from an ATX case

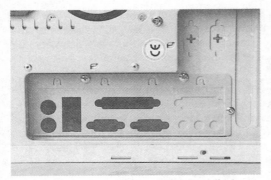

Fig.3.9 The new port cover plate installed on an ATX case

from the case, and they are also good at producing short-circuits if they get onto any of the circuit boards. If there are any dangerously sharp edges they must be removed, but otherwise do not bother. If you do have to file away any sharp edges try to thoroughly clean away any swarf. A damp rag does the job quite well, but the sticky side of adhesive tape or some Bostik Blu-Tack are probably the most effective ways of mopping up the swarf.

Having removed the panel you can simply leave a large hole in the rear panel, but it is better to fit one of the plates supplied with the case or the one supplied with the motherboard. Much neater results will be produced with a plate fitted on the rear panel (Figure 3.9). As pointed out previously, you may have to press out one or two small pieces of metal from the panel to make it match the connectors on the motherboard. Obviously this should be done before the motherboard is fitted in the case, and it is usually easier if it is done prior to fitting the plate on the case. Note that this can be necessary even when using the plate supplied with the

Fig.3.10 These days most of the plates are a push-fit into the case

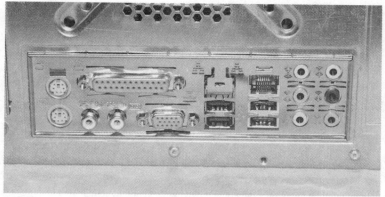

*Fig.3.11 A push-fit plate in position on the case. This is the plate
supplied with the motherboard, so it is a perfect match for
the port cluster*

motherboard. The board manufacturers often use the same plate design
with several boards that have a similar port layout.

The plates shown in Figures 3.7 and 3.9 are fixed to the case using a
couple of screws. Even with the more upmarket cases, this method is
falling from favour and many cases now use simple push-fit plates (Figure
3.10). The plates supplied with motherboards are invariably of this type.
The plates are pushed into place on the inside of the case, starting at
one end and pushing the whole thing into place. Many of these plates
are quite flimsy, so it is necessary to proceed carefully. There is otherwise
a risk of seriously distorting or buckling the plate.

Stand-offs

The next task is to install the stand-offs on which the motherboard will be
mounted. It is possible that these will be built into the chassis, or that
they will already be fitted to the chassis. This is unlikely though, and the
first part of the assembly process is to fit the stand-offs to the chassis. If
you look at the mounting holes in the motherboard and those in the
chassis you will find that there are many more in the chassis. This is
simply because the case is normally designed to take various types of
motherboard, large and small, old and new. Some of the holes in the
chassis probably have no relevance to any modern motherboards, and
others will probably not be relevant to the particular board you are using.

Fig.3.12 Two plastic stand-offs

The only sure way of telling which holes in the chassis should be fitted with stand-offs is to place the motherboard in position inside the case. With most cases it should be possible to fit the motherboard in place without any difficulty, but with some of the smaller cases it will be necessary to remove the 3.5-inch drive bay and (or) the power supply unit. Do not flex the board or use force to get it into position, as this could easily damage it beyond repair.

Methods of fixing the drive bay cages vary somewhat, but it usually involves nothing more than undoing one or two screws and sliding the cage out from the main assembly. It often takes a fair amount of force to get the cage free. With some cases the drive cages are not removable, but with these it should be possible to fit the motherboard with the cages in place. Once the motherboard is inside the case it can be moved around until all the holes in the board match up with holes in the case. Make a careful note of which holes in the case should be fitted with stand-offs, making a quick sketch if necessary.

It is possible that there will be some holes in the motherboard that have no counterparts in the case. This was quite normal with AT motherboards, but it is less likely to occur with the ATX variety. The extra holes can simply be left unused, and provided there are at least five mounting points spread well across the board it should be held in place adequately. Make sure that the board is well supported near the expansion slots, memory modules and the processor. A fair amount of pressure can be placed on the motherboards when an expansion card is fitted. The same is true when the PC is given a memory upgrade or the processor requires a replacement heatsink and fan.

A check through odds and ends of hardware supplied with the board might throw up a few plastic stand-offs that can be fitted into the underside of the motherboard, but have no provision for fixing to the chassis (Figure 3.12). These stand-offs are simply pushed into a mounting hole on the underside of the motherboard, and they can be used in any holes that have no counterparts in the case. They will avoid any tendency for the board to droop and possibly short circuit to the case. They will also effectively stiffen the board, reducing the risk of any damage occurring when fitting any expansion cards, memory modules, etc.

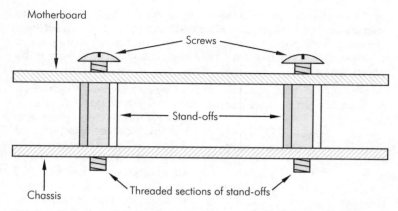

Fig.3.13 The most common form of stand-off for motherboards

Different types

There are several types of stand-off used with motherboards. Probably the most common stand-off at present is the hexagonal type that has a threaded section at the base which screws into the threaded holes in the chassis. The motherboard is then bolted to the stand-offs (Figure 3.13). These should be screwed quite firmly into the chassis, but with computers

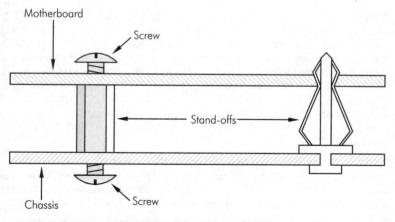

Fig.3.14 These two types of stand-off are quite common

it is not a matter of tightening everything as hard as you can. In order to avoid sheared threads you should tighten things enough to prevent them from easily coming apart again, but no more. In the absence of a suitable nut-driver for the stand-offs a pair of pliers should enable them to be tightened properly.

A similar type of stand-off is fixed in place by a screw, as in Figure 3.14. There are also plastic types that clip into the motherboard and then slide into cutouts in the chassis, and this type is also depicted in Figure 3.14. These operate in conjunction with one or two metal stand-offs that enable the board to be bolted in place, and provide an electrical connection from the earth rail of the motherboard to the case. The slide-in approach can be a bit awkward in practice with some of the stand-offs tending to buckle under the board rather than sliding nicely into place. If necessary, slide the motherboard back out again and try again, and do not simply leave the board supported by buckled stand-offs. They may fall out of position and permit the board to short-circuit to the case.

Fig.3.15 Two types of metal clip-in stand-off

Another type of stand-off clips into the case and the motherboard is then bolted to the stand-offs. A variation on this clip-in method has the motherboard slide into place under hooks on top of each stand-off. The hooked stand-offs have to be used in conjunction with one or two screw types so that the motherboard is reliably fixed in place. Both types are shown in Figure 3.15. It is increasingly common for cases to have some of the stand-offs pressed or welded into the base panel of the case. This type of stand-off can only used at places where every motherboard has a matching mounting hole, so some other form of stand-off has to be used as well.

A range of stand-offs have been covered here, but there are a few other types in use. They are mostly variations on the types described here. It should not be too difficult to work out how other types of stand-off are used, and this is not one of the more difficult aspects of building a PC.

Be careful not to fit metal stand-offs to the chassis at any points where there are no matching mounting holes in the motherboard. Doing so could result in connections on the underside of the board being short-circuited to the case. Once the stand-offs are in place the motherboard should be mounted inside the case to ensure that everything fits correctly. When you have established that everything is all right the motherboard should be removed so that the processor and memory can be installed, and (where appropriate) the motherboard can be configured via the DIP-switches and jumpers.

Configuration

Some motherboards do not require any configuration at this stage of the proceedings, but are instead configured using the BIOS Setup program. In fact most of these boards configure themselves using probing techniques to determine what processor is fitted, and manual configuration is only needed if you do not agree with the default settings for some reason. If you are not using one these "jumperless" boards it will be necessary to use DIP-switches or jumpers to set up the board to suit the processor.

In some cases there is the option of configuring the board using jumpers or the BIOS. Selection is unusually via a jumper on the motherboard, but the default setting is usually for configuration via the BIOS. The option of manual configuration is mainly included for those wishing to over-clock the processor. If it works, over-clocking provides extra speed, but it takes the processor beyond its rated limits. In most cases it also takes other components beyond their normal working limits, including the memory, support chips, and probably the graphics adaptor as well. Whether it is worth the effort and risk to the affected components depends on your need for processing speed, but over-clocking is certainly not the place to start. Where there is the option of automatic configuration it is best to use it.

Manuals for pieces of electronic equipment and computer software tend to get ignored, and are only read as a last resort. This is not an option when dealing with motherboards, and it is essential to read through the manual and constantly refer to it for vital pieces of information. You will certainly need to study the instruction manual for details of how to set it up to suit the particular processor you are using. It is quite possible that you will need to do nothing, and that the BIOS will sort it all out. However, the only way to be certain of this is to read the relevant part of the manual.

The parameters that are set via the jumpers or switches depend on the type of motherboard in use. The processor and motherboard clock speeds sometimes have be set, and the two are linked. The correct clock rate for the motherboard is set, and then a multiplier is used to produce the required clock frequency. As a couple of examples, an Athlon XP2000+ processor actually operates at about 1.66GHz, and with the motherboard operating at 133MHz (0.133GHz) a multiplier value of 12.5 (133 x 12.5 = 166.25). A Pentium 4 operating at 2.4GHz with a 133MHz bus frequency would require a multiplier value of 18 (133 x 18 = 2394).

As will be apparent from the first of these examples, the mathematics is not always perfect. In most cases the actual processor clock frequency will be slightly lower than its nominal value, or the motherboard bus speed will be fractionally higher (133.33MHz instead of 133MHz for example). It does not really matter which, and there will be no noticeable difference in performance between clock rates of (say) 2.394GHz and 2.4GHz. Matters can be confused slightly by different parts of the system operating at different frequencies. For example, the memory often operates at double or more the basic frequency of the motherboard. The processor's clock multiplier is relative to the basic motherboard frequency, and not any higher frequencies such as those used by memory or the graphics adapter.

Clock rates

Fig.3.16 An IBM/Cyrix processor marked with the system frequency and multiplier

As pointed out previously, there is a slight complication with the processor frequency for the AMD Athlon XP chips in that their actual clock frequencies are lower than the name of the processor would suggest. In fact, this is common to all of the recent AMD processors, including the Athlon 64 and Sempron chips. This is not a new phenomenon, and some of the Cyrix chips use the same system, where a figure in the name gives the speed in terms of an equivalent Pentium processor. Matters were complicated by the fact that there was more than one version of some Cyrix chips, with each version requiring a different clock frequency. There are also some instances of AMD and Intel processors where two chips having the same clock frequency require a different setup in order to work properly. It is important to check the motherboard manufacturer's web site to ensure compatibility with the processor you intend to use. It is then equally important to make sure that you order the correct processor!

An automatic detection system should correctly identify any processor and set the correct multiplier, etc. The only proviso is that the BIOS must be sufficiently up to date to recognise the processor. Using the very latest processor with a motherboard that has been in the retailer's warehouse for some months runs a slight risk of the BIOS not being sufficiently up to date.

Fig.3.17 Modern processors are usually devoid of information such as operating frequencies and voltages

When using a recently introduced processor it is especially important to make sure that the motherboard you are using is fully compatible with it. Updating the BIOS of a modern motherboard is not difficult, but it requires the board to be in a fully working PC.

At one time it was common for processors to have the bus frequency and multiplier marked on the top of the chip, and the correct core voltage was usually indicated as well (Figure 3.16). This information is not usually included on modern processors (Figure 3.17), but it should be included in the instruction booklet provided with the chip. Also, the instruction manual for the motherboard will probably have a chart showing the correct settings for the compatible processors. Wherever possible it is best to make life easier and simply opt for automatic detection. This also removes the slight risk of getting things wrong and damaging the processor.

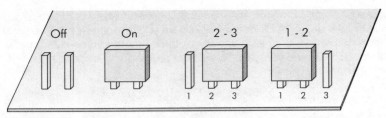

Fig.3.18 The two types of jumper normally used on motherboards

Core voltage

Conventionally, logic circuits operate from a 5-volt supply, but in order to get the highest possible performance it is common practice for other supply voltages to be used in parts of the computer. Memory circuits and some sections of the processor often operate at 3.3 volts, and the main processor circuits often work at a somewhat lower voltage. A supply voltage as low as 1.5 volts is often used for modern processors. This core voltage might have to be set via jumpers or DIP-switches, although this is unlikely provided you are using a modern motherboard. The instruction manual for the motherboard should give the correct settings for all the usable processors, and this information should be supplied with the processor. Again, it is best to use automatic detection and setting whenever possible.

Clear CMOS

There may be other settings to make, but these additional parameters vary a lot from one motherboard to another. One virtually standard feature is a jumper that enables the CMOS memory to be disconnected from the backup battery. By default this should be set so the board functions normally, with the backup battery ensuring that the BIOS is free from amnesia, with the correct drive parameters, etc., being used each time the computer is switched on. Setting this jumper to the "off" position for a few minutes wipes the CMOS memory of all its contents. With the jumper restored to the "on" setting the computer is able to function again, but it is a matter of starting "from scratch" with the CMOS memory settings.

In effect, this jumper provides a means of resetting the CMOS memory. This would be probably only be necessary if someone started to use the password facility and then forgot his or her password. The only way of getting the computer to boot if this happens is to clear the current set-up from memory. The next time the computer is started it uses the default settings, which means that it starts up without implementing the password facility. Unless there is a good reason to do so, it is best not to use any BIOS password facility.

Note that it is not necessary to clear the CMOS memory in this way if you manage to make a complete mess of the BIOS settings. From within the BIOS Setup program it is usually possible to revert to one or two sets of default settings, and then do any necessary "fine tuning". Provided the computer can be persuaded to get as far as the initial testing routine, it should be possible to enter the BIOS and select the Standard Defaults option. It is not necessary to clear the CMOS memory before using the motherboard for the first time.

Fig.3.19 The "ON" marking on a DIP-switch

There can be other jumpers or DIP-switches to set such things as the motherboard's bus frequency, to disable the built-in audio system, and this type of thing. You really have to read the manual for the motherboard to determine what jumpers or DIP-switches have to be set up correctly, if any. The modern trend is towards as much as possible being set using auto-detection methods, or via the BIOS Setup program. Many motherboards only have one switch or jumper that can be used to power-down the CMOS memory. Boards of this type are certainly preferable for those building their first PC.

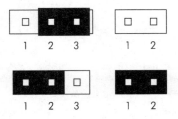
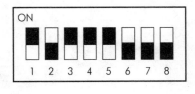

Fig.3.20 Some switch and jumper diagrams are clearer than others

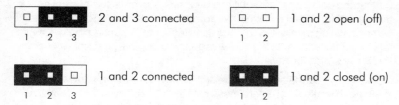

Fig.3.21 An explanatory diagram for jumper settings

Setting up

Actually setting any jumpers or switches should not give any major problems. There are two types of jumper, which are the straightforward on/off type and the two-way variety. The on/off type has two pins and you fit the jumper over the pins to connect them together ("on") or do not fit the jumper at all ("off"). This simple scheme of things is shown in the left-hand section of Figure 3.18. It is common practice to fit the jumper on one of the pins to provide the "off" setting. If you should need to change the setting at a later time you then know exactly where to find a jumper. The jumpers are minute and are likely to get lost if you store them somewhere other than on the motherboard.

The second type of jumper block has three pins, and the jumper is used to connect the middle pin to one of the outer pins, as shown in the right-hand section of Figure 3.18. The jumper is connecting together two pins, as before, and the jumpers are exactly the same whether they are used on a two-pin block or a three-pin type.

DIP-switches are normally in blocks of four or eight switches, but not all the switches in a block will necessarily be utilized. They are a form of

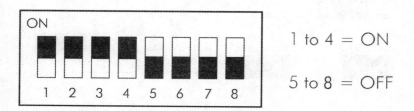

Fig.3.21 An explanatory diagram for DIP-switches

Socket Locked

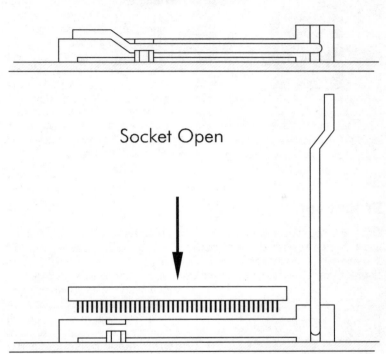

Socket Open

Fig.3.23 The ZIF socket is opened by raising the lever

slider switch, and are more or less a miniature version of the switches
often used in small electronic gadgets such as cassette recorders and
personal stereo units. The block of switches is marked with "on" and
(or) "off" legends (Figure 3.19) to make it clear which setting is which.

The motherboard's instruction manual normally includes a diagram
showing the correct switch or jumper settings for a given processor. There
is a slight problem here in that these diagrams are open to
misinterpretation. In the two examples of Figure 3.20, which pins do the
jumpers connect and which switches are in the "on" position. My guess
would be that the black blocks represent the jumpers and the control
knobs on the switches, but there is no way of telling for sure without
some further assistance. The manual should provide this assistance in

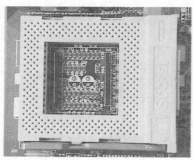

Fig.3.24 The socket is polarised by having a "missing" hole in one corner

the form of another diagram showing exactly how the switch or jumper setting diagrams should be interpreted. These diagrams will be something like Figure 3.21 and 3.22. Never rely on guesswork when setting jumpers and DIP-switches. Mistakes are unlikely to result in any damage, but it is not worth taking the risk. Carefully study the instruction manual for the motherboard and get things right first time.

Processor

Once any necessary configuring of the board has been completed the processor can be fitted into its socket. This is much the same for AMD and most Intel processors. Both makes of processor fit into a ZIF (zero insertion force) socket on the motherboard. Conventional integrated

Fig.3.25 The "missing" pin is marked on the top surface of the chip

circuit holders, even when used with integrated circuits that have only a few pins, are something less than easy to use. It is often quite difficult to squeeze the integrated circuits into them. The AMD and Intel chips have literally hundreds of pins. For example, some of the Intel chips use Socket 775 motherboards, and the Socket 775 name refers to the number of pins. So does the 939 in AMD's Socket 939 chips!

Getting a chip of this size into a holder could be bordering on the impossible, but the situation is greatly eased by the use of ZIF

sockets. The holder has a lever that is raised to the vertical position in order to open the socket (Figure 3.23). The lever normally has to be pulled outwards slightly in order to unlock it before it can be raised. With

*Fig.3.26 The missing pin of this Socket 775 Pentium 4 is indicated by a
          triangle (top right-hand corner)*

the socket open the processor should simply drop into place without
any difficulty. Returning the lever to its original position then locks the
processor in place.

The processor must be fitted with the correct orientation, and with modern
socket processors it impossible to fit a processor the wrong way round.
If you look at the socket for an Intel processor you will find that there are
three corners that have provision for a pin on the processor, and one
that does not (Figure 3.24). It is this missing hole in the socket that
prevents the processor from fitting into it unless the processor has the
correct orientation. If you look at the upper surface of the processor you
will find a dot in one corner, and that corner of the casing will probably
be chamfered as well (Figure 3.25). If you match that corner of the chip
with the missing hole in the socket, the processor should drop easily
into place. Figure 3.26 shows an Intel Socket 775 Pentium 4, and this
has a triangle at one corner of the chip to indicate the position of the
"missing" pin.

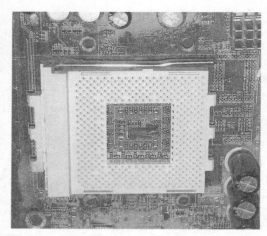

Fig.3.27 Things are done differently with AMD's Socket A

Socket A, as used for the old AMD Athlon and Duron processors, does things slightly differently. There are two corner holes "missing" from the socket and the corresponding pins of the processors are also absent. Figure 3.27 shows one of these sockets and it is the top and bottom left-hand corners that have the two "missing" holes. Confusingly perhaps,

Fig.3.28 The AMD Socket 939 has several "missing" pins

Fig.3.29 The orientation of an Athlon 64 is indicated by a small triangular marking (bottom left-hand corner)

the processor itself still has only one proper corner marker, but there might be a smaller mark near the other corner. The main marker corresponds to the top left-hand corner of the socket as viewed in Figure 3.27. In other words, you have to look for the "missing" hole next to the lever of the ZIF socket. Alternatively, just look at the underside of the processor to see which two corners do not have a pin.

The Socket 939 version of the Athlon 64 has a number of "missing" pins, as can be seen from the socket itself (Figure 3.28). It still uses what is really just the same "missing" pin approach to ensure that the processor will only fit into the socket if it is given the correct orientation. The processor has a triangular marking (Figure 3.29) that matches up with the similar marking on the socket. This marking does not show up very well in Figure 3.28, because it is quite small and is only lightly moulded into the plastic body of the socket. However, it is "present and correct" in the bottom left-hand corner of the socket. Figure 3.30 shows the processor in the socket, with the lever lowered so that the processor is locked in place

Fig.3.30 An Athlon 64 processor fitted to a Socket 939 motherboard

Modern AMD microprocessors use AM2 motherboards, but fitting a processor in an AM2 socket is essentially the same as fitting one in a Socket 939. The socket has "missing" holes and a gold or silver triangle to show the correct orientation for the processor. Figure 3.31 shows the socket with the triangle in the top right-hand corner. Figure 3.32 shows an Athlon 64 X2 processor, and this also has the triangle in the top right-hand corner. Figure 3.33 shows an Athlon 64 X2 processor fitted into its socket.

As mentioned previously, the Intel Socket 775 chips use a slightly unconventional approach with the socket in the processor and the pins on the motherboard. This does not really matter a great deal in practice, and the difference is not obvious when fitting the chip. Something which is obvious, is that the "socket" on the motherboard has a protective cover for the pins (Figure 3.34). This is hinged and can be raised when the locking lever is raised (Figure 3.35). The plastic part of the cover must be removed (Figure 3.36), and this is simply a matter of pressing it out of place. Next the processor is fitted in place (Figure 3.37). Although the

Fig.3.31 An AM2 socket has the "missing" holes and triangle in one corner

Fig.3.32 An Athlon 64 X2 processor has the triangular marking

Fig.3.33 An Athlon 64 X2 processor fitted in its socket

standard anti-static handling precautions will be taken when dealing with the processor, it is still advisable to avoid touching the contacts on the underside of this component whenever it is necessary to handle this component. Finally, the remaining part of the cover is lowered over the processor and the lever is used to lock the processor and cover in place (Figure 3.38).

Although the current processors use a few variations on the basic scheme of things, they all use what is essentially the same method of getting the processor into its socket the right way round. Look carefully at the processor and the socket, and the correct orientation for the chip should be obvious. Provided you obtain a retail boxed processor, any unusual aspects of fitting this component should be described in the instruction leaflet supplied with it.

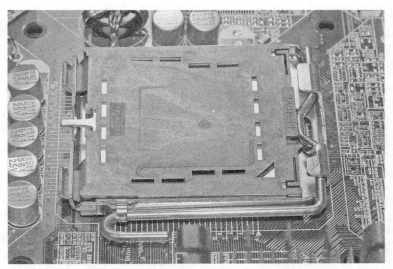

Fig.3.34 Socket 775 has a plastic cover to protect the pins

Fig.3.35 Here the hinged cover has been raised

Fig.3.36 The plastic cover must be removed

Be careful

When fitting a processor, bear in mind that it should drop into place very easily. It might take a certain amount of manoeuvring to get it into just the right position, but it should then drop into place without any problems. Make sure that the locking lever is fully raised prior to fitting the processor, and move it right back to its original position once the processor is in position. If the processor will not fall into place, check that its orientation is correct. If it still fails to drop into place it is likely that one of the pins has become bent out of position. If the damage is not of your doing, it should be possible to get the processor replaced under guarantee.

Probably the vast majority of problems with bent pins are due to "driver error", with the chip being dropped, or an attempt being made to fit it into the socket the wrong way round. This is definitely a case of prevention being better than cure. Handle processors carefully and never try to force one into its socket. A zero insertion force socket has been given that name for a very good reason. When correctly in place, the weight of

Fig.3.37 Here the processor has been placed in position

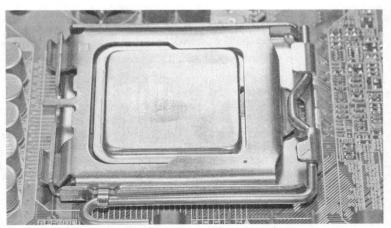

Fig.3.38 The cover has been closed and locked in place

Fig.3.39 Socket 478 is rather different to previous processor sockets

the processor is usually sufficient to make it drop into place, and it should certainly require nothing more than a gentle push to get it into position. Using anything more than slight pressure risks damaging the processor.

In the past it was usually possible to fix a "bent" processor by looking closely at all the pins and using the blade of a small screwdriver to carefully straighten any that were seriously bent out of place. This might still be possible, but it is a task that has become more difficult as processors have "sprouted" more and more pins. If you have an unusable processor I suppose that there is not a great deal to lose by trying to straighten any bent pins. Proceed very carefully and gently though, because the processor will certainly be a total write-off if one of the pins is broken off. Fortunately, the pins on modern processors are quite short and strong, so there should be no problems with bent pins unless the device has been seriously mistreated.

Fig.3.40 A 2.4GHz Pentium 4 processor fitted in its socket

Note that the Socket 478 version of the Intel chips have what is more or
less a conventional socket, with the pins on the processor and no cover
on the socket. Socket 478 still looks rather different to a conventional
processor socket though (Figure 3.39). It is surrounded by black plastic
"fence" which is used to fit the heatsink and fan assembly in place. The
processor is fitted and locked into place in standard fashion though.
Figure 3.40 shows a Pentium 4 processor fitted in its socket. Athlon
Socket 939 motherboards also have some plastic attachments to facilitate
fixing the heatsink to the board (see Figure 3.30).

Heatsink

With the processor in place the heatsink and fan are then fitted. With
Socket A chips, fitting the heatsink and fan can be rather fiddly and in
some cases you may find that the heatsink does not clip securely in

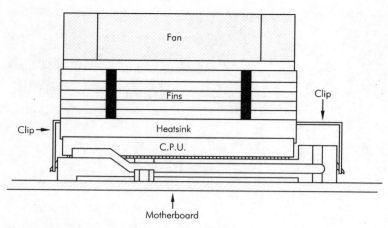

Fig.3.41 The heatsink and fan clip to the ZIF socket

place. The side-on view of Figure 3.41 shows the simple method of fixing that seems to be used for all Socket A heatsinks. Fitting the heatsink is just a matter of fitting one end of the spring clip on the heatsink under one of the plastic retaining clips on the socket. Without letting this end slip out of position, the other end of the clip is then secured on the other side of the socket. With some combinations of heatsink and processor it is a rather tight fit, but once the heatsink is actually in place it should stay there and work efficiently.

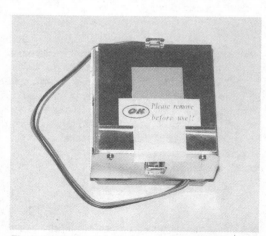

Fig.3.42 There is usually a protective covering on the pad of heatsink compound

If the heatsink is a loose fit it may not work very well, and there is a real risk that before long it will become dislodged. If you look carefully at the clip that secures the heatsink to the motherboard you will probably find that part of the clip can be removed and repositioned further up the main section of the clip. Using this second position should result in the heatsink and fan being held in place much more securely.

Fig.3.43 The pad of heatsink compound

With the heatsinks for modern processors, particularly the faster types, there may be a pad of a rather sticky rubber-like material on the underside of the heatsink. At one time this was often included on top of the processor, but these days it is only included on the heatsink. The pad is usually protected by a tear off strip of paper (Figure 3.42), and this should be removed just before the heatsink is fitted on the processor. Figure 3.43 shows the pad on the underside of the heatsink, and Figure 3.44 shows the heatsink and fan safely installed on an AMD XP2000+ processor.

The purpose of the pad is to ensure that there is a good thermal connection between the processor and the heatsink. Some processors consume quite high power levels and could overheat if there is an inefficient thermal contact with the heatsink. Do not remove the pad and be careful not to damage it. Doing either of these could seriously reduce the efficiency of the heatsink, and could even result in the processor overheating. If it becomes necessary to remove the heatsink at some time in the future, use a fresh pad or a smear of heatsink compound to ensure a good thermal contact when the heatsink is replaced.

Socket 478

The method of mounting the heatsink described previously is the one used for Socket A boards, but the Pentium 4 Socket 478 boards use a different type of heatsink. The heatsink does not clip onto the socket.

Fig.3.44 The heatsink and fan clipped into place

Around the processor there is a black plastic mounting bracket with a post in each corner, and the heatsink clips onto this. Refer back to the photographs of Figures 3.42 and 3.43 where the bracket can be clearly seen. The heatsink itself (Figure 3.45) is relatively large, and dwarfs the processor, but Pentium 4 processors run relatively cool because of this. The heatsink has two locking levers, one at each end.

Fitting the heatsink onto the motherboard is very easy, and it simply presses down into place on the black plastic mounting bracket. If it is reluctant to fit into place you probably have one or both of the levers in the locked position, and correcting this should enable it to be pressed down into place. The levers are set to the locked position once the heatsink has properly clipped into place. The levers operate a cam mechanism that forces the heatsink down onto the processor. Figure 3.46 shows the heatsink locked into place, and one of the cams can be seen in the side-on view of Figure 3.47.

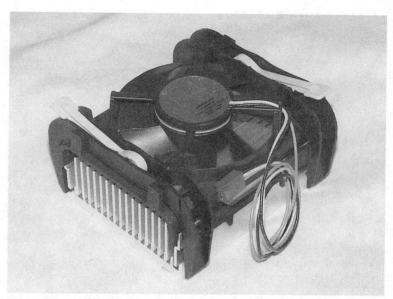

Fig.3.45 A heatsink and fan for a Pentium 4 processor

Fig.3.46 The heatsink clipped onto the plastic holder

Fig.3.47 One of the cams can be seen in this side-on view of the heatsink in position

Fig.3.48 A Socket 939 heatsink is similar to a Socket A type

Socket 939

The method of fixing the heatsink to a socket 939 motherboard is not a great deal different from the Socket A method, but it takes things a stage further. Like Socket 478 motherboards, the Socket 939 variety have a plastic "fence" around the processor, and the heatsink attaches to this rather than to the socket itself. If you refer back to Figure 3.30, the "fence" can be seen around the socket. The two large bolts to either side of the socket are used to securely clamp two plastic clips to the motherboard.

A Socket 939 heatsink fits onto these in much the same way as a Socket A type clips onto its socket. Figure 3.48 shows one side of

Fig.3.49 There is a lever on one side of the heatsink

Fig.3.50 The heatsink clamped into position

Fig.3.51   There are four fasteners on the underside of a Socket 775 heatsink

a Socket 939 heatsink, which has a simple spring-clip. There is a slightly more complex clip on the other side of the heatsink (Figure 3.49), complete with a small plastic lever. Initially though, it fits onto the "fence" in the usual way. Getting the heatsink in position can be a bit awkward. The obvious approach is to fit the simple clip first and then the one with the lever, since the lever makes it easier to get a firm grip on this one. In practice the heatsink often fits into place much easier if the clip with the lever is fitted first.

Once the heatsink is in place it will be a fairly loose fit and will not work efficiently. It is clamped tightly onto the socket and processor by moving the lever down from a vertical position (Figure 3.50). Note that the lever should be vertical when the heatsink is initially clipped into place. Note also, that the heatsink will only be clamped in place correctly if the lever is lowered in the right direction. There is a thumb-grip mould into one side of the lever, and this side should be facing upwards once the heatsink is clamped in position

Some Socket 939 heatsinks can be used with AM2 motherboards. However, with the more usual arrangement the heatsink pushes into place on four mounting clips and is then locked in place by a lever. This is essentially the same as the system used for Socket 478 heatsinks.

Socket 775

As pointed out previously, Socket 775 processors are unusual in that they have what is effectively the socket in the processor and the pins in what is inappropriately called the "socket". Another unusual aspect of these processors is the hinged cover plate. The way in which the heatsink and fan are fixed in place is equally unconventional. The underside of a Socket 775 heatsink is shown in Figure 3.51, and a view of the top is shown in Figure 3.52. In the underside view it is possible the see the pad of heatsink compound in the middle of the heatsink. Always take great care not to damage this pad when handling a heatsink. It is also

Fig.3.52 *The top side of a Socket 775 heatsink*

possible to see a white plastic fastener at the end of each of the four "legs". There are four holes in the motherboard to take these fasteners. As can be seen from the example shown in Figure 3.53, these are just simple holes drilled in the motherboard, and the business part of system is on the heatsink.

In order to fit the heatsink in place it is just a matter of aligning the four fasteners with the holes in the motherboard, and then pressing down on each of the four "legs" to fit the fasteners into place. A "click" should be heard as each one locks into place. The method usually recommended is to press two diagonaly opposite "legs" into place simultaneously, but this can be a bit difficult with some heatsinks. With this

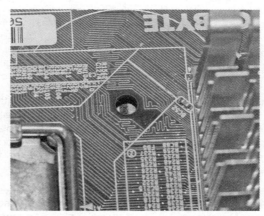

Fig.3.53 *Each fastener clips into a hole in the motherboard*

Fig.3.54 A heatsink and fan fitted to a Socket 775 motherboard

type of thing you often have to "play it by ear" and use a little common sense. Once all four fastenings have been fitted it is advisable to pull on the heatsink to check that it is not loose at one corner. If one of the fasteners fails to lock in place, check its alignment and try again. Figure 3.54 shows a Socket 775 heatsink that is correctly locked in place on a motherboard. Note that once in place it is not possible to remove the heatsink simply by pulling it free. There is a slot for a screwdriver at the top of each "leg", and about a quarter of a turn in a counter-clockwise direction should free each one so that the heatsink can be easily lifted from the motherboard.

Currenty there are several different methods of fixing heatsinks in place, and the manufacturers seem to come up with a steadly flow of new types. Retail boxed processors are supplied with an instruction leaflet that explains how the heatsink is fitted in place, so if in doubt you can always refer to this. A heatsink obtained separately from the processor should also be supplied complete with fixing instructions, but some lack worthwhile fitting instructions. Clearly it is essential to be very careful when buying a processor and heatsink separately, as it would be very easy to end up with a heatsink that did not match the fixing method used by the motherboard. Buying a retail boxed processor, complete with heatsink and fan, is a much safer option, and should not be significantly more expensive.

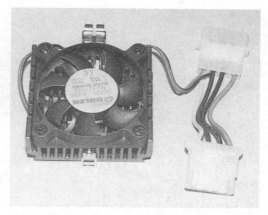

Fig.3.55 This fan taps off power from a 5.25-inch drive's power lead

Fan

The cooling fan will require a 12-volt supply, and there are two normal ways of obtaining this. In the past the most common method was to obtain power from one of the 5.25-in. disc drive supply outputs of the power supply unit. There will not always be a spare output of this type, but the fan will almost certainly be fitted with a lead that has two connectors (Figure 3.55). One of these connects to the output of the power supply and other connects to a 5.25-in. drive. This enables a single output of the power supply to provide power to both the cooling fan and one of the drives. If you use this method of powering the fan it is obviously not connected to the power supply until the motherboard has been finally installed in the case.

Fig.3.56 A three-pin fan connector

The alternative method, and by far the most common one these days, is to power the fan from the motherboard. Virtually all modern motherboards

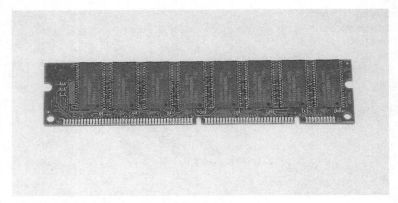

Fig.3.57 A 256 megabyte non-DDR DIMM

have a small three-pin connector that can supply 12 volts to the cooling fan, and most processor cooling fans are now fitted with this type of connector. The fans fitted to the heatsinks for Intel processors sometimes have a four-way connector, and the motherboard might have a matching four-pin type. The four-way connectors used on the fans are compatible with three-pin motherboard connectors, so there should be no great problem if the motherboard only has a three-pin type. There is no need to worry about getting fan connectors fitted the right way round, because they will only fit with the correct orientation. If the fan is powered in this way it should be connected to the motherboard as soon as it has been fitted on the processor.

On the face of it, a two-way connector is adequate to provide power to a fan. The third connection is used to send a signal from the fan to the motherboard so that the BIOS or an application program can monitor the speed of the fan. The general idea is for a warning to be given if the speed of the fan is too low or no fan is detected. In fact the BIOS might prevent the computer from starting if no fan is detected.

Modern motherboards often have more than one power supply output for a fan. If this should be the case the motherboard's instruction manual should indicate which output to use for the processor's fan. It is important to use this one for the processor's fan, and it is definitely not a good idea to leave it unused. The motherboards will sense that there is not an operating fan connected on the processor fan's output, which could cause warning alarms to sound or prevent the PC starting The same problem can arise if the fan is powered from a 5.25-inch drive supply. The safest option is to power the fan from the correct output on the motherboard.

Fitting memories

The next stage is to install the memory on the motherboard. Modern motherboards mostly use some form of DIMM (dual in-line memory module). Whether it is pre DDR memory or the latest DDR3 type, the memory will still be in the form of one or more DIMMs. Fitting DIMMs is very easy, and it is impossible to fit them the wrong way round because the DIMM's circuit board has a polarising "key". This is just an off-centre notch cut in the circuit board that matches a bar in the DIMM socket. Refer back to Figure 2.17 in chapter 2 for a photograph of a DDR DIMM. The key is apparently in slightly different position depending on the supply voltage of the module and the type of RAM fitted, and there are two keys in some DIMMs. Figure 3.57 shows a non-DDR DIMM that has a second notch. These differences should make it impossible to fit a DIMM of the wrong type.

Because one notch and bar are well off-centre it is easy to determine which way around the module should go. The module simply drops into place vertically and as it is pressed down into position the plastic lever at

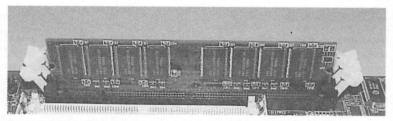

Fig.3.58 Here the DIMM is only partially slotted into place

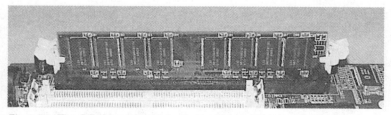

Fig.3.59 The DIMM pushed into the holder and locked in place

each end of the socket should start to close up. Pressing both levers into a fully vertical position should securely lock the module in place, if the levers do not snap into this position anyway. Make sure the levers are pulled fully outwards before you try to fit the DIMM. Figures 3.58 and 3.59 respectively show a DIMM that is ready to be pushed down into place, and one that is locked in place. To remove a DIMM, simply press the two levers outwards as far as they will go. This should unlock the memory module so that it can be lifted free of the socket.

RIMMS were the standard type of memory for early Pentium 4 systems, but you will not need to use these unless you obtain a really old motherboard. Installing RIMMs is much the same as fitting DIMMs, and the same basic method of locking and unlocking is used. With DIMMs it is permissible to have unused memory holders, and a single DIMM can be used even if the motherboard has three or four memory sockets. With RIMMs it is necessary to have all the sockets occupied, so a Continuity Module has to be used in any holders that are not fitted with RIMMs. It is essential to read the appropriate section of the motherboard's instruction manual when dealing with the memory, but it is especially important when RIMMs are used. Make sure that everything it strictly in accordance with the recommendations of the motherboard's manufacturer.

Dual channel

Most new motherboards now support dual channel operation. Do not confuse double data rate (DDR) with dual channel operation. DDR technology is used to produce faster memory modules. Dual channel operation is a method of using memory modules more efficiently, and in most cases the memory modules will be of the DDR variety. The processor tends to deal with data faster than it can be written to and read from memory, causing "bottle-knecks" and a reduction in the speed of the system. Dual channel memory uses the simple concept of adding a second memory channel so that when one is busy the processor can use the other. In theory anyway, this enables two "bog standard" memory modules to operate rather like one ultra-quick module.

Although it is possible to use a single DIMM on most motherboards, this is not possible if you have a motherboard that supports dual channel operation and you wish to utilise this facility. If an odd number of memory modules are used on a dual channel board, either single channel operation will be obtained or part of the memory will be left unused.

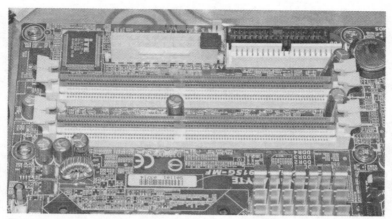

*Fig.3.60 Two colours are often used for the DIMM holders of
motherboards that support dual channel operation*

Dual channel motherboards often have the holders for the memory
modules in two different colours (Figure 3.60). The usual scheme of
things, as in this example, is for a pair of memory modules to be fitted in
two holders of the same colour. It does not normally matter whether you
use holders one and three (red in this case), or holders two and four
(blue on this motherboard). Provided you use two holders of the same
colour, dual channel operation should be obtained. However, it is
advisable to check the relevant section of the motherboard's instruction
manual just in case there are any restrictions you need to be aware of.

In general, and apart from the limitations imposed by dual channel
operation, modern motherboards are not fussy about which memory
holders are used. If a board has four DIMM holders and the memory will
be provided by a single DIMM, it does not matter which DIMM holder is
used. Practical experience suggests that things in the real world are not
as simple as this. Using memory in the higher numbered DIMM holders
and leaving the lower numbered holders empty does seem to cause
occasional problems. The system can become very unreliable, the video
card can have problems of fail to work at all, and so on. It is probably
advisable to populate the lower numbered holders first, and where
appropriate leave the higher numbered holders empty.

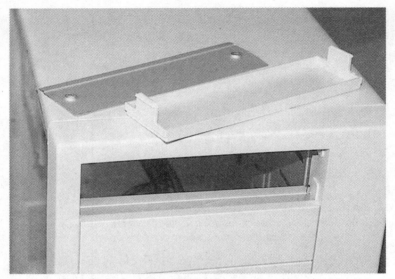

Fig.3.61 The metal plate and plastic cover removed from a drive bay

Drives

Once the memory modules have been fitted and the motherboard is installed in the case, the next step is to install the drives in the drive bays. There are plastic covers over the external drive bays, and these must be removed at the positions where drives are to be fitted. These are easily pushed out from the rear, but there will probably be a slight snag here in the form of a metal plate behind each plastic cover. These plates are partially cut from the case, and must be removed from any bays where externally accessible drives will be fitted. They can usually be left in place where other drives, such as the hard drive or drives, will be fitted.

They are removed in the same way as other blanking plates in the case. Remove the plastic cover first. There are usually a couple of holes in the metal plate so that you can push out the plastic cover from the rear by poking a screwdriver through one of these holes. With a bit of pushing and shoving it should be possible to turn the plate through about 30 degrees or so, although it can take a while to get the blanking plate completely free. You can then get hold of one edge, and with a bit of waggling the plate should soon break away from the case.

Fig.3.62 There are four mounting holes in each side of a 5.25-inch drive

With the plate and plastic cover removed (Figure 3.61) the bay is ready for the drive to be fitted. Note that with some of the more expensive cases the metal plates are held in place by two or four screws, so check for these before trying to break the plates free.

It is likely that there will be more drive bays than drives, leaving some of the bays unused. It does not really matter too much which bays you leave unused, but where possible it is probably better to arrange things so that there is an unused bay between drives. Spacing out the drives often makes installation slightly less fiddly, and it can also make them easier to use. Another factor is that many modern drives get quite hot when they have been in use for a while. Spacing them out as much as

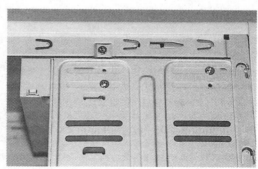

Fig.3.63 Two fixing screws per side will hold a drive in place

131

Fig.3.64 The enclosed side of a hard disc drive is usually the top

possible makes it easier for the air to circulate and should help to keep the drives cool.

With modern cases there should be no difficulty in fitting the drives since they mostly slot direct into the bays. Suitable fixing screws should be supplied with the case, and will probably be included with some of the drives as well. It is best to use only the screws supplied with the drive or case, as they are suitably short. Screws even slightly longer might penetrate too far into the drive and cause severe damage. Where appropriate, the fixing screws that are supplied with a drive should always be used, since they will presumably be a perfect fit for the drive. Some of the screws supplied with the case should do the job perfectly well though.

There are usually four mounting holes in each side of 5.25-inch drives (Figure 3.62), but it is only necessary to use two fixing screws in each side (Figure 3.63). Initially leave the screws slightly loose, and then manoeuvre the drive precisely into the right position so that its front panel is flush with the case's front panel. Then tighten the screws, being careful not shift the drive out of position.

Fig.3.65 A circuit board is usually visible on the underside of the drive

Drive access

Depending on the design of the case you are using, it may or may not be possible to gain adequate access to both sides of the 3.5-inch drive bays. If necessary, remove the 3.5-inch bays from the case, fit the drives, and then replace the drive bays complete with the drives. With most cases, extricating the 3.5-inch bays only requires one or two screws to be removed, and then the bay can be slid away from the main casing. If this proves to be impossible it may be necessary to have the drives only secured to the bays on one side. This is not a desirable state of affairs, but it should hold the drives in place adequately.

Some cases give better access to the underside of the 3.5-inch bays when the motherboard is not in the case, but you may then find it difficult to install the motherboard with the 3.5-inch drives fitted. You have to use your initiative when dealing with this type of thing, or you will simply end up going round in circles. Try to avoid the embarrassing mistake of fitting one or more of the externally accessible drives upside-down.

Fig.3.66 Only two mounting holes per side will match up with holes in the drive bay

3.5-inch hard disc drives usually have a metal covering on one of the large surfaces (Figure 3.64) and a circuit board visible on the opposite surface (Figure 3.65). The metal covering is on what is usually the top of the drive. There is usually a minimum of three mounting holes in each side of the drive, but when the drive is fitted in the drive bay it is likely that only two holes will match up with the holes or slits in the bay (Figure 3.66). However, two mounting bolts per side are more than adequate.

It might be necessary to move the drive backward and forward to get the mounting holes in the drive to match up with those in the drive bay. It is more likely that there will be a range of positions where a match is obtained. Where there is a choice, always mount the drive as far forward as possible. The 3.5-inch drives tend to obscure the motherboard to some extent, but mounting them as far forward as possible minimises this problem. Modern cases often have internal bays going right down to the base panel, and using the very low bays can also help to minimise this problem.

The more upmarket cases are sometimes designed to have the 3.5-inch drives only bolted in place on one side. Any case of this type should be supplied complete with one mounting rail per 3.5-inch drive bay. It is unusual for the guide-rails to have provision for fixing screws, and most of them simply clip onto the side of the drive. The drive and guide-rail assembly is then slid into the drive bay and held in place by two screws that fit into place on the side that does not have the guide-rail. The other side of the drive is supported by the guide-rail, which clips into the case reasonably securely.

I think it is as well to repeat the warning that mounting bolts should not be tightened using the maximum force you can muster. Obviously the bolts need to be tightened sufficiently to reliably hold the drives in place for several years, but the "hammer and tongs" approach can result in screw threads being sheared. It is best to err on the side of caution. After all, if a screw should eventually work loose it only takes a few seconds to tighten it again.

Cabling

It is best to complete the cabling next, prior to installing the expansion cards (which tend to get in the way and make it difficult to fit the cables). The motherboard should be supplied complete with a basic set of connecting cables. For a budget ATX board this will probably just be a data cable for the floppy disc drive and another one for the IDE drives. Both of these cables will support two drives, but in the case of the IDE drives you may prefer to buy a second cable so that the hard disc and the CD-ROM drive can be operated from separate IDE ports.

In fact it is definitely a good idea to do so. As pointed out previously, this should give faster data transfers from the hard disc which will be free to operate in the fastest mode that both the drive and the motherboard support. Using some form of CD-ROM drive on the same interface would probably result in the hard disc drive operating in a more basic mode such as UDMA33, with a consequent slow-down in transfer rates. Also, transfers between the CD-ROM drive and the hard disc are likely to be faster with the two drives on different IDE interfaces. If you should settle for a single cable, the drives can normally be connected to the IDE1 or the IDE2 interface, but the convention is to use the IDE1 port. Some motherboards will only boot from devices on IDE1, so this is the safe option.

If the hard disc drive is an ordinary IDE type it will presumably operate in a "turbo" mode such as UDMA133, and it will need the special cable that supports UDMA66 operation and beyond. The IDE cable supplied with the motherboard will almost certainly be of this type. A second IDE cable might be supplied with the motherboard, but this is by no means certain. If there are two IDE cables of different types, the one having 80 connecting wires is used with the hard disc drive, and the one having 40 thicker wires is used with the CD-ROM drive, etc. If you have to buy an

IDE cable for use with CD-ROM drives, etc., on the second IDE interface, a 40-way cable will suffice, but an 80-way type should work perfectly well.

When using two modern hard disc drives they can both be connected to IDE1, and they should both provide fast data transfers. If one of the hard disc drives is an older and slower unit it is better to connect it on IDE2. It is otherwise likely that the old drive will result in the faster hard disc drive being reduced to a slower operating mode by the presence of the older drive.

IDE connectors

In theory the IDE connectors are polarised and can only be fitted the right way round. In practice some of the connectors, especially the ones

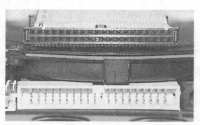

on cheaper motherboards, are rather basic and are not properly polarised. The plugs on the motherboards and drives should each have a cutout in the plastic surround, and this should match up with a protrusion on each plug. Figure 3.67 shows an IDE socket (top) and a matching plug (bottom), and the polarising keys are clearly visible.

Fig.3.67 IDE and floppy drive connectors are polarised

Some manufacturers take a "belt and braces" approach, and there may also be a missing pin on the plug and a blocked hole in the socket. If you look carefully at Figure 3.67 you will see that the connectors have the missing pin and blocked hole. Cables that have this method of polarisation are only suitable for use with motherboards that have the missing pin. This will not be a problem when using the cables supplied with the motherboard or if you buy standard IDE cables. It could be a problem if you try to use a cable removed from a defunct PC. However, it is usually quite easy to drill out the blocked hole using a very small drill bit.

If you find that it is possible to fit the connectors either way round it is still quite easy to determine the correct method of connection. Computer data cables are made from a ribbon-like cable, which, unsurprisingly, is actually called ribbon cable. This is grey in colour, but there is a red mark or pattern running along one edge of the cable. This is the lead that connects pin one on one connector to pin one on the other connector.

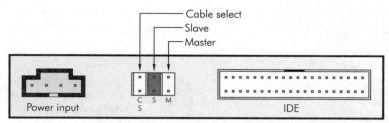

Fig.3.68 The configuration jumpers for a CD-ROM drive are buried in the connectors at the rear of the unit

The instruction manuals for the motherboard and drive should have diagrams that show the position of pin 1 on each connector. In fact pin one is usually marked on the actual components, although you will probably have to look carefully to find these markings. Make sure that the red lead always matches up with pin one on the drives and motherboard, and the drives will be connected correctly. These days some of the more upmarket motherboards are supplied with "round" IDE cables that use conventional multi-way cable rather than the ribbon variety. Pin one of each connector should still be clearly marked though.

Drive configuration

The two devices on an IDE port are called the "master" and "slave" devices. It does not matter which drive you connect to which connector on the IDE cable. Jumpers on the device itself control the role of an IDE device. If there is only one device on an IDE port it is normally set up as the master, but the system should work just as well if it is set as the slave device. The hard disc drive used to boot the system is normally the master device on IDE1.

The more or less standard arrangement for the

Fig.3.69 There is a jumper setting diagram on most hard disc drives

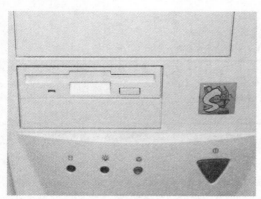

Fig.3.70 The conventional method of fitting
a 3.5-inch floppy disc drive

jumpers on a CD-ROM drive is shown in Figure 3.68. The jumper is used to bridge the two "S" terminals if it is to be the slave device or the "M" terminals if it is to be the "master" drive. Some IDE cables have the connectors marked something along the lines of "Master", "Slave", and "Motherboard". The idea is to select

the "CS" (cable select) option, and the device at the opposite end of the cable to the motherboard is then set as the master device. The one fitted to the connector in the middle of the cable becomes the slave device.

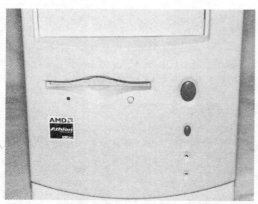

Fig.3.71 This case hides the floppy drive
behind a fascia

Hard disc drives normally operate using a similar arrangement, but when used as a master device some drives are not quite as straightforward as this. A different jumper configuration can be needed depending on whether or not there is a slave device on that IDE port. The Master setting is then only used if there is a slave device on the same

IDE interface as the hard drive. The alternative setting, which will be called something like the Sole setting, is used if the hard disc is the only drive on that IDE interface.

You should always check the instruction manuals of IDE drives to see if there are any unusual aspects to the configuration, and then proceed accordingly. Retail boxed drives are usually supplied with a detailed instruction manual, but the OEM units are usually "bare" drives. Instruction manuals for hard disc drives are usually available from the manufacturer's web site. The vast majority of modern drives have a configuration diagram or chart marked on the actual drive (Figure 3.69), and this is usually the only installation information you will require.

Serial ATA

Drive configuration with Serial ATA drives is very straightforward. They do not require any! Serial ATA operates on the basis of having an individual interface for each drive. They also have small and polarised connectors that are easy to use. At one time it was common for motherboards to have a few Serial ATA ports and two ordinary IDE types as well. This made it possible to use (say) a couple of hard disc drives and two CD/DVD drives without using the serial interfaces.

The more usual arrangement these days is to have something like four Serial ATA ports, but just one IDE type. The idea is to use the serial ports for hard disc drives and any other fast drives that have this type of interface, and to use the IDE interface only if there are slower drives that use this type of interface. In practice this generally means using the Serial ATA ports for hard disc drives and the IDE interface for CD and DVD drives. Alternatively, it is possible to use the Seial ATA for all the drives, including suitably equipped CD and DVD types.. Using IDE ports for all the drives will probably not be a practical proposition. Drives having the right type of interface should be readily available, but there will probably not be sufficient IDE channels to accommodate them properly.

RAID controller

It has been assumed here that the motherboard has two IDE interfaces. Some motherboards have a built-in RAID (Redundant Array of Inexpensive Discs) controller, giving two or more additional IDE interfaces. This used to be an expensive addition to a motherboard, but it is increasingly common for mid-price and even budget motherboards to sport this feature. It is not essential to use the additional IDE ports, and they can simply be ignored. The section of the BIOS that handles the input and

Fig.3.72 There are three mounting holes in each side of a 3.5-inch floppy disc drive

output circuits usually has a setting that permits the RAID controller to be switched off.

RAID controllers are also to be found on motherboards that have SATA disc interfaces. Some motherboards have IDE ports for drives that will be used normally, and a couple of SATA ports for hard drives that will be used as a RAID array. In some cases the two SATA ports can only be used with two drives set to operate as a RAID array. They can not be used with a single drive or two drives operating independently.

There are various RAID operating modes that enable additional hard disc drives to be used in various ways. Apparently the basic idea is to permit two or more hard disc drives of relatively low capacity to operate as one huge disc drive. This has potential advantages, including a possible speed increase,, but "small" hard drives currently offer capacities of 40 to 120 gigabytes, which is more than adequate for most purposes! Another operating mode (RAID 1) has data written to two hard disc drives simultaneously, and it can then be read from either drive. If one drive

Fig.3.73 Two mounting bolts per side will hold a floppy drive in place

fails, the other effectively becomes a backup device that should still have perfect copies of all your files.

Using a RAID controller really goes beyond the scope of this book, and it is probably something that is best avoided when building your first PC. If you use a motherboard that has a RAID controller it might be best to switch it off or ignore it initially. Once the PC has been built and tested you can always add an extra disc or two and try out the RAID controller. Unfortunately, the RAID documentation provided with motherboards is often limited or even absent, but there is plenty of information on this subject available on the Internet. Some motherboards have a sort of second BIOS that is accessed by operating the Tab key during the initial start-up sequence. This additional BIOS is used to set the required RAID mode.

Floppy drive

Like CD-ROM and DVD drives, a 3.5-inch floppy drive requires a drive bay that has external access. Many cases only have one 3.5-inch drive bay with external access, which is usually the top one, so there may be

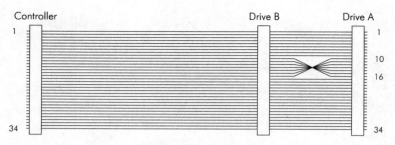

Fig.3.74 The arrangement used for a PC floppy disc data cable

no choice but to use this bay for the floppy drive. Where appropriate, the plastic cover and metal plate covering the front of the drive bay must be removed. The conventional way of fitting a floppy disc drive is to have the front of the drive flush with the front panel of the case, as in Figure 3.70.

It is increasingly common for modern cases to use the alternative method of having a sort of plastic fascia on the front of the case, with the drive fitted behind it (Figure 3.71). The drive's disc eject button is operated via a button built into the front of the case. Most cases will take ordinary 3.5-inch floppy drives, but some require a drive having a somewhat simplified front section. It is probably best to avoid this type of case unless you are sure that a matching floppy drive can be obtained, or a suitable drive is supplied with the case.

A 3.5-inch floppy disc drive usually has three mounting holes per side (Figure 3.72). The one nearest the front is a bit difficult to spot in Figure 3.72, but it is unlikely that there will be matching hole for this in the drive bay. The other two are used to hold the drive in place, and the drive bays usually have slits (Figure 3.73) that permit the drive to be positioned so that its front panel is flush with the front of the case. If the case is a type that has a plastic fascia, simply mount the drive as far forward as it will go.

Floppy cabling

Connecting the floppy disc drive tends to cause a certain amount of confusion due to the unusual method of cabling used. The standard PC floppy disc drive cable consists of a length of 34-way ribbon cable, which is fitted with 34-way edge connectors and IDC connectors at the floppy drive end. 3.5-inch floppy drives require the IDC connectors, and 5.25-

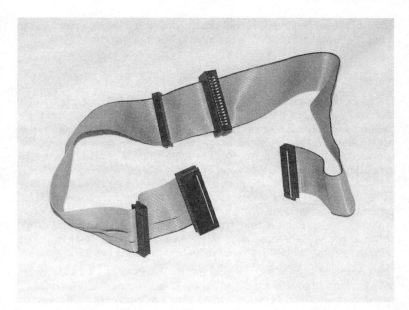

Fig.3.75 A floppy disc cable having two sets of drive connectors

inch types connect to the edge connectors. The connector at the motherboard end is a 34-way IDC connector. Most cables are for twin drives, and therefore have two sets of drive connectors, which is some four in total. The maximum number of floppy drives that can be used is two and not four.

In a standard floppy drive set-up, the two connectors would be wired in exactly the same way. Pin 1 at the controller would connect to pin 1 of both drives, pin 2 would connect to both of the pin 2s, and so on. On the face of it, the two drives will try to operate in unison, with both trying to operate as drive A. In practice this does not happen, because there are jumpers on the drives which are set to make one operate as drive A, and the other as drive B. This is essentially the same as the master and slave system used for drives connected to an IDE interface.

The jumper blocks are normally in the form of four pairs of terminals marked something like "DS0", "DS1", "DS2", and "DS3" (or possibly something like "DS1" to "DS4"). The instruction manual for the disc drive (in the unlikely event of you being able to obtain it) will make it clear which of the many jumper blocks are the ones for drive selection. Drive A has the jumper on "DS0", while drive B has it on "DS1".

Strange twist

Things could actually be set up in this fashion in a PC, but it is not the standard way of doing things. Instead, both drives are set as drive B by having the jumper lead placed on "DS1". The so-called "twist" in the cable between the two drive connectors then reverses some of the connections to one drive, making it operate as drive B. This may seem to be a strange way of doing things, but there is apparently a good reason for it. If you obtain a PC disc drive, whether for use as drive A or B, the same drive configured in exactly the same way will do the job. This avoids the need for dealers to stock two different types of drive, which in reality is exactly the same type of drive with a slightly different configuration. In fact these days most drives sold for use in PCs do not have the jumper blocks, and are hard-wired to act as drive B.

The computer will still work if you get the connections to two floppy drives swapped over, but the one you required as drive A will be drive B, and vice versa. The connector at the end of the cable couples to drive A, while the other one connects to drive B. Figure 3.74 shows this general scheme of things, and Figure 3.75 shows a floppy disc cable that has two pairs of drive connectors. Getting the floppy drive cable connected to the new drive should be straightforward, because the connectors should be polarised, so that they can not be fitted the wrong way round. In reality matters are not always as straightforward as this.

The connectors used for 3.5-inch drives are much the same as the ones used for IDE drives, but with 34 pins instead of 40. Like the IDE connectors, they are not always properly polarised. Some floppy drives unhelpfully have two polarising keys so that the data lead can be connected either way round. Floppy drive cables use the same system as the IDE variety, with pin 1 indicated by a red lead. If the connectors are not properly polarised, check the pin numbering on the drive and the motherboard and make sure that the red lead connects to pin 1 at both ends of the cable. It can be difficult to locate the pin numbering on floppy drives, but there are usually at least a couple of numbers marked to show which end of the connector has pin 1.

5.25-inch floppy drives have a different connector to the 3.5-inch variety. A simple edge connector system is used, and this is similar to an expansion card and an expansion slot. The connector on the drive is just part of its main printed circuit board, and the connector on the lead

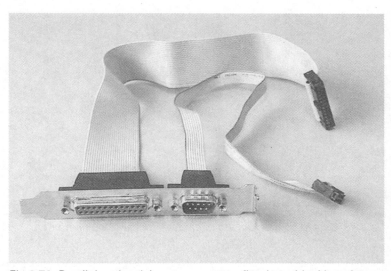

Fig.3.76 Parallel and serial port connectors fitted to a blanking plate

is a bit like a miniature expansion slot. These connectors are properly polarised, and the necessary "key" is just a small metal rod on the edge connector, which fits into a slot in the connector on the drive. Note that many modern floppy disc cables do not have the connectors for 5.25-inch drives. It may be

necessary to do some searching for a suitable lead in the unlikely event that you wish to include a 5.25-inch drive in a PC. Because floppy drives are little used these days, and systems with two floppy drives are very rare, many of the floppy cables supplied with motherboards only have the connector for drive A.

Fig.3.77 The port connectors are often like smaller versions of IDE connectors

Fig.3.78 Simple connectors are often used for the ports on modern motherboards

Termination resistors

Floppy disc drives used to be supplied with a block of removable resistors, or resistors that could be switched out of circuit. The idea was to have these termination resistors connected into circuit on the drive at the end of the cable, but not on any drives along the way. Modern floppy disc drives for use in PCs do not seem to have these resistors, or if they do there is no way of cutting them out of circuit. Consequently you will not have to bother with these resistors unless you are using an old floppy drive in your new PC. The resistors should then be switched out or removed if the drive is used as drive B (the one connected to the middle of the cable).

Without an instruction manual for the disc drive it could be difficult to deactivate the resistors. A search of the drive's circuit board will probably bring to light a small component mounted in a socket so that it can be removed easily, and this will probably be the termination resistors. Alternatively there might be a switch or a jumper with markings that suggest it is for deactivating the termination resistors. If not, the drive probably does not have these resistors and it can then be used as is.

Ports

AT motherboards do not have "proper" on-board connectors for the serial and parallel ports. Instead, the basic connectors on the board are wired to sockets mounted on the rear of the case, or in blanking plates that are fitted behind any vacant expansion slots. The boards were normally supplied with connectors and leads for the serial and parallel ports, and possibly connectors and leads for the mouse port as well. Figure 3.76 shows a blanking plate fitted with connectors for one serial and one parallel port.

As explained previously, ATX motherboards make things much easier by, as far as possible, having the connectors for the ports mounted on the motherboard and accessible through cut-outs in the rear of the case. With the early ATX motherboards there was usually no need for any connectors mounted on blanking plates. However, the proliferation of ports on modern motherboards has resulted in a return to ports provided in this fashion. For example, additional USB ports are sometimes provided in this way, as are Firewire ports. Also many motherboards still

Fig.3.79 *The individual connectors are marked with their functions*

have the electronics to provide legacy ports such as the serial and game types, but these ports are often omitted from the main port cluster. Instead they are provided by backplates and leads, which are optional extras in some cases.

At the motherboard end of the cables the connectors are usually small IDC types, like the disc drive connectors. In Figure 3.77 the three smaller connectors near the top are for off-board ports, and the one below them is a floppy drive port. The connectors should be polarised, but if not you will have to use the red lead to pin 1 method. Pin 1 might be indicated on the motherboard itself, but if not there should be a diagram in the instruction manual that shows pin 1 of every connector on the board. It is worth remembering that the motherboard's instruction manual gives concise connection information for all the onboard connectors, and should be able to solve problems when connecting anything to the motherboard.

There has been a trend towards the use of simple connectors that just consist of a few pins on the motherboard. These are usually polarised by having a "missing" pin. In Figure 3.78 a connector is fitted to the pair of USB ports on the left. The "missing" pin can be seen in the top left-hand corner of the connector for the set of unused USB ports on the right. Essentially the same connector is often used for other types of port such as Firewire. A different "missing" pin is used for each type of port, making it is impossible to fit (say) a pair of USB connectors to what is actually a pair of Firewire ports. This method of connection is not completely foolproof though. Make sure that the connector is aligned properly with the pins on the motherboard, and not one set of pins out of position.

As pointed out previously, some or all of the connectors and leads needed to implement additional ports are sometimes optional extras. If you wish to use these facilities and suitable leads are not supplied with the motherboard you must be sure to obtain the correct lead and connector set. There are often minor differences from one manufacturer to another, and in some cases the connectors at the motherboard end are completely different. In others they are the same but wired differently. Buy leads that are specifically designed for use with the particular motherboard you are using, and connect them in accordance with the instructions in the motherboard's instruction manual.

Fig.3.80 An ATX power connector fitted on
a motherboard

Some motherboards have connectors for additional USB ports and (or) a second set of audio connectors, but they are not primarily intended for use with brackets mounted at the rear of the PC. Instead, they are intended for use with cases that have provision for USB and (or) audio sockets mounted on the front panel. The majority of modern cases have this feature, a few have support for Firewire as well. Front panel audio and USB sockets are very useful, and it is well worth implementing this facility.

Unfortunately, it can be a bit awkward to connect the front panel connectors to the motherboard. Due to a lack of standardisation of the motherboard connectors, the cases often have the leads terminated in a number of one-way connectors rather than (say) a 10-way

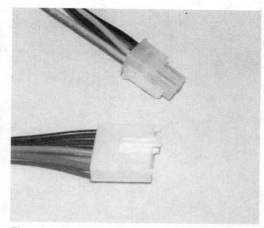

Fig.3.81 The two additional connectors needed for a Pentium 4 motherboard

connector. This produces what is often a substantial number of leads coming from the front of the PC, with a huge number of individual connectors. It provides great versatility though, and it should be possible

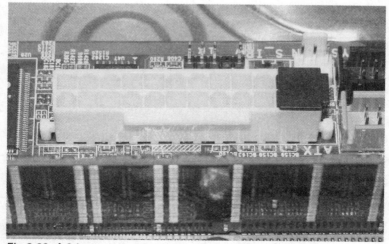

Fig.3.82 A 24-way power connector fitted with a plastic cover

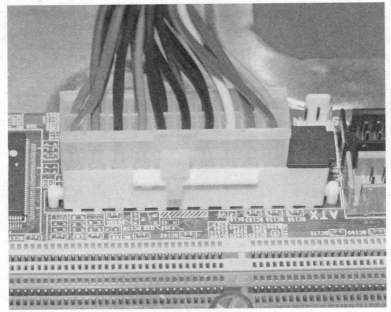

Fig.3.83 A 20-way power connector fitted to a 24-ATX 2.0 connector on the motherboard

to connect the front panel sockets to any motherboard that supports this feature and uses simple pin-type connectors. These days, this means practically all motherboards.

The connectors on the leads are marked with their functions (Figure 3.79), and the instruction manual for the motherboard should have diagrams that shows the functions of each pin of every connector. This makes it reasonably easy to find the matching pin on the motherboard for each of the case's connectors. Getting it all connected properly is a bit fiddly though, and it is easy to accidentally free one connector while fitting the next one. With a little patience the job should soon be completed. Make sure that no errors are made, and be especially careful with the USB ports. USB ports carry a 5-volt supply, and getting this wired incorrectly could damage any peripheral device connected to the port. If you are not sure what you are doing, leave the front panel USB ports unconnected. Even if you do know what you are doing, it is advisable to test each of the front panel USB ports using something cheap and expendable, such as an old USB mouse.

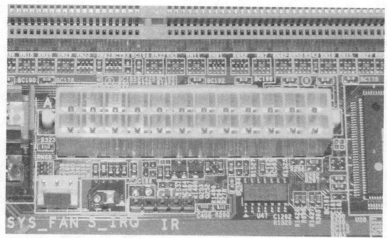

Fig.3.84 The 24-way connector with the cover removed

Power supply

The original PC power supply was an AT type that had two power connectors and conventional on/off switching. Modern PCs use an ATX power supply that has a conventional on/off switch, but in normal use the power is left switched on. Like many current items of electronic equipment, when in the "off" state a PC is really in a sort of low-power standby mode. It is switched off by shutting down Windows, but this leaves the power supply operating in a limited fashion. Operating the on/off switch on the front panel sends a signal to the power supply via the motherboard, which results in the PC powering up.

The two connectors of the old AT supplies were replaced by a single 20-way connector when ATX supplies were introduced. This made connecting an ATX power supply to the motherboard somewhat easier, and avoided the possibility of getting two connectors accidentally swapped. An ATX power connector is polarised, so it can not be fitted the wrong way round. Figure 3.80 shows an ATX power lead connected to a motherboard. Some of these connectors can be reluctant to fit into place, but with firm pressure it should do so. The power connector is a locking type, and the lever mechanism on the connector must be operated in order to pull it free of the motherboard.

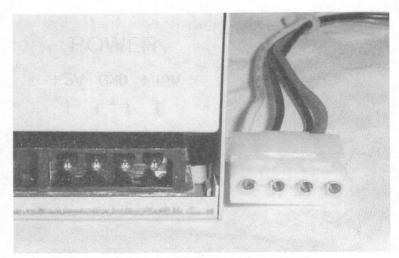

Fig.3.85 The 5.25-inch power connectors are polarised

Power supplies for Pentium 4 motherboards have two additional connectors (Figure 3.81). If you are building a PC based on a motherboard that requires the additional power sources it is clearly essential to buy a case that has a suitably equipped power supply, but any modern supply should have them. Both the additional power connectors are properly polarised so there is no risk of connecting them the wrong way round. The two extra power connectors on the

Fig.3.86 The power lead connected correctly to a 3.5-inch floppy drive

motherboard will not necessarily be close to the main power input, but they should be easy to spot. The larger of the two additional connectors seems to be little used these days. Just ignore it if there is no matching connector on the motherboard. The smaller of the two additional power connectors now seems to be used by most motherboards, including those that take AMD processors. Again, if there is no matching connector on the motherboard, simply leave it unused.

Some motherboards are now designed for use with ATX 2.0 power supplies.

Fig.3.87 The 3.5-inch floppy disc power connectors

These have a main connector that looks very similar to the usual 20-way ATX type, but it is actually a bit larger and is a 24-way type. No doubt plenty of ATX 2.0 power supplies will become available in due course, but at the time of writing this they are "a bit thin on the ground". However,

Fig.3.88 A dual serial ATA power adaptor lead

153

many motherboards that have a 24-way power connector can be used with the normal 20-way type.

The motherboard sometimes has a plastic cover that blocks four terminals at one end of the power connector (Figure 3.82). With this in place it is possible to fit and use an ordinary 20-way ATX power connector, as shown in Figure 3.83. With the cover removed (Figure 3.84) the connector is a standard ATX 2.0 type that can be used with a 24-way power connector. With anything like this it is advisable to consult the motherboard's instruction manual rather than jumping to conclusions. The manual should give clear information about the board's supply requirements.

With a modern power supply there should be more than ample power leads for the disc drives. The larger connectors are the ones for the 5.25-inch drives and 3.5-inch hard drives. Figure 3.85 shows the power port of a 5.25-inch drive or hard drive together with a matching connector of the power supply. Getting this type of connector into place can require a substantial amount of force. It can require even more effort to remove one again. I normally advise people not to use the "hammer and tongs" approach with computer equipment, but you have to be prepared to use a certain amount of brute force with this type of connector. Due to their shape it is impossible to fit these connectors the wrong way round.

The smaller connectors for the 3.5-inch drives are also polarised, and it should need relatively little force to connect them to the drives. Figure 3.86 shows a 3.5-inch power connector fitted to a floppy drive. If you find it difficult to fit these plugs into the drives you either have them up-side-down or out of alignment with the connectors in the drive. The concave side of the connector faces downward and the convex surface faces upwards.

There can be problems with the terminals on the floppy drive's connector getting bent slightly upwards, making it impossible to fit the power connector on the supply lead. Pressing the terminals down slightly should permit the supply to be connected. Make sure that you get the floppy power connector fitted just right. Mistakes here can have dire consequences for the power supply and (or) the floppy drive. Figure 3.87 shows the connector on the drive, and the connector on the power lead the right way up, ready to be fitted to the drive.

Serial ATA Power

Serial ATA drives sometimes have standard 5.25-inch power connectors in addition to their own miniature type, but most only have the miniature power port. Unfortunately, by no means all PC power supplies have any serial ATA power connectors. Where a drive has a 5.25-inch power port, using it will probably be the best option. In most cases it will be necessary to power serial ATA drives from 5.25-inch power leads via an adaptor. The example shown in Figure 3.88 enables two serial ATA drives to be powered from a single 5.25-inch power lead. Serial ATA power leads are polarised and usually fit into place with a minimum of fuss.

Connector block

The motherboard will have a connector block that accepts leads from various items on the case (Figure 3.89). This block is a common cause

of confusion for newcomers to PC building because the facilities of the case never seem to perfectly match up with those of the motherboard. A typical set of connectors for an ATX case is shown in Figure 3.90. There may be some features of the case that are not supported by the motherboard, and there will almost certainly be several motherboard features that the case is unable to accommodate.

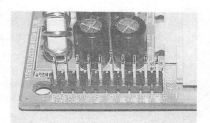

Fig.3.89 A typical connector block

This is something where you have to take a down to earth attitude, and provided a few basic features are implemented on both, which they will be, that is all that is needed to get your new PC operating successfully. These are the functions that you should be able to implement:

Power LED

This connects to what is usually a green LED on the front of the case that switches on whenever the computer is operating. Note that an LED, unlike an ordinary light bulb, will only work if it is connected with the right polarity. The instruction manual for the motherboard will have a diagram showing the functions of the

Fig.3.90 A typical set of connectors for an ATX case

various pins in the block, and this with have a "+" sign on one of the pins that connects to the power LED. The connectors on the leads that connect to the LEDs, etc., will be marked with their functions, and the connector for the power LED might have its polarity marked. If not, it is usually the white lead that is the "–" connection and the coloured lead that is the "+" one. There is little risk of a LED being damaged if it is connected with the wrong polarity, so you can use trial and error if necessary.

IDE activity LED

This is sometimes called the hard disc light, and in days gone by it would probably only switch on when the hard disc was active. However, this light actually switches on when any IDE device is active, and these days there will normally be other IDE devices such as CD-ROM drives and CD writers. Where a PC has serial ATA drives, this LED will operate when these or any IDE drives are active. This LED must be connected with the right polarity. Again, trial and error can be used if necessary.

Reset switch

This is the switch on the front panel that can be used to reset the computer if it hangs up. Its lead can be connected either way round. Some users prefer not to connect this switch, so that it is not possible to accidentally reset the computer. However, without the reset switch the only means of providing a hardware reset is to switch the computer off, wait at least a couple of seconds, and then switch on again.

Loudspeaker

This is the lead for the computer's internal loudspeaker, which is little used in modern computers. This loudspeaker is normally used to produce one or two beeps at start-up to indicate that all is well or a different set of beeps if there is a fault. The leads on this connector will probably be red and black, but it can actually be connected either way round and it is not polarised.

Power switch

As explained previously, with an ATX power supply the on/off switching is controlled via a signal from the motherboard. The on/off switch on the front panel connects to the power supply via the motherboard and the supply's main power output lead. Pressing the power switch turns on the computer, pressing it again switches off the computer, and so on. This switch appears to operate like a normal power switch, but note that the computer will be in the off state if the mains supply is removed and then reinstated.

Also note that this switch might not switch off the PC once it has booted into the operating system. Depending on the operating system and the way it is set up, the power switch might turn off the PC, place it into a standby mode, or have no effect. This lead can be connected either way round.

These are some of the functions that might be implemented on the motherboard, but they are non-essential:

Keylock

It used to be standard practice for PCs to have a key that could be used to operate a special type of switch fitted on the front panel. This switch enabled the keyboard to be switched off, thus preventing anyone from tampering with the PC while you were not looking. This feature was never very popular, and when control of PCs was partially handed over to the mouse it failed to fulfil its intended task anyway. It is probably not worth implementing even if this feature is supported by the case.

Temperature warning

Because modern PCs contain a lot of components that get quite hot it is now very common for some sort of temperature monitoring and warning feature to be included on motherboards. Exactly what happens when something in the PC starts to get too hot varies from one motherboard to another, but the internal loudspeaker will probably start to "beep", a warning LED might start flashing, or the PC might even switch itself off. If there is an output for a temperature warning LED and the case has a spare LED indicator, I would recommend implementing this feature. Note that the LED will only work if it is connected the right way round. Most facilities of this type have the LED normally switched on, and it flashes when an excessive temperature is detected.

Suspend switch

This switch can be used to enable and disable the power management function. This is probably something you can live without, which is just as well since few cases have the necessary switch. There is sometimes an output for a LED which operates in conjunction with this feature. With modern motherboards the suspend feature is not usually implemented, but there is often an output for a "suspend" or "message" LED. This is activated when the operating system is placed into the standby mode.

Fig.3.91 The expansion cards are bolted to the rear of the case

There may well be other functions available, and it is a matter of consulting the motherboard's instruction manual for details of any additional features. However, unless the case has some spare switches and (or) LEDs any "extras" will only be of academic interest. The modern trend is for cases to have a minimum of switches and indicator lights, leaving plenty of space for drives, front panel audio and USB connectors, etc.

On the cards

By this stage the PC is nearly complete, and the only major task remaining is to fit the various expansion cards. Some advocate having only the essential cards installed initially, with others being added once the PC has been completed and the operating system has been installed. Windows 95 was notorious for installation difficulties with several expansion cards installed. The installation process tended to go round in circles with the drivers being installed, the computer resetting, the drivers being installed again, and so on. This does not seem to be a major problem with Windows 98 and beyond, and I have no qualms about fully completing the PC before installing the operating system.

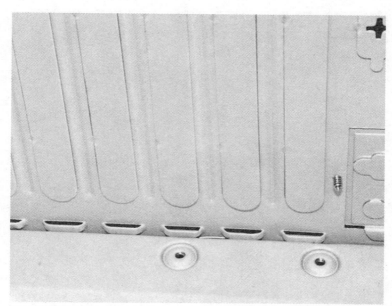

Fig.3.92 The brackets on the expansion cards should fit into holders in the rear of the case

Not that a typical PC actually has much in the way of expansion cards these days. There could be no need for expansion cards if the motherboard has integrated sound and graphics.

Before the cards can be fitted it is necessary to remove the blanking plates in the rear of the case for the particular slots you will be using. Cases used to be supplied with blanking plates that were held in place by screws, but only a few up-market cases still

Fig.3.93 A notch in the front of an AGP card enables it to be locked in place

Fig.3.94 The locking lever on an AGP expansion slot

use this method. The more usual method is for the blanking plates to be partially cut out. Those that are not required are simply broken away from the main case. Some cases have blanking plates that can be unclipped. Provided this is done carefully, it is usually possible to clip them back in place again, should the expansion card be removed at some time in the future.

The expansion cards should fit into place without having to push too hard. If a moderate amount of force fails to get one or more of the cards into position it is likely that the motherboard is slightly out of alignment with the case. Try slackening the motherboard's mounting screws slightly, fitting a couple of expansion cards, and then tightening the mounting screws again. It should then be easy to fit any remaining expansion cards, remembering to bolt the metal bracket of each card to the rear of the case (Figure 3.91).

If it is still difficult to fit one or two of the expansion cards the most likely cause of the problem is the metal bracket at the rear of the offending

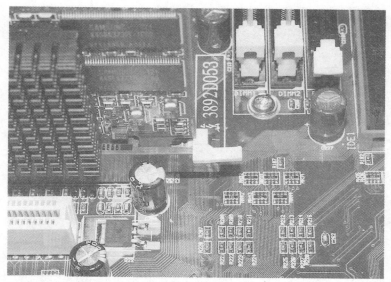

Fig.3.95 An AGP card locked into position in the expansion slot

card or cards. If you look at the rear of the case you will notice that there
are receptacles to take the bottom sections of the mounting brackets
(Figure 3.92). With some expansion cards it is necessary to carefully
bend the lower section of the mounting bracket backwards so that it
engages with the receptacle in the case. Everything should then slot
nicely into position.

AGP cards

Unless the motherboard has integrated video circuits, an AGP or 16X
PCI Express video card will presumably be used. Fitting either type of
card is slightly different to fitting a PCI type. There is a locking lever at
the front of the expansion slot, and the locking mechanism is much like
the one used on memory sockets. Unlike a memory socket, the locking
mechanism is only included at one end of the connector. It is quite
common for expansion cards to ride up slightly at the front when the
mounting bolt is tightened. The connector of an AGP or 16X PCI Express
card has so many terminals in such a small space that even a small

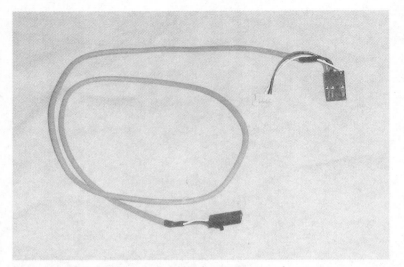

Fig.3.96 A CD-ROM audio lead having two types of connector

degree of tilt can prevent it from connecting to the motherboard properly. The purpose of the locking mechanism is to ensure that the card can not ride up slightly at the front.

Any modern AGP card should have a cut-out in the front edge of the connector to take the locking mechanism (Figure 3.93). Initially the locking lever on the AGP slot should be in the open (down) position, as in Figure 3.94. When the card is pushed into its expansion slot the lever should automatically move up and into place (Figure 3.95), but if necessary it can be given a little manual assistance. Essentially the same system is used for 16X PCI Express cards. Be aware that some motherboard manufacturers use their own methods for clipping video cards in place. Consult the motherboard's instruction manual if the video slot seems to have a non-standard locking mechanism. Make sure that the locking mechanism is fully released before trying to remove a video card.

Note that some motherboards can be rather fussy about the video cards that they will work with reliably. In particular, some motherboards lack proper compatibility with some 2x/4x AGP boards. The problem seems to stem from the fact that 2x operation uses higher signal voltages than 4x operation, but some video boards do not adjust to low voltage operation in the 4x mode. If you are using a motherboard of this type

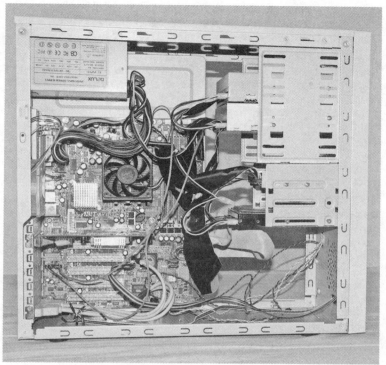

Fig.3.97 An interior view of the completed Athlon 64 (Socket 939) PC

there will probably be a warning sticker on the AGP slot itself as well as warnings in the instruction manual. Make sure that the video card is a compatible type if you use one of these boards, since a mistake could result in damage to the motherboard. Provided you use a modern motherboard and AGP card they should both support 8x operation, and there should be no problem.

Audio cable

These days most CD-ROM drives are supplied complete with an audio cable that can connect the audio output at the rear of the drive to the audio input of the soundcard. This enables audio CDs in the CD-ROM drive to be played through the computer's speakers. This lead is not needed if you will only play audio CDs through headphones connected direct to the CD-ROM drive, or if you are not interested in playing audio CDs at all. On the other hand, you may as well fit it anyway just in case you need to use this facility at some future time.

The connector at the soundcard end of the cable will almost certainly be a type that is compatible with SoundBlaster cards. Most other soundcards now use the same type of connector, or have two audio input connectors including one SoundBlaster compatible type. There is still a slight risk that the cable will not be compatible with your soundcard, and you will then have to seek out a cable of the correct type. Some PC audio cables have both types of soundcard connector (Figure 3.96), guaranteeing compatibility with the soundcard. There should be at least one audio input on the motherboard if it is a type that has integrated audio. The connector will almost certainly be a standard SoundBlaster type.

These days it is quite normal for a PC to have two CD-ROM drives of some kind, such as a CD-RW drive and a DVD type. Two audio inputs are needed in order to permit both drives to play CDs via the computer's sound system. Modern soundcards often have several audio inputs, and should be able to accommodate two CD-ROM drives. Integrated audio systems sometimes have two or three audio inputs, but some have only one audio input port. Unfortunately, only one CD-ROM drive can be used with the PC's sound system if there is only one audio input available.

You then have what is basically a complete PC base unit. There may be one or two other leads that need to be connected, such as cables from the soundcard or modem to the motherboard, but this is dependent on both items of equipment supporting some extra features, and you wishing to implement them. Where necessary, add any extra cables in accordance with the instructions in manuals for the items of equipment concerned. The motherboard will probably have a power output for a fan fitted at the front or rear of the case. Practically every PC case has provision for a fan, but they are not always fitted as standard. If no fan is supplied with the case it is advisable to fit one. In fact with most processors it is essential, since the temperature inside the case will otherwise become too high, making it impossible to keep the processor's temperature down to an acceptable level. A fan at the rear of the case is usually quieter and more efficient than one at the front. Where there is a choice, I would definitely recommend fitting the fan on the rear panel.

Fig.3.98 An interior view of the Pentium 4 (Socket 775) PC, which uses two serial ATA hard disc drives. It still has quite a clutter of cables, including an IDE type for the CD and DVD drives

Tidying up

The interior of the finished PC can look a bit untidy, but things are not as bad as they used to be. ATX motherboards have helped to reduce the amount of cabling and this greatly reduces the amount of clutter inside the PC. I made two PCs while producing this book. One is based on a 3.0GHz Athlon 64, and the other is a slightly more expensive (but possibly slower) PC based on a 2.8GHz Pentium 4. Interior views of these PCs are shown in Figures 3.97 and 3.98 respectively.

Results can certainly be made much neater by fixing the cables to convenient points on the case rather than just leaving them dangling. It is definitely a good idea to secure each cable in at least one place if the PC will be transported several miles or more. It is otherwise of relatively little importance. Double-sided adhesive pads represent the easiest way of fixing the cables to the case, drive bays, or whatever.

It is best not to get carried away with this sort of thing. I once bought a PC that had received a glowing review in a magazine, and it had been particularly complemented for the tidiness of its cables. The interior of the PC was indeed very neat, but there were major problems each time I tried to upgrade any of the hardware. The very neat cabling was effectively barring access to the drives, memory, expansion cards, and just about everything else inside the PC. It was necessary to carefully cut one or two cables free each time a change was made to the hardware. Tidy up the cabling by all means, but do not get carried away.

Testing

With the minor cabling completed the base unit of the computer is finished. Before connecting the mouse, keyboard, and monitor it is definitely a good idea to thoroughly check everything, making sure that all the cables are connected correctly and that none have been accidentally dislodged when working on the unit. None of the connectors lock into place, and it is very easy to dislodge one connector while fitting another. Also check that the expansion cards are fitted into their slots properly.

It is not possible to boot from the hard disc until it has been properly prepared, so initially try booting from something like an MS-DOS boot disc. Better still, use a Windows 98 or ME start-up disc as this can provide CD-ROM support, and it will enable you to check that the CD-ROM drive is working properly. When the computer is switched on it should go through the normal BIOS start-up routine. By default it will probably be set to auto-detect the IDE devices, and it will probably list the drives that are detected.

If nothing happens, or there is any sign of a malfunction, switch off at once and recheck the entire wiring, etc. Assuming all is well, let the computer go through its boot-up routine so that you can check that it is more or less working correctly. If it is, the next step is to go into the ROM BIOS Setup program and configure the CMOS memory correctly. This is covered in the next chapter. Tips on getting troublesome PCs sorted out are provided in chapter 6.

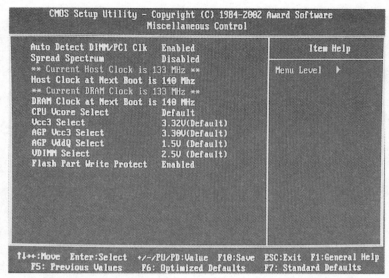

Fig.3.99 This section of the BIOS permits over-clocking to be used

Over-clocking

Over-clocking is sometimes referred to as the "free upgrade", and it is the practice of using electronic components beyond their maximum speed rating. By no means all motherboards support any form of over-clocking. With those that do, the motherboard's instruction manual usually contained one or two disclaimers, saying something along the lines that the board has the ability to use over-clocking, but the manufacturer does not condone this practice. This may seem rather two-faced, but the manufacturer is basically saying that the board has the overclocking facility, but you use it at your own risk.

Modern processors often have the clock multiplier locked, and the motherboard is unlikely to provide any means of altering this setting. Consequently, the only way of using over-clocking is to increase the basic clock frequency of the system. This usually boosts the operating frequency of the memory, video card, etc., and not just the processor. While this gives a greater increase in speed than simply boosting the clock frequency of the processor, it reduces the chances of over-clocking being usable. If any component in the system is unable to support the

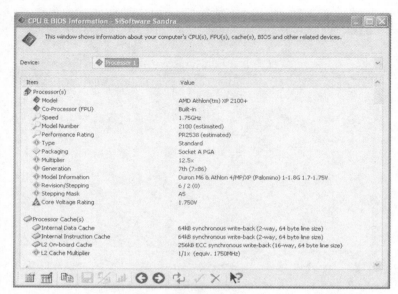

Fig.3.100 The system is indeed operating at a higher clock frequency

higher frequency caused by over-clocking, then the PC will fail to operate reliably. Some motherboards have clever overclocking facilities that enable the processor frequency to be raised without altering some of the other operating frequencies, such as those used by the expansion slots.

Over-clocking the motherboard's chipset is unlikely to damage anything, but good reliability can not be guaranteed. The same is true of the memory modules. Over-clocking the processor is a bit more dubious since it increases its power consumption and causes it to operate at a higher temperature. This might necessitate the use of a bigger heatsink, and even with a larger heatsink it is a dubious practice with a processor that runs quite hot at its normal operating frequency. There are now some very elaborate cooling systems available for overclocked processors, but these are aimed at experienced users. Unless you really understand what you are doing, serious overclocking is likely to produce a fast but short-lived PC.

Where over-clocking is supported, it is usually possible to increase the basic clock frequency in one megahertz increments via the BIOS Setup

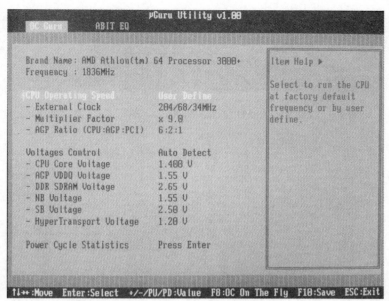

Fig.3.101   This BIOS provides a range of settings for overclocking

program.   Figure 3.99 shows the relevant section of the BIOS Setup program for the Athlon XP2000+-based PC. As an experiment I tried overclocking the Athlon XP2000+-based PC by raising the system bus frequency from 133MHz to 140MHz. I also tried the same thing with a PC based on a 2.4GHz Pentium 4. In both cases no reliability problems were apparent, and the components all ran quite cool.

Figure 3.100 shows a diagnostics program running on the Athlon XP2000+ PC, and it correctly shows the increased processor clock frequency. In fact the higher clock frequency has caused the program to identify the processor as an Athlon XP2100+. Although this method of over-clocking will usually provide some increase in speed, it will not turn a slow PC into a fast one, and in this example the increase in clock frequency is a very modest five percent or so. Trying for a much more significant increase in speed gives little chance of success unless you use fast and relatively expensive components such as high-speed memory modules. An elaborate heatsink for the processor might also be needed. In many cases the money could be used more effectively on a faster processor or more "bog standard" memory.

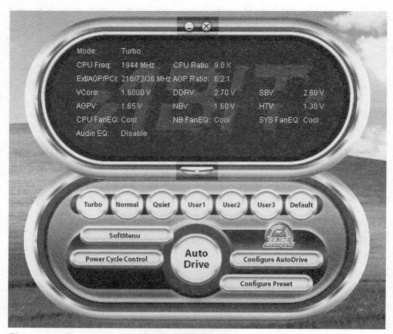

*Fig.3.102 This program was supplied with the motherboard, and
enables a range of frequencies and voltages to be changed*

The BIOS Setup program of some modern motherboards enables various
clock frequencies and voltages to be altered (Figure 3.101) Some are
even supplied with a Windows program that provides similar features
without the need to enter the Setup program (Figure 3.102) It is definitely
not a good idea to "play" with this type of thing unless you really know
what you are doing.

Bear in mind that if you should damage a processor by over-clocking it,
or if it should fail for any reason while it is not being used within its normal
operating parameters, it will almost certainly not be covered by the
guarantee. If you experiment with over-clocking techniques you do so
entirely at your own risk. New PC builders would be well advised to do
everything "by the book", and not risk problems trying to stretch any
item of hardware beyond its normal limits.

Points to remember

Try to get a mental picture of how everything fits together before you actually start assembling the PC. Also make sure that you have everything you need including small items such as bolts and stand-offs.

Although most people only refer to instruction manuals as a last resort, this is not an option with the manual for the motherboard. Read it through carefully so that you can determine what configuration is needed for the particular processor you are using. It should also explain any special features that the board supports.

Do not rush construction of the PC. Proceed carefully, double-checking everything as you go, and the completed PC should work first time.

Unless the case limits access and makes it impossible, fit the processor, the processor's heatsink and fan, and the memory modules before fitting the motherboard in the case. Any configuration switches or jumpers should always be set up before fitting the motherboard in the case. Working on the motherboard is much easier before it is fitted in the case, because it is much more accessible. With smaller cases, fitting the motherboard is often easier if the 3.5-inch drive bay assembly is removed from the case first.

The motherboard must be mounted on stand-offs so that the connections on the underside of the board are held well clear of the case. Otherwise short-circuits will occur and the motherboard could be damaged. There will probably be more mounting points on the case than the motherboard can handle, but there should still be sufficient mounting holes in the board to enable it to be properly supported over its entire area.

It is sometimes easier to mount the 3.5-inch drives if the drive bay is removed, the drives are fitted in the bay and then the whole drive and bay assembly is fitted in the case. Two mounting bolts per side are sufficient to securely fix the drives in place.

Most of the cables are properly polarised and will only fit the right way round. If one of the data cables is not properly polarised, refer to the instruction manuals to find pin 1 of the connector on the motherboard and the connector on the drive. The red lead of the data cable carries the pin 1 to pin 1 connection. The end of the cable having the "twist" connects to the floppy disc drive, and the other end connects to the motherboard.

The functions provided on the motherboard's connector block will probably not match up exactly with the functions supported by the case. The power switch. reset switch, IDE activity LED, and power LED are the only ones that are really needed. Note that the front panel LEDs will only operate if they are connected the right way around.

To complete the PC fit the expansion cards, followed by any cables that connect to these cards. There will usually be an audio cable to connect the CD-ROM or DVD drive to the soundcard. With modern motherboards it is usually possible to implement more ports via one or more backplates and (or) the connectors on the front of the case. Be careful to connect everything correctly when wiring the front panel sockets to the motherboard.

Have a final and thorough check of the completed PC before it is switched on and tested. Check that you have not accidentally dislodged one lead while fitting another.

4

The BIOS

Essentials

Before you can go on to install the operating system and applications it is essential to set up the BIOS correctly. A modern BIOS Setup program enables dozens of parameters to be controlled, many of which are highly technical. This tends to make the BIOS intimidating for those who are new to PC building, and even those who have some experience of PC construction.

However, it is not necessary to go through the BIOS setting dozens of parameters in order to get the PC to perform satisfactorily. The BIOS should be customised to suit the particular motherboard it is fitted to, and it should set sensible defaults. In order to get the PC running well it is usually necessary to do nothing more than set a few basic parameters such as the time, date, and some drive details. Some "fine tuning" of a few other parameter might bring benefits, but is not essential.

We will therefore start by considering the BIOS essentials before moving on to consider some of the other features that can be controlled via the BIOS. A detailed description of all the BIOS features would require a large book in itself, so here we will concentrate on those that are of most importance.

BIOS basics

Before looking at the BIOS Setup program, it would perhaps be as well to consider the function of the BIOS. BIOS is a acronym and it stands for basic input/output system. Its basic function is to help the operating system handle the input and output devices, such as the drives, and ports, and also the memory circuits. It is a program that is stored in a ROM on the motherboard. These days the chip is usually quite small and sports a holographic label to prove that it is the genuine article (Figure 4.1). The old style ROM is a standard ROM chip, as in Figure 4.2. Either way its function is the same.

Fig.4.1 The BIOS is a program stored in a ROM chip

Because the BIOS program is in a ROM on the motherboard it can be run immediately at start-up without the need for any form of booting process. It is the BIOS that runs the test routines at switch-on, or the POST (power on self test) as it is known. With these tests completed successfully the BIOS then looks for an operating system to load from disc. The operating system appears to load itself from disc, which is a bit like pulling oneself up by ones bootlaces. It is said to be from this that the term "boot" is derived. Of course, in reality the operating system is not loading itself initially, and it is reliant on the BIOS getting things started.

Another role of the BIOS is to provide software routines that help the operating system to utilize the hardware effectively. It can also store information about the hardware for use by the operating system, and possibly other software. It is this second role that makes it necessary to have the Setup program. The BIOS can actually detect much of the system hardware and store the relevant technical information in memory.

However, some parameters have to be set manually, such as the time and date, and the user may wish to override some of the default settings. The Setup program enables the user to control the settings that the BIOS

Fig.4.2 An older style ROM BIOS chip

stores away in its memory. A battery powers this memory when the PC is switched off, so its contents are available each time the PC is turned on. Once you have set the correct parameters you will probably not need to deal with the BIOS Setup program again unless you do some drastic upgrading.

Entry

In the past there have been several common means of getting into the BIOS Setup program, but with the motherboards available to amateur builders at present there is only one method in common use. This is to press the Delete key at the appropriate point during the initial testing phase just after switch-on. The BIOS will display a message, usually in the bottom left-hand corner of the screen, telling you to press the "Del" key to enter the Setup program. The instruction manual should provide details if the motherboard you are using has a different method of entering the Setup program.

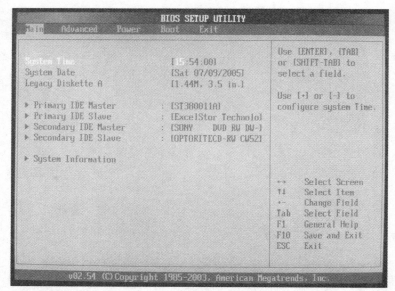

Fig.4.3 This AMI BIOS has five sections that are accessed via the tabs

The manual should also have a section dealing with the BIOS. It is worth looking through this section to determine which features can be controlled via the BIOS. Unfortunately, most motherboard instruction manuals assume the user is familiar with all the BIOS features, and there will be few detailed explanations. In fact there will probably just be a list of the available options and no real explanations at all. However, a quick read through this section of the manual will give you a good idea of what the BIOS is all about. A surprisingly large number of PC users who are quite expert in other aspects of PC operation have no real idea what the BIOS and the BIOS Setup program actually do. If you fall into this category the section of the manual that deals with the BIOS should definitely be given at least a quick read through.

There are several BIOS manufacturers and their BIOS Setup programs each work in a slightly different fashion. With motherboards available to the do-it-yourself builder it is probably the ones from Award, Phoenix, and AMI that are most likely to be encountered. At one time the AMI BIOS had a Setup program that would detect any reasonably standard mouse connected to the PC. With the aid of a mouse it offered a simple form of WIMP environment, although keyboard control was still available.

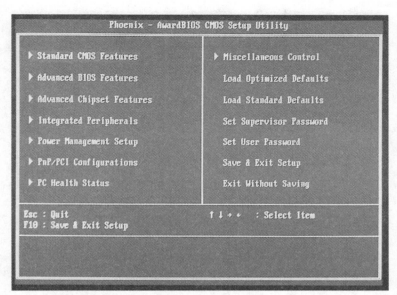

Fig.4.4 The main menu of a Phoenix-Award BIOS

This system seems to have been dropped, and a modern AMI BIOS uses a more conventional approach with tabs at the top of the screen providing access to the various sections of the program (Figure 4.3). The required tab is selected via the keyboard and not using a mouse. The Award BIOS is probably the most common and as far as I am aware it only uses keyboard control. Figure 4.4 shows the main menu for a modern Phoenix-Award BIOS.

Apart from variations in the BIOS due to different manufacturers, the BIOS will vary slightly from one motherboard to another. This is simply due to the fact that features available on one motherboard may be absent or different on another motherboard. Also, the world of PCs in general is developing at an amazing rate, and this is reflected in frequent BIOS updates. The description of the BIOS provided here has to be a representative one, and the BIOS in your PC will inevitably be slightly different. The important features should be present in any BIOS, and it is only the more minor and obscure features that are likely to be different. The motherboard's instruction manual should at the least give some basic information on setting up and using any unusual features.

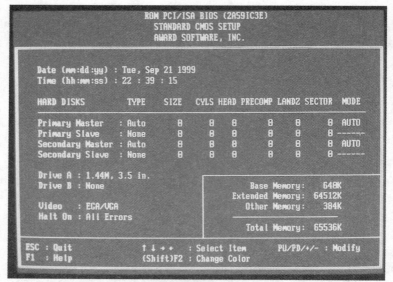

```
                    ROM PCI/ISA BIOS (2A59IC3E)
                         STANDARD CMOS SETUP
                       AWARD SOFTWARE, INC.

   Date (mm:dd:yy) : Tue, Sep 21 1999
   Time (hh:mm:ss) : 22 : 39 : 15

   HARD DISKS          TYPE   SIZE    CYLS HEAD PRECOMP LANDZ SECTOR   MODE

   Primary Master   : Auto     0       0   0       0     0       0    AUTO
   Primary Slave    : None     0       0   0       0     0       0    -----
   Secondary Master : Auto     0       0   0       0     0       0    AUTO
   Secondary Slave  : None     0       0   0       0     0       0    -----

   Drive A : 1.44M, 3.5 in.
   Drive B : None                             Base Memory:    640K
                                          Extended Memory:  64512K
   Video   : EGA/VGA                          Other Memory:    384K
   Halt On : All Errors
                                             Total Memory:  65536K

   ESC : Quit              ↑ ↓ → ←  : Select Item      PU/PD/+/- : Modify
   F1  : Help            (Shift)F2 : Change Color
```

*Fig.4.5 An example of a Standard CMOS Setup screen. Not every
BIOS now permits manual entry of drive parameters*

Standard CMOS

There are so many parameters that can be controlled via the BIOS Setup
program that they are normally divided into half a dozen or so groups.
The most important of these is the "Standard CMOS Setup" (Figure 4.5),
which is basically the same as the BIOS Setup in the original AT style
PCs. The first parameters in the list are the time and date. These can
usually be set via an operating system utility these days, but you may as
well set them from the Setup program while you are in that section of the
program. There are on-screen instructions that tell you how to alter and
select options. One slight oddity to watch out for is that you often have
to use the Page Up key to decrement values, and the Page Down key to
increment them.

With virtually any modern BIOS a help screen can be brought up by
pressing F1, and this will usually be context sensitive (Figure 4.6). In
other words, if the cursor is in the section that deals with the hard drives,
the help screen produced by pressing F1 will tell you about the hard
disc parameters. It would be unreasonable to expect long explanations

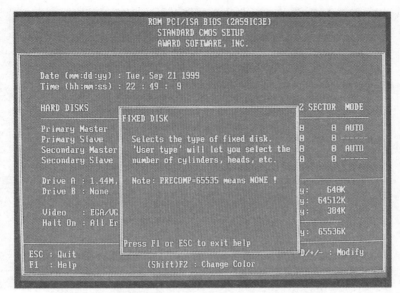

Fig.4.6 Pressing F1 will usually bring up a brief Help screen

from a simple off-line help system, and a couple of brief and to the point
sentences are all that will normally be provided.

Drive settings

The next section is used to set the operating parameters for the devices
on the IDE ports, including any serial ATA ports. For the sake of this
example we will assume that the hard disc is the master device on the
primary IDE channel (IDE1), and that the CD-ROM is the master device
on the secondary IDE channel (IDE2). Note that CD-RW and DVD drives
are straightforward CD-ROM drives as far as the BIOS is concerned.
The additional features of these drives are provided by applications
software such as Nero and Power DVD. Windows XP has some built-in
support for CD-RW drives, but this is the operating system providing the
extra features and not the BIOS.

If the manuals for the drives provide the correct figures to enter into the
CMOS memory, and they certainly should do so in the case of hard disc
drives, you can enter these figures against the appropriate device. In
this case the hard disc drive is the "Primary Master". A modern AMI

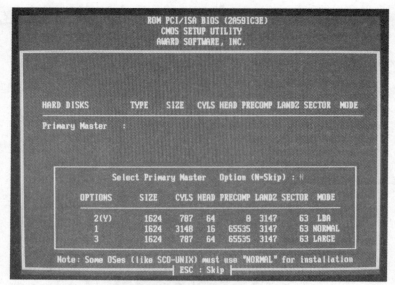

Fig.4.7 An IDE automatic detection screen in operation

BIOS should have a setting specifically for a CD-ROM drive, and this can be used for the "Secondary Master" device. Simply setting everything at zero usually works where no CD-ROM setting is available. There are no primary or secondary slave drives, so simply enter "None" for these.

If you do not know the appropriate figures for your drives it does not really matter, because there is always an "Auto" option. If this is selected, the BIOS examines the hardware during the start-up routine and enters the correct figures automatically. This usually works very well, but with some drives it can take a while, which extends the boot-up time.

There is an alternative method of automatic detection that avoids this delay. If you go back to the initial menu you will find a section called "IDE HDD Auto Detection" (Figure 4.7), and this offers a similar auto-detection facility. When this option is selected the Setup program examines the hardware on each IDE channel, and offers suggested settings for each of the four possible IDE devices. If you accept the suggested settings for the hard disc drive (or drives) they will be entered into the CMOS RAM. There may actually be several alternatives offered per IDE device, but the default suggestion is almost invariably the correct one. After using this auto-detection facility it is a good idea to return to the "Standard CMOS Setup" page to check that the settings have been transferred correctly. Also, make sure that "None" is entered for the drive type where appropriate.

The last parameter for each IDE drive is usually something like Auto, Normal, LBA (large block addressing), and Large. Normal is for drives under 528MB, while LBA and Large are alternative modes for drives having a capacity of more than 528MB. Modern drives have capacities of well in excess of 528MB, and mostly require the LBA mode. The manual for the hard drive should give some guidance here, or you can simply select Auto and let the BIOS sort things out for itself.

Some users get confused because they think a hard drive that will be partitioned should have separate entries in the BIOS for each partition. This is not the case, and as far as the BIOS is concerned each physical hard disc is a single drive, and has just one entry in the CMOS RAM table. The partitioning of hard discs is handled by the operating system, and so is the assignment of drive letters. The BIOS is only concerned with the physical characteristics of the drives, and not how data will be arranged and stored on the discs.

Non-standard IDE

If you are using IDE devices other than hard discs and an ordinary CD-ROM drive it is advisable to consult the instruction manual for these drives to find the best way of handling their BIOS settings. As pointed out previously, CD-RW and DVD drives are normally entered into the BIOS as normal CD-ROM drives. A modern operating system such as Windows XP should then recognise and install the drive, but only as a simple CD-ROM type. Some additional software, which is usually but not always supplied with the drive, will be needed in order to exploit the additional capabilities of these drives. It is a good idea to obtain a drive that comes complete with some bundled software since the extra cost is minimal, and buying the software separately can be quite expensive.

Other drives such as LS120 and Zip drives often have some specific support in the BIOS. It may even be possible to boot from these devices, although not necessarily with all operating systems. The instruction manuals for the drives should give detailed instructions on how to integrate them with any common BIOS.

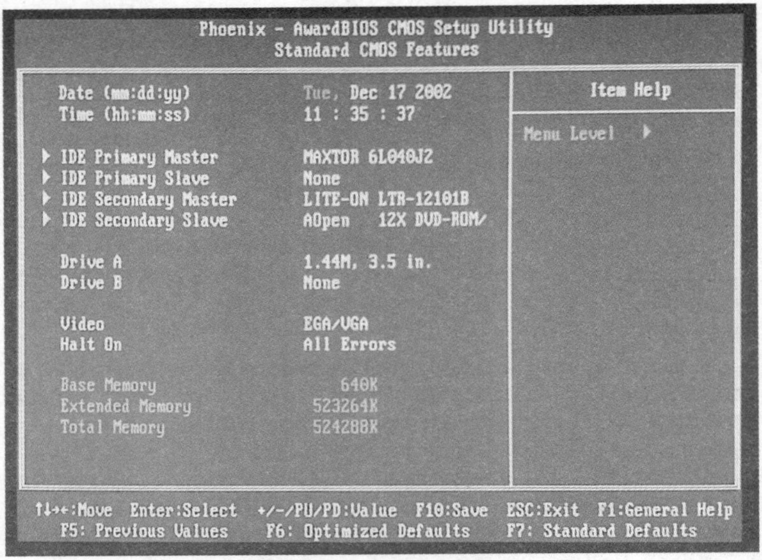

```
                Phoenix - AwardBIOS CMOS Setup Utility
                        Standard CMOS Features

     Date (mm:dd:yy)          Tue, Dec 17 2002          Item Help
     Time (hh:mm:ss)          11 : 35 : 37
                                                   Menu Level   ▶
   ▶ IDE Primary Master       MAXTOR 6L040J2
   ▶ IDE Primary Slave        None
   ▶ IDE Secondary Master     LITE-ON LTR-12101B
   ▶ IDE Secondary Slave      AOpen   12X DVD-ROM/

     Drive A                  1.44M, 3.5 in.
     Drive B                  None

     Video                    EGA/VGA
     Halt On                  All Errors

     Base Memory                  640K
     Extended Memory          523264K
     Total Memory             524288K

  ↑↓→←:Move  Enter:Select  +/-/PU/PD:Value  F10:Save  ESC:Exit  F1:General Help
     F5: Previous Values    F6: Optimized Defaults    F7: Standard Defaults
```

Fig.4.8 *This Standard CMOS screen only permits automatic detection
of the IDE devices*

Auto-only

There is a trend towards automatic detection with no manual override.
With the Phoenix-Award BIOS shown in Figure 4.8 the Page Up and
Page Down keys permit parameters such as the time and date to be
changed, but they have no effect on the IDE drive types. The BIOS
automatically detects the drives, displays its findings in the Standard
CMOS page, and sets the correct parameters. As most users opt for
automatic detection anyway, the lack of manual control is not likely to be
of any importance. On the other hand, if you should happen to use an
IDE device that the BIOS can not identify, it will probably be unusable
until a BIOS update becomes available.

Floppy drives

The next section in the "Standard CMOS Setup" is used to select the
floppy disc drive type or types. All the normal types of floppy drive are
supported, from the old 5.25-inch 360k drives to the rare 2.88M 3.5-inch
type. You simply select the appropriate type for drives A and B. Select

"None" for drive B if the computer has only one floppy drive. In days gone by you had to enter the amount of memory fitted, but with a modern BIOS the amount of memory is automatically detected and entered into the CMOS RAM. The "Standard CMOS Setup" screen will report the amount of memory fitted, and will display something like Figure 4.9.

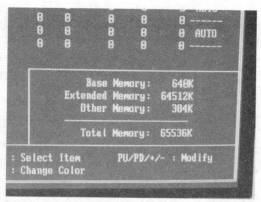

Fig.4.9 *The BIOS reports the memory it finds. The user can not alter these settings*

Note that there is no way of altering the memory settings if they are wrong. If the BIOS reports the wrong amount of RAM there is a fault in the memory circuits, and the correct amount will be reported if the fault is rectified. Sometimes what appears to be an error is just the way the amount of memory is reported by the BIOS. For those who are new to computing the way in which the amount of memory is reported can seem rather strange. It should look very familiar to those who can remember the early days of IBM compatible PCs. The original PCs had relatively simple processors that could only address one megabyte of RAM, but only the lower 640k of the address range were actually used for RAM. The upper 384k of the address range was used for the BIOS ROM, video ROM, and that sort of thing.

Modern PCs can address hundreds of megabytes of RAM, but the lowest one megabyte is still arranged in much the same way that it was in the original PCs. The BIOS therefore reports that there is 640k of normal (base) memory, so many kilobytes of RAM above the original one megabyte of RAM (extended memory), and 384k of other memory. This "other" memory is the RAM in the address space used by the BIOS, etc.

The final section of the standard Setup enables the type of video card to be specified, and the degree of error trapping to be selected. The BIOS will probably detect the video card and set the appropriate type, which for a modern PC will presumably be a EGA/VGA type. It might be possible to select the old CGA and mono adaptors, but these are obsolete and

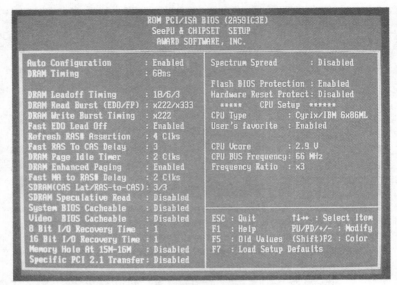

Fig.4.10 This screen provides control over the chipset features

not used in modern PCs. The error trapping controls the way in which the computer responds to errors that are found during the BIOS self-testing routine at switch-on. The default of halt on all errors is probably the best choice, particularly when you are testing a new PC. Once the PC has been fully tested and is running properly you may prefer to alter this setting, but I would not bother.

Chipset

Setting up the standard CMOS parameters is probably all you will need to do in order to get the computer running properly, but it is a good idea to look at the options available in the other sections of the Setup program. There will be a section called something like Chipset Setup or Advanced Chipset Setup (Figure 4.10), which controls things such as the port and memory timing. There are so many parameters controlled by a modern BIOS that a multi-level menu system is sometimes used. In the example of Figure 4.11 the DRAM timing option produces the submenu of Figure 4.12. You can "play" with these settings in an attempt to obtain improved performance, but higher speed may well produce lower reliability. Results

184

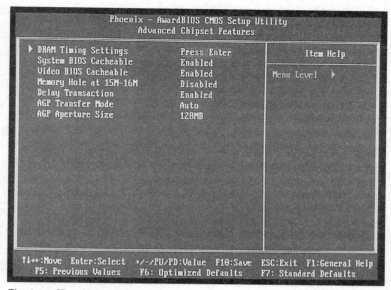

Fig.4.11 The Chipset Features menu might contain some submenus

should be quite good if you simply leave this section with the auto configuration enabled.

If you make a complete "dogs breakfast" of these settings it is possible that the PC could become unusable. This is not as drastic as it sounds because you can always go back into the BIOS and select the default settings from the initial screen. There will probably be an option to return to the "old" settings, which usually means the settings saved prior to the last time the BIOS Setup program was used. I suppose it is conceivable that changes made in the BIOS could render the computer unable to start up at all. I think that this is highly unlikely, but remember that the contents of the CMOS memory can always be wiped clean using the appropriate jumper on the motherboard. No matter how badly you scramble the BIOS settings it should always be possible to get back to the default settings and then "fine tune" things from there.

It is worth remembering that no changes are made to the settings unless you opt to save the changes when exiting the Setup program. If you know you have made a complete mess of things, simply exit the Setup program without saving the changes. The PC will then reboot, the Setup

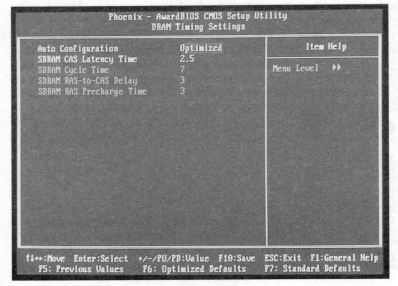

Fig.4.12 This is the DRAM Timings submenu

program can be entered again, and you can start from scratch with the changes.

If the PC is fitted with SDRAM, one of the timing settings will be the SDRAM CAS Latency. The default setting will probably be suitable provided the Standard Default settings are used. If the Optimised Default settings are used, or a low figure is set manually, make sure that the DIMMs used are up to the task. Trying to use memory modules beyond their ratings is not usually successful and can produce major problems when running applications programs.

The AGP Aperture Size controls the amount of system memory that is set aside for use with a graphics adaptor for such things as texture storage. The default value should be a sensible one for the amount of system memory installed in the PC and the amount of video memory fitted to the AGP card. There are various formulas for calculating the optimum setting, and you can try these if maximum video performance is important. In most cases any change in performance will be quite small.

The amount of memory allocated by default might seem to be large relative to the total amount of system memory. However, bear in mind that it is actually the maximum size that is being set. The actual amount of memory used depends on the video activity, and system memory is only used when it is essential to do so.

Cache

There are various BIOS address ranges listed or there may be just a list of BIOS names. There is the option of enabling or disabling shadowing of each one. By default the video BIOS will be shadowed, and possibly the video RAM as well, but the system BIOS and any others listed will probably not be cached. Shadowing of a BIOS is where it is copied into the computer's RAM and then run from there. The top 384k of the base memory is given over to the main BIOS, plus any other device that needs its own BIOS. In a modern PC this part of the memory map is occupied by RAM, but this RAM is normally disabled.

When shadowing is enabled, the relevant block of RAM is activated, and the contents of the BIOS at that address range are copied into it. The point of this is that the RAM is faster than the ROM used for the BIOS, and using shadowing should speed up operation of the video card. Usually the only peripheral that has its own BIOS is the video card, but shadowing of other parts of the top 384k of memory can be enabled if necessary. If you have a peripheral device that will benefit from this treatment its manual should say so, and specify the address range that must be shadowed.

Power Management

Most operating systems and all modern motherboards seem to support some form of power management facility. In other words, the computer goes into some form of standby mode if there is no mouse or keyboard activity for a certain period. Most motherboards can also be switched to and from a standby mode via a peripheral such as a modem, and this also comes under the general heading of power management. A modern BIOS usually has a section dealing solely with power management (Figure 4.13).

The Power Management Setup will probably be set to Disabled, and with some operating systems this is probably the best way to leave it. A lot of power management features can be controlled via the operating system these days, and you can sometimes get into a situation where the BIOS and the operating system are both trying to rule the power

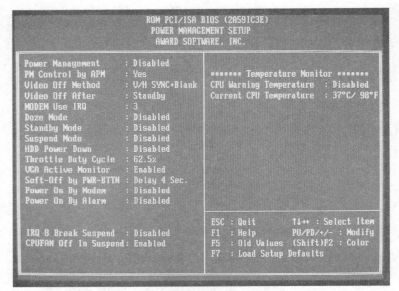

```
                    ROM PCI/ISA BIOS (2A59IC3E)
                     POWER MANAGEMENT SETUP
                     AWARD SOFTWARE, INC.

 Power Management     : Disabled
 PM Control by APM    : Yes          ******* Temperature Monitor *******
 Video Off Method     : V/H SYNC+Blank  CPU Warning Temperature  : Disabled
 Video Off After      : Standby       Current CPU Temperature  : 37°C/ 98°F
 MODEM Use IRQ        : 3
 Doze Mode            : Disabled
 Standby Mode         : Disabled
 Suspend Mode         : Disabled
 HDD Power Down       : Disabled
 Throttle Duty Cycle  : 62.5%
 VGA Active Monitor   : Enabled
 Soft-Off by PWR-BTTN : Delay 4 Sec.
 Power On By Modem    : Disabled
 Power On By Alarm    : Disabled
                                    ┌─────────────────────────────────
                                    │ESC : Quit        ↑↓→← : Select Item
 IRQ 8 Break Suspend  : Disabled    │F1  : Help        PU/PD/+/- : Modify
 CPUFAN Off In Suspend: Enabled     │F5  : Old Values  (Shift)F2 : Color
                                    │F7  : Load Setup Defaults
```

Fig.4.13 A typical Power Management Setup screen

management roost. Where possible I totally disable this feature and
only enable it if there is good reason to do so.

These days it is not uncommon for the motherboard to support more
than one standby mode. The idea seems to be that the computer
progressively shuts down the longer it is left unused. It will typically go
from normal operation into the "doze" mode, followed by the "standby"
and "suspend" modes. Operating the mouse or keyboard should always
result in the computer returning directly to the "normal" mode, but it may
take a few seconds to become fully operational if the motor of the hard
disc has been switched off. Due to the high rotation speed of a hard
disc it takes several seconds for it to reach its normal operating speed.

The BIOS Setup program will probably permit adjustment of the delay
times before each standby mode is entered, plus other details such as
whether the processor fan is switched off when the "suspend" mode is
entered. Of course, all this type of thing is only relevant if the power
management feature is enabled. You may wish to "fine tune" the power
management feature at a later time, but when initially setting up a PC it is
probably best not to get deeply embroiled in this type of thing.

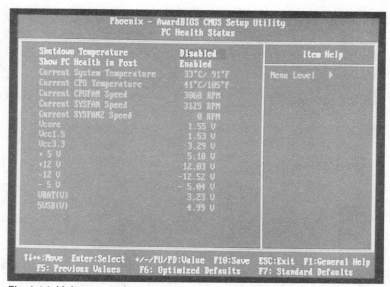

Fig.4.14 Voltages and temperatures can be monitored via the PC Health Status screen

If the motherboard supports some form of external power management, and you wish to use this feature, it will have to be enabled in this section of the BIOS. Any feature of this type is always disabled by default. Any feature of this type will, of course, only operate if it is properly supported by the peripheral device or devices, and any extra cabling that it needed is properly installed.

Monitoring

Most motherboards now support at least a basic over-temperature detection circuit for the processor, and there are often various CPU threshold temperatures that can be selected. Figure 4.14 shows a typical BIOS screen that provides temperature and voltage monitoring. This screen usually shows the system temperature (the temperature inside the PC's case) in addition to the processor's temperature and various operating voltages. If the CPU goes above the selected temperature a warning can be produced, and the PC usually shuts down as well. It is probably best to activate this feature and simply leave the threshold temperature at its default setting.

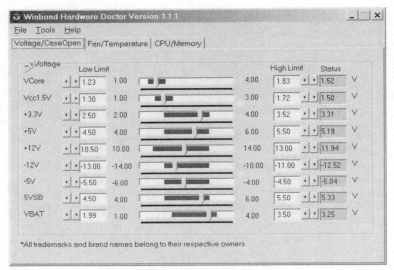

Fig.4.15 Many motherboards are supplied with a monitoring program that runs under Windows

The normal operating temperature varies considerably from one type of processor to another. In general, the processor should operate below about 50 degrees Celsius. However, some AMD chips seem to operate quite happily at around 60 degrees while many Intel chips settle down at around 40 degrees or even less. Unless you know what you are doing it is not a good idea to alter the default alarm temperatures.

Note that many motherboards are supplied complete with so-called health monitoring software that enables parameters such as the CPU temperature, fan speeds, operating voltages, etc., to be monitored while running Windows. It is well worthwhile installing any bundled software of this type. Figure 4.15 shows the main window of the Winbond Hardware Doctor program while it is monitoring a Pentium 4-based PC. A range of voltages are measured by this window, including the core voltage of the processor and the main 5-volt supply.

Whether monitoring via the BIOS or a Windows program, do not be surprised if the measured voltages are slightly different to the nominal voltages. There is a tolerance of plus and minus 5 percent or more on most voltages, and the measuring circuits will produce small errors that

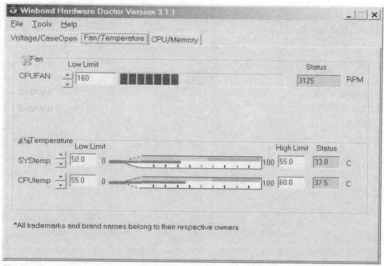

Fig.4.16 Further screens allow more parameters to be monitored

effectively widen the tolerance ratings. Another window of the Hardware Doctor program enables the processor's temperature, the system temperature, and the speed of the processor's fan to be monitored (Figure 4.16). Most of these monitoring programs can sound an alarm if (say) an excessive temperature is detected.

CPU settings

If the motherboard is one that uses software control to set the correct parameters for the PC there could be a separate page for this (Figure 4.17), but it is sometimes included in the chipset settings or in a miscellaneous section. The BIOS will automatically detect the processor type and should set the correct core voltage, bus frequency, and processor multiplier values. It is advisable to check that the BIOS has correctly identified the processor and set the correct values. It should be possible to set the correct figures manually if the BIOS makes a mistake, although it is very unlikely that it would do so. Otherwise, it should only be necessary to exercise manual control if over-clocking is to be tried (see chapter 3).

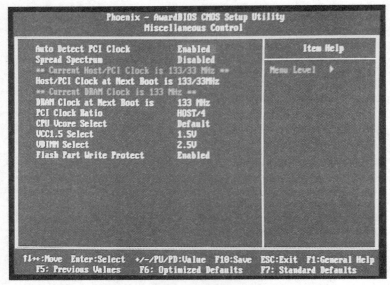

Fig.4.17 The CPU Settings menu of the Phoenix-Award BIOS

Note that any changes you make to the CPU settings may be ignored unless you activate an override setting. Also, with any modern Intel or AMD processor the motherboard will automatically set the correct multiplier value by reading information from the processor itself. It is not normally possible to set the multiplier manually even if the override setting is activated. The BIOS may seem to accept the new multiplier value, but when you exit the BIOS and reboot the computer it will operate with multiplier value set by the chip.

PNP/PCI

Unless you know what you are doing it is not a good idea to mess around with the PNP/PCI settings (Figure 4.18). The initial screen might be lacking in options (Figure 4.19), but things like the IRQ assignments will be tucked away in submenus like the one of Figure 4.20. The defaults should work perfectly well anyway. There will be the option of selecting "Yes" if a PNP (Plug-N-Play) operating system is installed or "No" if a non-PNP type is installed. Windows 95 and 98 are PNP operating systems, and the obvious setting is "Yes" if you will use either of these. In practice I

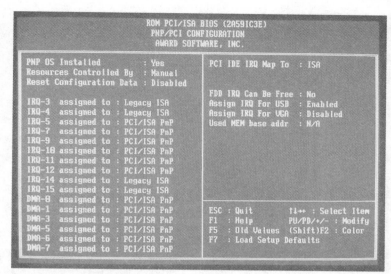

Fig.4.18 The PNP/PCI Configuration menu

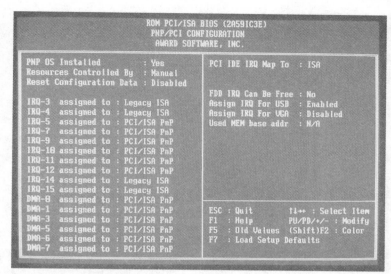

Fig.4.19 The PNP/PCI menu might rely on submenus

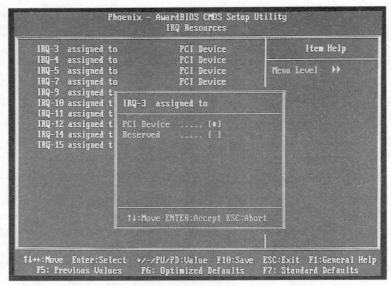

Fig.4.20 The IRQ Resources submenu

have sometimes encountered problems if "Yes" is selected when using Windows 95. Assuming that a modern operating system such as Windows XP is used, there should be no problem if "Yes" is selected.

It should only be necessary to alter the IRQ (interrupt request) settings if there are problems with hardware conflicts. While this problem was not exactly unknown in the past, the widespread use of PCI expansion cards and USB external peripherals has greatly eased the problem. It is definitely not a good idea to alter these settings unless you know exactly what you are doing. With this type of thing it is much easier to make matters worse than it is to cure a problem.

Integrated Peripherals

The Integrated Peripherals section (Figure 4.21) provides some control over the on-board interfaces. In particular, it allows each port to be switched on or off, and in the case of the serial and parallel ports it also enables the port addresses and interrupt (IRQ) numbers to be altered. This can be useful when trying to avoid conflicts with hardware fitted in

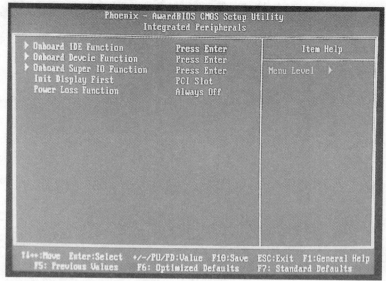

Fig.4.21 The Integrated Peripherals menu will probably use submenus

the expansion slots, but is unlikely to be necessary with a modern PC. The number of integrated peripherals on current motherboards is such that the options in this section of the BIOS will largely be handled by sub-menus.

With the example BIOS the serial and parallel ports are covered by the Super IO submenu (Figure 4.22). There will be various parallel port modes available, but with a modern BIOS it is unlikely that there will be a Standard (output only) mode. The choices will probably be SPP, EPP, and ECP, which are all bi-directional modes. For most purposes either SPP or EPP will suffice. Only set ECP operation if you use the port with a device that definitely needs this mode. There might be further options, such as a mode that can provide both EPP and ECP operation, and a choice of ECP versions. It is unlikely to matter which version is selected, but the relevant one should obviously be selected if the instruction manual states that a peripheral requires a certain ECP version.

If the motherboard supports infrared communications it may be possible to switch serial port two (COM2) between normal operation and infrared operation. When set to infrared operation it is possible for the PC to

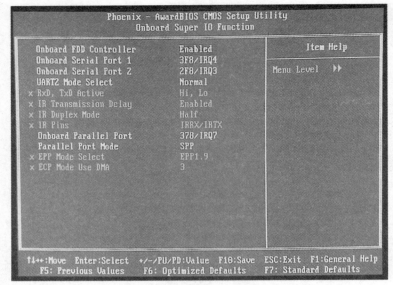

Fig.4.22 This is the Onboard SuperIO Function submenu

communicate with suitably equipped notebook computers and digital cameras that support infrared communications. However, the correct hardware add-on is needed on COM2 before this cordless communication will be possible.

This dual role for serial port two seems to be less common these days and most motherboards now have entirely separate hardware to implement the IrDA facility. It is likely that the BIOS Setup program will give some control over the settings for this port, but simply accept the default settings. Only change the settings if this port is used with a piece of equipment that requires changes to be made. If any changes should be required, the instruction manual for the device concerned should explain exactly what needs to be altered.

The Onboard IDE Function submenu (Figure 4.23) enables the IDE controllers to be switched on and off and permits the modes to be set manually. Auto operation will be selected by default, and manual control should only be contemplated if the automatic mode selection fails for some reason. This is very unlikely to happen.

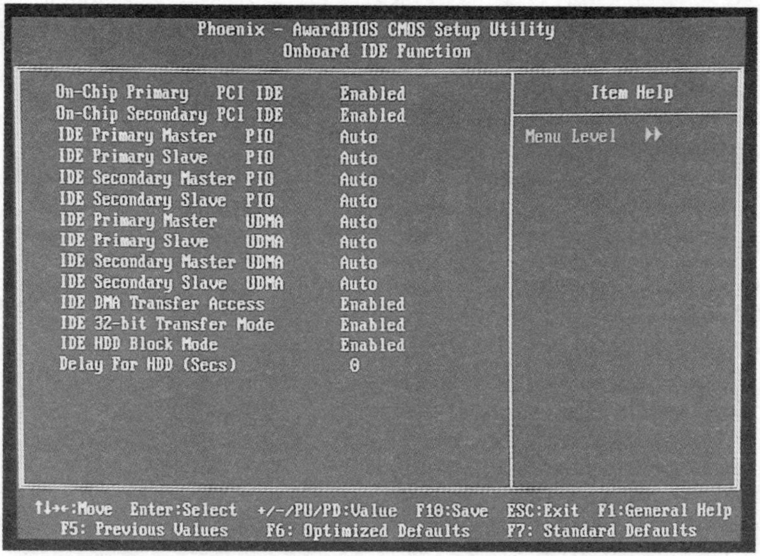

```
          Phoenix - AwardBIOS CMOS Setup Utility
                  Onboard IDE Function

 On-Chip Primary   PCI IDE      Enabled          Item Help
 On-Chip Secondary PCI IDE      Enabled
 IDE Primary Master   PIO       Auto       Menu Level   ▶▶
 IDE Primary Slave    PIO       Auto
 IDE Secondary Master PIO       Auto
 IDE Secondary Slave  PIO       Auto
 IDE Primary Master   UDMA      Auto
 IDE Primary Slave    UDMA      Auto
 IDE Secondary Master UDMA      Auto
 IDE Secondary Slave  UDMA      Auto
 IDE DMA Transfer Access        Enabled
 IDE 32-bit Transfer Mode       Enabled
 IDE HDD Block Mode             Enabled
 Delay For HDD (Secs)           0


 ↑↓→←:Move  Enter:Select  +/-/PU/PD:Value  F10:Save  ESC:Exit  F1:General Help
   F5: Previous Values    F6: Optimized Defaults    F7: Standard Defaults
```

Fig.4.23 The Onboard IDE Function submenu. Automatic detection should set suitable operating modes

Onboard Device

The Onboard Device submenu (Figure 4.24) covers an assortment of onboard hardware. Many motherboards now have a built-in RAID interface with two additional IDE ports. This was once an expensive option, but it is a feature that is now found in quite low-cost motherboards. This means that your chosen motherboard may well come complete with a RAID interface that you do not actually need. It is unlikely that leaving the RAID hardware switched on will cause any major problems, but the boot process will be lengthened while the BIOS looks for absent drives on the RAID ports. It is therefore a good idea to switch off the RAID hardware if it is not needed.

If there is a built-in audio system there will probably be the option to disable it in this section of the BIOS. This should not be necessary unless a PCI soundcard will be used. In theory it should be possible to have both sound systems installed, but in practice there could be difficulties. Since having both audio systems installed is unlikely to bestow any advantages, it is advisable to disable the built-in sound circuits.

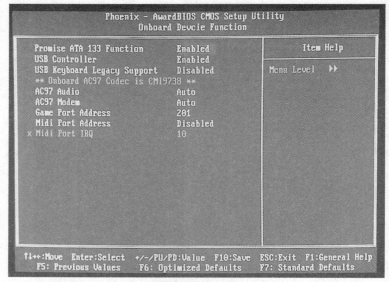

Fig.4.24 The Onboard Device Function menu. The Promise ATA 133 Function controls the built-in RAID controller

Similarly, it is probably best to disable the integral USB ports if a USB expansion card is used for some reason.

It is only necessary to alter the game and MIDI port addresses and the MIDI port IRQ setting in the event that hardware conflicts occur. This is unlikely to be a problem with a modern PC. Note that the MIDI port is often disabled by default. This is a common cause of problems, with users finding that they can not output data to the MIDI port. Indeed, with the port disabled it will not be listed by Windows as an output option. If you are going to use the MIDI port or might use it in the future, it is a good idea to enable it from the outset.

BIOS Features Setup

The BIOS Features Setup (Figure 4.25) controls some useful features, but once again the default settings should suffice. Note that the larger menus, which will probably include this one, can not show all the settings simultaneously. A sort of scrollbar appears down the right-hand edge of the section that contains the settings, and this indicates which section of

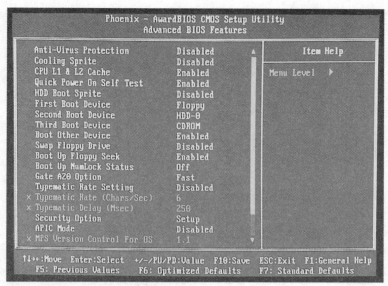

Fig.4.25 The Advanced BIOS Features menu

the page is being displayed. It is not possible to scroll the page using the scrollbar and the mouse. The up and down cursor keys are used to do this. Figure 4.26 shows the scrolled version of the BIOS Features Setup screen. Once into the menu system, the right-hand panel of the screen indicates the current menu level.

Returning to the BIOS features, the internal and external caches must be enabled if the computer is to operate at full speed. There are various boot sequence options, and eventually you might like to select C Only. In the meantime the boot sequence must include drive A if Windows 95, 98, or ME is to be installed on the PC. This is the drive that the computer must boot from until drive C is made bootable. It is advisable to have drive A as the first boot drive. There is otherwise a slight risk that the boot process will stall when the BIOS tries to boot from a blank hard disc drive.

Most other operating systems, including Linux and Windows XP, can be and normally are installed from a bootable CD-ROM. Any modern BIOS should have the option to use the CD-ROM drive as a boot drive, and this option must be selected if you intend to use this method of installation.

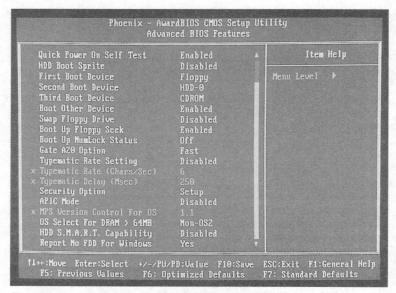

Fig.4.26 Here the menu has been scrolled down to reveal further options

The drives might be referred to as A, B, C, etc., in the BIOS Setup program, but these days different terminology is often used. In the example BIOS the hard drives are referred to as HDD-0, HDD-1, etc. Assuming drive C is the hard disc that will be used as a boot drive, it is HDD-0 (not HDD-1). To avoid possible confusion, this drive should be used as the master drive on the primary IDE interface.

Other drives are referred to by suitable names, such as CD-ROM, Floppy, and ZIP-100. If there are two of these drives of the same type, the BIOS will probably try to boot from the drive with the highest priority and ignore the other one. The primary IDE interface is searched first, followed by the secondary IDE interface. As one would expect, the master drive takes precedence over the slave device on the same interface.

If this option is present, make sure that the IDE HDD Block Mode is enabled, because the hard disc performance will be relatively poor if it is not. In a modern BIOS this function might be in the Onboard IDE Function submenu. After boot-up the NumLock key is normally on, but there is a useful option that enables it to be switched off after boot-up.

Floppyless

There are usually several options relating to the floppy disc drive or drives. One of these enables drives A and B to be swapped over. I am not sure why it would ever be necessary to have drive A operate as drive B and vice versa, but this facility is there if you should need it. Although at one time a floppy disc drive was an essential part of a PC, this is no longer the case. Other forms of removable disc are available, and with some operating systems it is now possible to install the system from a bootable CD-ROM. This removes the need to boot initially from a floppy disc.

The problem with leaving out the floppy disc drive is that the BIOS will produce an error message each time that the computer is booted. There should be an option called something like Floppy Seek or Boot Up Floppy Seek, and by disabling this option the BIOS will not check for a floppy drive, and the error message will be suppressed. In some cases there might be a setting called something like Report No FDD for Windows, and could be necessary to set this to No as well.

The Rest

Other sections of the BIOS Setup program allow you to select a user password that must be entered before the PC will boot-up, load standard or optimised default settings, save the new settings and exit, or exit without saving any changes to the settings. Being able to load the standard set of default settings is clearly useful if you experiment a little too much and end up with totally unsuitable settings. It is worth repeating that no settings are actually altered unless you select the Save and Exit option. If you accidentally change some settings and do not know how to restore the correct ones, simply exiting without saving the new settings will leave everything untouched. You can then enter the Setup program again and have another try.

Flash upgrade

If you look through the specifications for motherboards you will often encounter something like "Flash upgradeable BIOS" or just "Flash BIOS". In days gone by the only way of upgrading the BIOS was to buy a new chip, or pair of chips as it was in those days. Some of the ROMs used to store the BIOS were actually re-programmable, but only by removing them from the PC and putting them into a programmer unit. This was not a practical proposition for most users. New BIOS chips were very difficult to obtain and you were usually stuck with the BIOS supplied with the motherboard.

The rate at which modern computing changes makes it beneficial to upgrade the BIOS from time to time in order to keep PCs up to date, and not just to accommodate a major upgrade such as a change of processor. The BIOS sometimes has to be updated to cure compatibility problems with certain items of hardware. There could even be one or two minor bugs in the original BIOS.

With a modern BIOS there is no need to replace the BIOS ROM chip or to remove it from the motherboard for reprogramming. The ROM for a modern BIOS can be electronically erased and reprogrammed while it is still on the motherboard. This is why it is possible to download a new BIOS and a "blower" program and upgrade the BIOS. Of course, an upgrade of this type is dependent on the motherboard having the BIOS in Flash memory. However, there is little likelihood of a new motherboard lacking support for the Flash method of upgrading the BIOS. It is many years since I last used a motherboard that lacks this facility.

Write protection

If you get an error message such as "Flash type unrecognised" during the upgrade, this does not mean that the BIOS is a non-reprogrammable type. It usually just means that the Flash memory is write-protected, making it impossible for the upgrade program to alter its contents. Write protection is used as a means of preventing viruses and other malicious programs from corrupting the BIOS and rendering the PC unusable. It would be prudent to check for write-protection before trying to upgrade the BIOS.

The manual for your PC or its motherboard should give instructions for disabling this facility. In some cases the write protection is provided via a switch or jumper on the motherboard. These days it is more usual for this facility to be controlled via a setting in the BIOS itself (Figure 4.27), but you may have to do some searching to find the appropriate menu. There should be no difficulty in upgrading the BIOS once the write-protection has been switched off. Having completed the upgrade it is a good idea to enable this facility again, so that the BIOS is protected from attack.

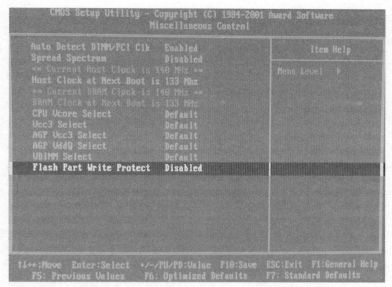

*Fig.4.27 The BIOS can not be upgraded unless write protection
            is disabled*

Risk factor

It is only fair to point out that a BIOS upgrade is a bit risky. For a start,
you need to be absolutely certain that the data file you are using is the
correct one for your motherboard. Using the wrong BIOS data file could
easily render the computer unusable, and if it will not boot-up correctly it
is impossible to restore the original BIOS.

Another slight worry is that a power failure during the upgrade could
leave the PC with a BI (half a BIOS)! With an incomplete or corrupted
BIOS it is unlikely that the PC could be rebooted to restore the original or
complete the upgrade. It only takes a few seconds to carry out the
upgrade, so you would be very unlucky indeed if a power failure
interrupted the process, but there is a slight risk. A serious error when
upgrading the BIOS could necessitate the fitting of a complete new
motherboard.

The upgrade program usually has to be run from MS-DOS, and is very
simple to operate (Figure 4.28). After you have supplied the name of the
data file for the new BIOS (including any extension to the filename) the

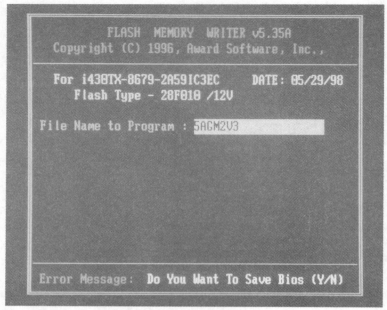

Fig.4.28 A typical Flash writer program in operation

program should give the option of saving the existing BIOS onto disc. It
is as well to do this so that you can revert to the original BIOS if the new
version proves to be troublesome. After you have confirmed that you
wish to continue with the upgrade the new data will be written to the
BIOS ROM chip. Do not touch the computer during the flash upgrade,
just stand back and let the upgrade program get on with it. The computer
is then ready for rebooting and checking to see if the new BIOS has the
desired effect.

Boot disc

The boot disc used when upgrading has to be a very basic type that
does not run some form of memory management software such as
EMM386. Making a suitable boot disc from a system running Windows
XP is very straightforward. Place a blank disc in the floppy drive, launch
Windows Explorer, and then locate drive A in Windows Explorer. Right-
click on the entry for drive A and select the Format option from the pop-

up menu. This produces the window for the Format program, which looks like the one in Figure 4.29. Tick the Create an MS-DOS Startup Disc checkbox and then operate the Start button. A warning message will probably appear, pointing out that any data on the disc will be lost. Operate the Yes button to continue and create the boot disc. Exactly the same method is used to make a boot disc when running Windows Vista,

When the formatting has been completed, copy the BIOS data file and upgrade program to the floppy disc. Leave the disc in the floppy drive and restart the computer.

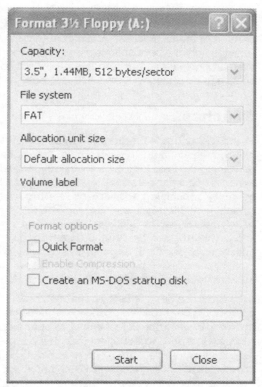

Fig.4.29 Making a boot disc in Windows XP

With luck the floppy drive will be used as the boot drive and you will be ready to proceed with the upgrade once the boot process has been completed. It is possible that the computer will simply boot into Windows. This occurs because the floppy drive is not set as the first boot disc in the BIOS. The BIOS therefore looks for the hard drive first, finds it, and then boots into Windows as normal. Restart the PC, go into the BIOS and set the floppy as the first boot disc, then save the changes and exit the BIOS Setup program. The computer should then boot into MS/DOS using the floppy disc in drive A.

Unfortunately, the Windows ME Format program does not provide a boot disc option. It is possible to make a Startup disc via the Control Panel and the Add/Remove Programs facility. However, this option results in various utilities being placed on the disc, and some of these could interfere with the upgrade process. Make sure that the Minimal Boot option is selected from the boot options menu during the initial boot process, and the memory management programs, etc., will not be run. It should then be safe to go ahead with the BIOS upgrade.

Switches

Most BIOS upgrade programs allow certain switches to be added after the command name. For example, it is possible to specify the file containing the data for the new version of the BIOS. Another common option is one that clears the CMOS memory of all the BIOS settings. It is generally considered advisable to use this switch, since some of the original settings might be inappropriate to the new BIOS. Using this switch means that the BIOS will have no setting when the PC is restarted, and you must enter the Setup program so that the Load Setup Defaults option can be selected. If necessary, the defaults can then be "fine tuned" to suit your requirements. The date and time will have to be reset, but this can be done from the Windows Control Panel.

If the BIOS has been updated correctly a new BIOS version number and date should be displayed on the initial screen at start-up. It is also likely that Windows will detect that there has been a change and respond with various messages to the effect that new hardware has been detected. Actually, it is just detecting the same old hardware and reinstalling the drivers for it. The change in BIOS presumably fools Windows into "thinking" that a different motherboard has been installed. Once this reinstallation has been completed the computer should perform much the same as it did before.

Some motherboards are supplied with a Windows program that permits the BIOS to be easily updated. In fact most motherboards now seem to be supplied with a program of this type. A facility such as this should make it much simpler and easier to upgrade the BIOS, but as always with a BIOS upgrade, make sure that the manufacturer's instructions are followed "to the letter".

Points to remember

The BIOS helps the operating system to deal with the hardware, particularly the drives and memory. It stores masses of information about the hardware in CMOS RAM which retains its contents when the computer is switched off. These can be controlled via the Setup program built into the BIOS.

The normal way into the BIOS Setup program is by pressing the Del (Delete) key during the initial startup routine. A message will appear on the screen at the appropriate time. If the BIOS you are using has a different method of entering the Setup program the motherboard's instruction manual should explain what to do.

It is essential to go into the BIOS to ensure that it is set up correctly. If you simply try to bypass this part of PC building it is unlikely that the PC will work really well, and it may well be impossible to get it working properly at all. Vital information required by the operating system may be missing.

Do not be intimidated by the BIOS Setup program. With a modern BIOS there are numerous parameters that can be adjusted, but to a large extent you can leave the BIOS to sort things out for itself.

As a minimum, set the time and date and check that the various drives (including any floppy drives) are properly installed. It is advisable to check to see if there are any memory settings that might need adjustment. It might be necessary to alter the boot sequence in order to get the operating system installed.

The manual provided with hard disc drive should give the correct parameters to enter into the Setup program, but satisfactory results should be obtained if you simply opt for automatic detection. With a modern BIOS there might not be a manual option.

If the BIOS detects the processor and sets the core voltage, bus frequency, and multiplier value, check that they are correct. Do not experiment with overclocking unless you know what you are doing and are prepared to foot the bill for any damage caused.

Read the section of the motherboard's manual that deals with the BIOS. Each BIOS is slightly different, and the only way to find out if the one you are using has some special features you should know about is to read through the manual.

It is worthwhile adjusting things such as the Numlock setting to suit your own preferences, so check through the available parameters for any that you can usefully customise.

You may need to alter the parallel port's operating mode if you use any advanced parallel port devices that require high-speed data transfers.

Remember to save the new parameters before exiting the Setup program. Alternatively, if you have made a mess of things you can exit without saving the scrambled settings.

It is very unlikely that "playing" with the BIOS settings will cause any damage to the hardware, and if things get into a complete mess you can always return to the default settings. However, simply playing around with settings to see what happens is not really a good idea.

Do not experiment with the flash memory writing program. A careless error here could easily render the computer unusable, and the only solution might be a replacement motherboard. A BIOS upgrade is something you only undertake if you really need to, and it is then essential to proceed with great care.

The Operating System

Which one?

There are actually several operating systems that can be used with PCs, but the only ones that are used to a significant extent are Windows and Linux. At the time of writing this there are two current versions of Windows for desktop PCs, which are Windows XP and Windows Vista. Of course, there are various versions of XP and Vista available, but the basic operating system is the same for all versions of XP. Similarly, all versions of Vista are essentially the same, but in its more expensive forms it offers more facilities.

There are two basic options if the cheapest possible operating system is required. One is to use the operating system from the PC that the new one will be replacing. This does, of course, assume that the new computer will replace an old PC which will be scrapped, and that the old PC is equipped with a worthwhile operating system. The old operating system will probably be a worthwhile proposition provided it is a version of Windows XP, but using any earlier form of Windows is unlikely to be a practical proposition. Using modern hardware with an obsolete operating system such as Windows ME is not usually possible due to the lack of suitable driver software for the hardware. Things like the soundcard, video system, and even much of the hardware on the motherboard will not function unless supported by the correct driver software.

Unfortunately, it is not safe to assume that the Windows XP operating from an old PC can be successfully transferred to a new PC. There should be no major problem provided the operating system is either a retail type or a normal OEM (original equipment manufacturer) version. These have the standard installation disc and can be installed in the normal way.

Some PCs, and particularly those from the larger manufacturers, are supplied with a bundled version of Windows that will not run on another

Fig.5.1 Use this window to select the correct language settings

PC. The computer's BIOS chip contains a pass code, and the operating system will only run if it finds this code. Since the pass code will not be found if the software is used on another PC, the operating system will refuse to load. While this restriction might seem to be a little unreasonable, bear in mind that the cost of bundled versions of Windows is relatively low, and the restrictions placed on the software are simply a reflection of this fact.

Linux is now available in a few hundred variations, some of which are free, but it is also on offer in normal commercial forms. The free versions usually have little or no support but usually include a wide range of application programs. In any commercial form there should be proper support from the manufacturer, and in general there are more and better application programs as well.

At one time it was often quite difficult to get Linux installed correctly and running as it should. Life is generally much easier with any of the modern versions that are intended for general use, which includes all the popular versions such as SUSE and Fedora. Even so, it is probably slightly more

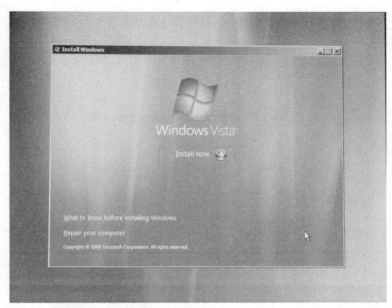

Fig.5.2 Select the Install Now option

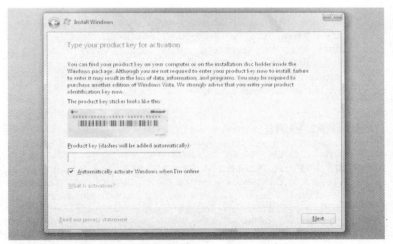

Fig.5.3 It is advisable to take this opportunity of entering your product code

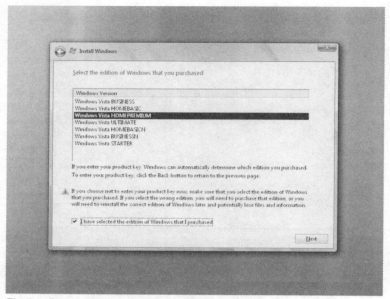

*Fig.5.4 Be careful to select the version of Vista that you have
purchased*

difficult to install than modern versions of Windows, and it can be very
difficult to sort things out if the installation goes seriously awry. A modern
distribution of Linux still represents a good choice for anyone aiming to
produce a working PC at a "rock-bottom" price, not the least because
there is usually an impressive array of free application software. Bear in
mind though, that Windows programs can not be used with Linux.

Installing Vista

Here we will concentrate on installing Windows Vista, which is the
operating system that most people choose for a new PC. Installing some
earlier versions of Windows involved a fair amount of preamble when
the hard disc drive was new, or for some other reason was blank. With
Windows Vista the installation process is relatively simple, and is very
similar whether the operating system is installed from scratch or on top
of an existing Windows installation. It is therefore largely the same whether
you use a new hard disc drive or one rescued from your previous PC.

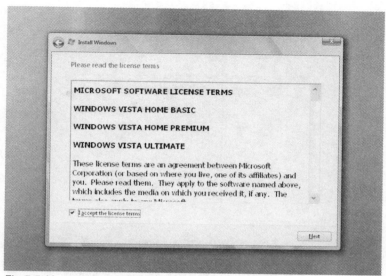

Fig.5.5 You must agree to the terms in order to proceed

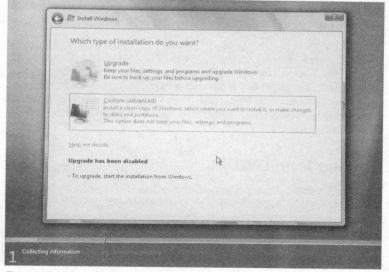

Fig.5.6 Choose the Custom (advanced) option at this window

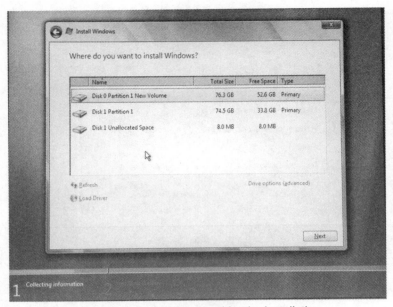

Fig.5.7 Select the drive that will be used for the installation

If Windows Vista is already on the hard disc it will be detected by the Setup program, which can then reinstall Windows Vista on top of the existing installation. Note that the versions of Windows Vista supplied with some PCs do not have the standard installation disc. The methods described here are only applicable if you have the standard Windows Vista installation disc. Such a disc is included when you buy the retail or OEM version of Vista.

Booting from DVD

Whether reinstalling on top of an existing installation or installing Windows Vista from scratch, the first step is to boot from the installation DVD. The BIOS must be set to boot from the DVD drive before it tries to boot from the hard disc. It is unlikely that the computer will attempt to boot from the DVD drive if the priorities are the other way around, and it will certainly not do so unless the DVD is set as one of the boot devices. If all is well,

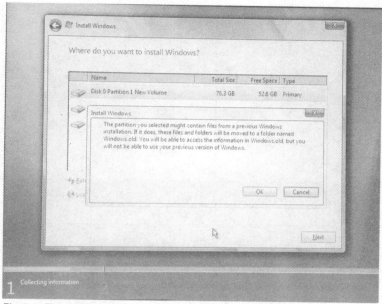

Fig.5.8 The old installation will be saved, but will not be used

a message will appear on the screen indicating that any key must be operated in order to boot from the DVD drive. This message appears quite briefly, so be ready to press one of the keys. The computer will try to boot from the hard disc if you "miss the boat". It will then be necessary to restart the computer and try again.

After various files have been loaded from the DVD, things should come to a halt with the screen of Figure 5.1. Here you use the three menus to set the installation language, the time and currency format, and the keyboard language or type. For a UK user these are normally set at English, English (United Kingdom), and United Kingdom respectively. Operating the Next button moves things on to the screen of Figure 5.2, where the "Install now" option should be selected. At the following screen (Figure 5.3) you have the option of entering your product key. It is not essential to do so at this stage, but it is definitely a good idea to do so. With a reinstallation it is also a good idea to opt for automatic activation by leaving the checkbox ticked.

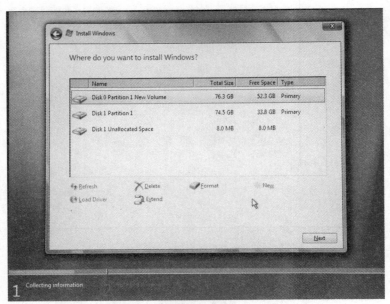

Fig.5.9 The advanced drive options have been activated

If a screen like the one in Figure 5.4 appears, use the list to select the version of Vista that you have purchased, and then tick the checkbox. The Next screen (Figure 5.5) is the usual licence agreement, and you have to tick the checkbox in order to agree with the licensing terms. Note that Windows Vista can not be installed unless you do agree to the licensing conditions. At the next screen (Figure 5.6) you supposedly have the choice of upgrading an existing Windows installation or installing a fresh one, but the upgrade option is unlikely to be active. This does not matter, because it is the "Custom (advanced)" option that is required in this case.

The available disc drives are listed at the next screen (Figure 5.7), where you select the drive that will be used for the Windows Vista installation. In this example it will be installed on Disk 0 Partition 1, but there is an obvious problem in that an existing installation is still present here. One option is to go ahead and install the fresh copy of Vista on this partition, but this will produce the warning message of Figure 5.8. This explains that the files associated with the existing Windows installation will be

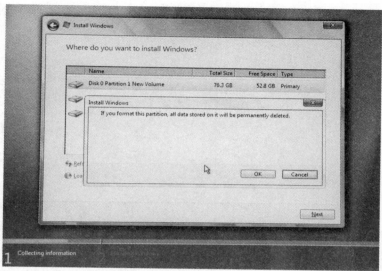

Fig.5.10 All the files on the drive will be deleted if it is formatted

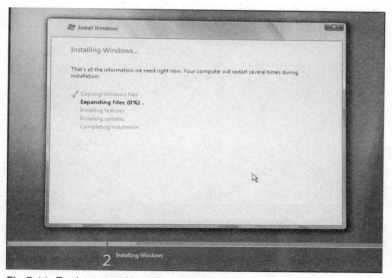

Fig.5.11 Each stage of installation is ticked as it is completed

217

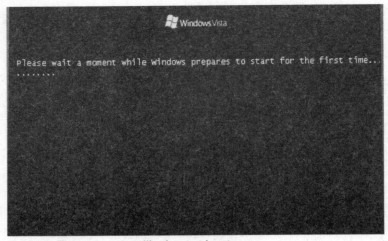

Fig.5.12 The computer will reboot at least once

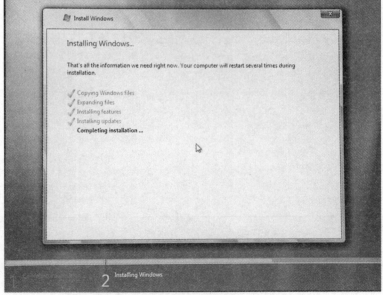

Fig.5.13 Installation has resumed and is nearing completion

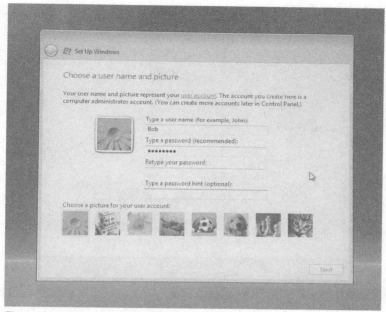

Fig.5.14 Supply a name for your account

moved to a folder called Windows.old, but the old version of Windows and the installed programs will not be usable.

You might prefer to do things this way provided the hard disc drive is large enough to take the old files and the new installation. Unwanted files can be deleted once the new installation is in place and fully operational. However, we will assume here that any existing operating system is not required and that Vista will be installed "from scratch".

Formatting

The Vista installation program includes a facility for formatting partitions, making it easy to wipe an existing partition of all existing files and folders. These facilities are accessed by operating the "Drive options (advanced)" link, which changes the screen to look like Figure 5.9. Where appropriate, make sure that the correct drive/partition is selected in the upper panel, and then operate the Format button in the lower section of the screen.

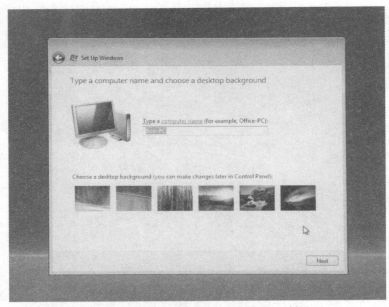

Fig.5.15 A network name for the computer is entered here

This will produce a warning message (Figure 5.10), which explains that all the files in the partition will be deleted when it is partitioned. This is, of course, exactly what is required in this case, but bear in mind that any data on the partition that has not been backed up will almost certainly be lost for ever once the formatting has started.

Operate the Next button once the partition has been formatted, and the installation of Windows Vista will then commence. The screen will change to show a list of tasks, and each one will be ticked as it is completed (Figure 5.11). Installation of a modern operating system takes a fair amount of time, so be prepared to wait several minutes while various tasks are performed. The computer will be restarted at least once during installation, and it is important that it is allowed to boot from the hard disc drive when this happens. Do not get it to boot from the installation DVD, or you will just end up going through the same steps over and over again with installation never being completed. The message of Figure 5.12 will be displayed if the computer reboots correctly from the hard disc drive.

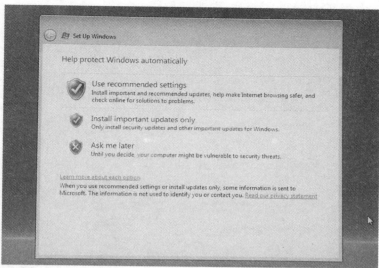

Fig.5.16 The screen is used to control automatic updates

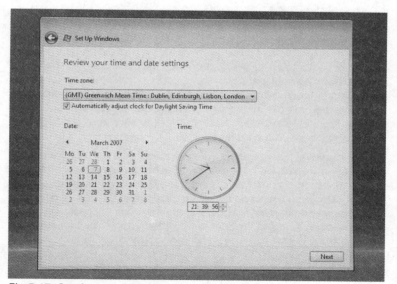

Fig.5.17 Set the correct time, date, and time zone

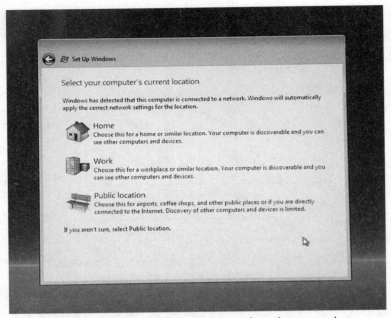

Fig.5.18 Choose whether the PC will be used at a home, work, or public location

The screen of Figure 5.13 will appear once the computer has rebooted, and the final stages of installation will then be completed. Although the installation process is largely automatic, it is still necessary for the user to enter some simple information. When the screen of Figure 5.14 appears, you have to select a picture to represent your account, and supply a name for your account.

It is not essential to use password protection, but it is probably best to do so. As usual, you will have to enter your choice of password into one textbox and then confirm that it is correct by entering it again in another textbox. An optional hint can be entered in another textbox, and the hint should be something that will help you to remember the password if you should happen to forget it. Bear in mind that you will be locked out of your account if you forget your password and do not manage to remember it.

The next screen (Figure 5.15) is used to enter a name for the computer, or the default name can be used. Do not confuse the account name and

Fig.5.19 This screen indicates that the setting up has been completed successfully

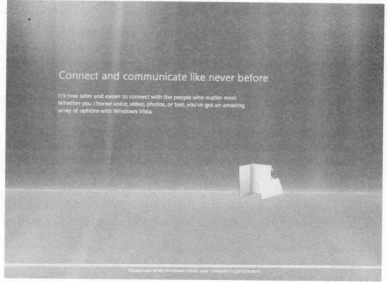

Fig.5.20 This is one of a series of information screens

Fig.5.21 Log on to the system in the usual way

the computer name. The name for the computer is the one that will be used to identify it if the computer is connected to a network. This name must therefore be different to the names used for any other computers on the network. It does not matter too much what name is used if the computer will not be used as part of a network. The account name given at the previous screen is the one used for your account on the computer. Other accounts can be added once Vista is installed and running properly, but this is not mandatory. The general idea is to have a different account for each user, so there is usually no point in having more than one account if there is only one user.

This screen is also used to select a background design for the Windows desktop. The first design in the row of thumbnail images will be used if you do not select one. Of course, the desktop's background is easily changed to just about anything you like once Vista has been installed, so it does not matter too much which design is chosen at this stage. There are three options at the following screen (Figure 5.16), which is where you select to have recommended updates installed, important

Fig.5.22 The computer has booted into the new Vista installation

updates, or neither at this stage. It is probably best to opt for at least important updates to be installed, but the automatic update settings can be altered once Vista is installed, so there is no need to make a final decision at this stage.

The next screen (Figure 5.17) allows the time, date, and time zone to be altered, if necessary. With a new motherboard in use it is unlikely that the existing settings will be correct, and this screen provides an opportunity to make any necessary adjustments. Tick the checkbox if you wish to have Vista automatically adjust the system clock for daylight saving. Things then move on to the screen of Figure 5.18 where you select Home, Business, or Public Location, depending on where the computer will mainly be used.

This completes the setting up procedure, which will be confirmed by the screen of Figure 5.19. Operating the Start button results in a series of information screens appearing, such as the example of Figure 5.20, while the installation is finalised. The usual log-on screen (Figure 5.21) will then appear if you opted to use a password. Log-on in the usual way,

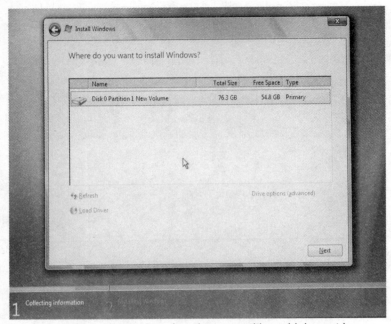

Fig.5.23 In this example there is only one partition which must be reformatted

and the Windows Vista desktop (Figure 5.22) should then be obtained. The desktop will appear straight away if no password was entered during the setting up procedure. Of course, it is just the bare desktop that is obtained when Vista is installed from scratch. In order to get the computer into full working order it is necessary to install all the application software, customise the Windows environment, copy your data files to the hard disc drive, etc.

From scratch

In this demonstration of installing Windows Vista the hard disc drive was already partitioned and formatted, making it slightly easier to install the operating system. If you use a brand new hard disc drive it will have the low level formatting performed at the factory, but it is unlikely that it will be supplied with any existing partitions or high level formatting already carried out for you. Apart from the low level formatting the disc will be blank, and the user has to add the required partitions and type of

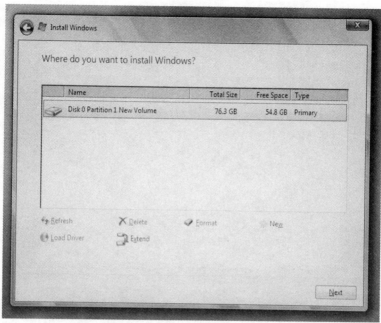

Fig.5.24 Activate the Format link to format the selected partition

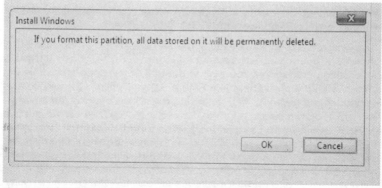

Fig.5.25 All files in the selected partition will be deleted

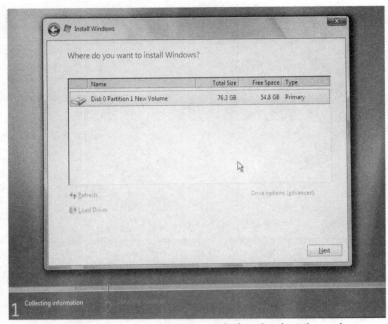

*Fig.5.26 Things look much the same as before back at the main
        screen*

formatting. It will also be necessary to repartition and format the disc if
you wish to start from scratch with a disc that has already been partitioned
and formatted Either way it is not difficult since the necessary utilities
are built into the Windows Vista installation program.

The installation process is exactly the same as the method described
previously, but only until the screen of Figure 5.7 is reached. If there is
an existing partition that you wish to remove or reuse from scratch, the
screen will look something like Figure 5.23. In order to remove this
partition it is a matter of first activating the "Drive options (advanced)"
link, which produces a screen like the one in Figure 5.24. There are two
ways of dealing with the existing partition, and the format option will
suffice if you intend to reuse the existing partition, with no changes being
made to the disc's partitioning. Make sure that the correct partition is
selected in the upper part of the window if there is more than one listed
here. Reformatting a partition will erase any existing data that it contains,
and a message to this effect will appear when the Format option is

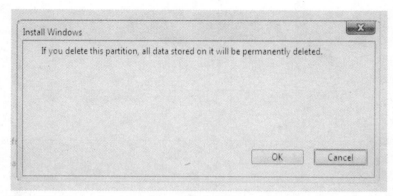

Fig.5.27 You are warned that any data in the selected partition will be erased

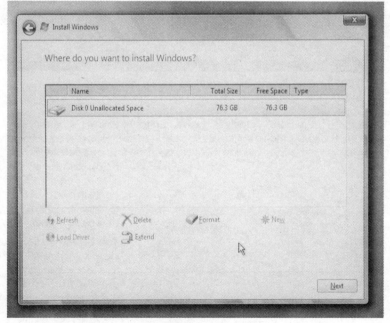

Fig.5.28 The disc is now "Unallocated Space"

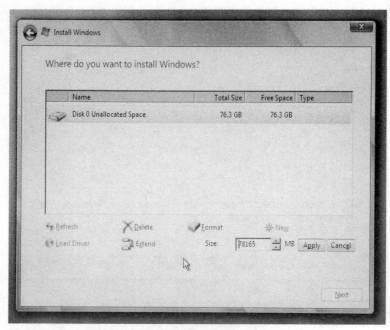

Fig.5.29 By default, one large partition will be produced

selected (Figure 5.25). Operate the Yes button if you are sure that you wish to proceed. Once the formatting has been completed you are taken back to the main screen, which will look much the same as before (Figure 5.26). However, the disc is now partitioned and formatted, but is otherwise empty.

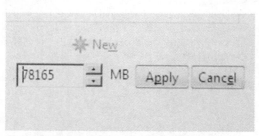

Fig.5.30 This textbox can be used to alter the partition's size

The Delete option is used if you would like to effectively start with a new and totally blank disc that has no partitions. It is probably only

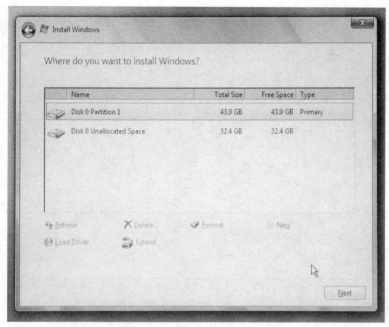

Fig.5.31 The new partition has been added successfully, but there is still some unallocated disc space

worthwhile using this method if it is necessary to change the existing partitioning of the disc, such as having two partitions instead of one. The warning message of Figure 5.27 appears when the Delete option is used, and this message simply points out that any data in the partition will be lost if you proceed. Again, if there is more than one partition listed on the main screen, make sure that the right one is selected. Operate the Yes button if all is well and you wish to proceed. Back at the main screen, the deleted partition will now be shown as "Unallocated Space" (see Figure 5.28). This is where things start if you use a new disc that has no existing partitioning.

Partitioning

In order to use the disc it must have at least one partition, and the partition or partitions must be formatted. The first task is to create the required partition or partitions. In this example two partitions will be used, but

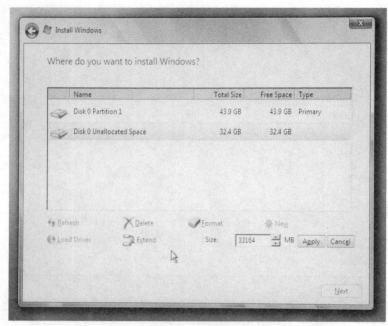

Fig.5.32 As before, the size of the partition can be specified

regardless of the number of partitions, the first step is to operate the New link in the bottom of section of the window. The screen then changes, with a textbox appearing in the lower section of the screen (Figures 5.29 and 5.30). Simply leave this unchanged if you wish to have a single partition on the disc that is as large as possible. If more than one partition is required, enter the size required for the first one. The size of the partition is specified in megabytes, and there are 1024 megabytes per gigabyte. In this example I specified a size of 4500 megabyes, which is just under 44 gigabytes.

This partition was created successfully (Figure 5.31), leaving a large amount of unallocated disc space for a second partition. The second partition is produced by selecting the unallocated disc space and repeating the procedure (Figure 5.32). It is not essential to accept the default size and use all the space for a single partition. As before, a smaller size can be specified leaving space for a third partition. Dividing a disc into three separate partitions can have advantages, but bear in

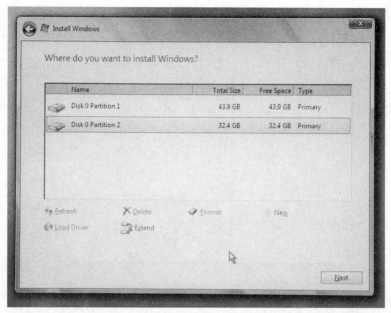

Fig.5.33 The disc now has two partitions and no unallocated space

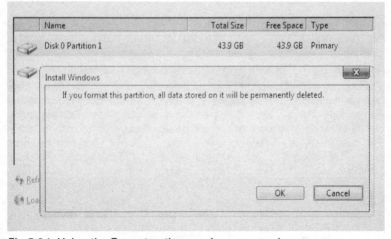

Fig.5.34 Using the Format option produces a warning message

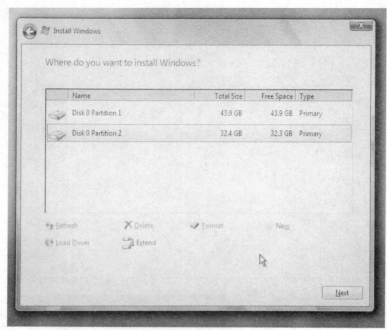

Fig.5.35 The main window looks much the same as before, but both partitions have been formatted

mind that it can also be inefficient and inconvenient in some circumstances. Do not partition a disc in this way just for the sake of it. Only do so if you have a good reason to do so. In this example I settled for two partitions that were produced without any problems (Figure 5.33).

The disc now has two partitions, but they are not usable until they have been formatted. Start by selecting the first partition and operating the Format link. This will produce a warning message (Figure 5.34) pointing out that any data on the partition will be erased by the formatting, but in this case there is no data to lose. However, make sure that the right partition is selected in cases where there is a partition that contains data. Having formatted the first partition, repeat the process to format any other new partitions. Things do not look any different back at the main window (Figure 5.35), but the disc is now ready for the Windows installation to proceed. Operating the Next button moves things on to the beginning of the installation process (Figure 5.36), and from here everything progresses in the manner described previously.

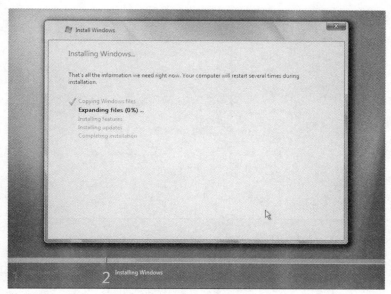

Fig.5.36 Windows Vista can now be installed in the normal way

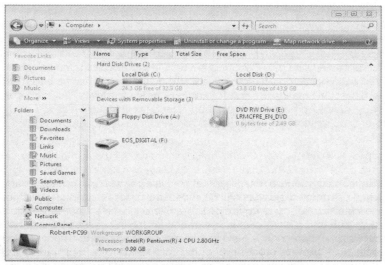

Fig.5.37 Partitions 1 and 2 are drives C and D in Windows

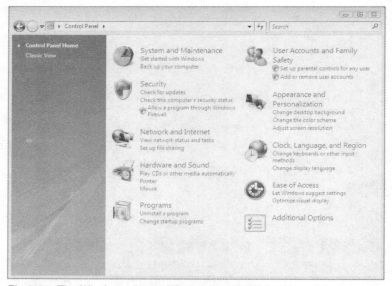

Fig.5.38 The Windows Control Panel (standard view)

With Windows installed it is a good idea to use Windows Explorer to check that any extra partitions are present and correct. In this example both partitions are present (Figure 5.37). Partition 1 is Disc C in Windows, and it contains the Windows Vista installation. Partition 2 is drive D, and as yet contains no data. Writing a few test files to this disc should confirm that it is functioning correctly. It is worth noting that Windows Vista has facilities for partitioning and formatting hard disc drives, so it is only necessary to produce one partition during the installation process. If preferred, any others can be added once Windows has been installed.

Video settings

The resolution and colour depth of the video system is usually set at something fairly basic when Windows XP and earlier versions of Windows are installed. You then have to go to the Control Panel to set the required resolution and maximum number of colours. In most cases this is not possible because only a generic video driver is installed. The range of resolutions provided by a driver of this type tends to be a bit limited, as does its performance. In order to get the video system working properly

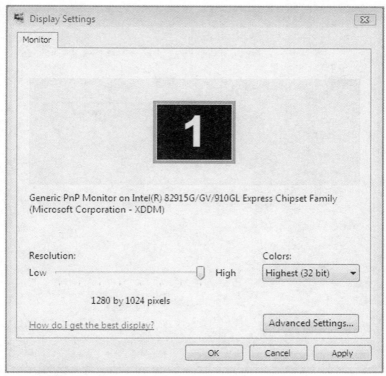

Fig.5.39 Use the slider control to set the screen resolution

it is therefore necessary to install the correct video driver software first, and then set the required parameters.

Essentially the same routine might be needed in order to get the video system working properly once Windows Vista has been installed. This will not necessarily be the case though. In this example the most up-to-date video driver was installed during the installation process, and the resolution was set at the optimum level for the flat screen LCD monitor. Presumably the monitor is a Plug-N-Play type, and the installation program set the resolution at the native level of the monitor.

Of course, Vista will not always be able to locate and install the optimum video driver. Its chances of success are quite good if you are using a

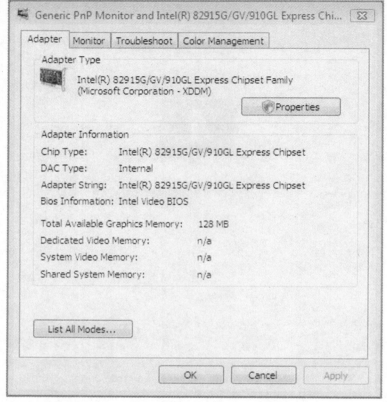

Fig.5.40 The Adapter section of the window will probably appear by default

video card that is a year or two old, but are rather less good if your PC is fitted with the latest card that has only just been released. Another point to bear in mind is that the installation program can not mind-read. It will apply settings which are likely to be the ones that most users will require, but it will not necessarily use the ones that you deem to be the most suitable. If you prefer something less than the highest available resolution so that the screen is easier to read, you will probably have to set the required resolution manually.

In order to adjust the video settings it is first a matter of going to the Start menu and launching the Windows Control Panel. With the Control Panel

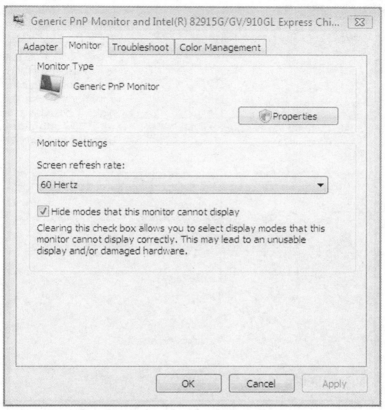

Fig.5.41 The menu offers a range of refresh frequencies

in the standard (Home) view (Figure 5.38), left-click the "Adjust screen resolution" link, which is in the "Appearance and Personalization" section. This produces the window of Figure 5.39 where the screen resolution can be adjusted via the slider control.

The colour depth is set via the "Colors" drop-down menu, but there will probably be just two options here. These will be 16-bit and 32-bit, with the latter probably being used by default. Using the 16-bit option gives over 65,000 colours, and this is adequate for most purposes. The 16-bit option is less demanding on the hardware, so it can be advantageous to use it if the computer has a relatively small amount of memory and (or) a

Fig.5.42 Operate the Yes button if this window is visible

processor that is not particularly fast.

The refresh rate of the screen is not usually too important with LCD monitors, but it is important to use the highest possible rate with CRT monitors. Using a low refresh

Fig.5.43 Operate the Update Driver button

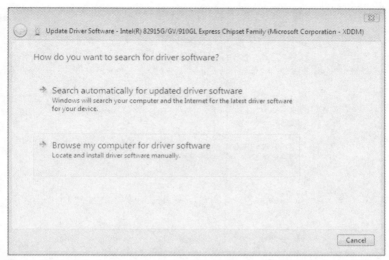

Fig.5.44 Just the computer or the computer and the Internet can be searched for more up-to-date drivers

frequency tends to give noticeable screen flicker with CRT monitors. The refresh frequency can be adjusted by operating the Advanced Settings button, which produces a new window (Figure 5.40). This will probably show the Adapter section by default, but in this case it is the section under the Monitor tab (Figure 5.41) that is required. The pop-down menu should offer a few options at higher frequencies than the current setting, and it is a matter of using trial and error to find the optimum setting. This is the highest setting that enables the monitor to produce a proper picture.

The small window of Figure 5.42 appears when a new setting is selected and the Apply button is operated. At least, it will do so provided the monitor is capable of supporting the selected refresh frequency. If this window does appear, and a stable picture is obtained, operate the Yes button. If not, the original refresh rate will be restored after six seconds, and you will not be stuck with an unusable video system. You can then try again using a lower refresh frequency. Note that the maximum scan rate for a CRT monitor generally reduces as the screen resolution is increased. Consequently, the higher the screen resolution used, the lower the scan rate that will have to be set.

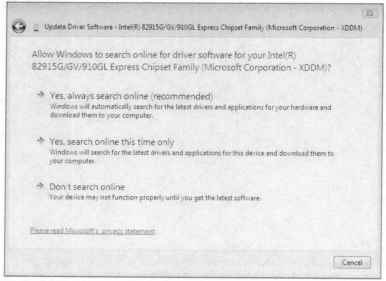

Fig.5.45 The choices here govern future searches for drivers

Video driver

The video system will not provide optimum results unless the driver software is the proper type for the video card, and it is the most up-to-date version of the software. If your PC or video card was supplied complete with video driver software for Vista, this can be installed in accordance with the manufacturer's instructions. It is possible that this software will be older than the version already installed, but you will then get an onscreen message to that effect and the installation will not go ahead.

Although Windows has facilities for installing driver software, these are not necessarily used when installing device drivers. In fact it seems to be quite normal for hardware manufacturers to "do their own thing" in this respect. Therefore, whenever you install hardware drivers, read the manufacturer's installation instructions and follow them "to the letter". There is no point in trying to install drivers through the official Windows route when the driver software is designed for some other method. The most common installation method these days is to run a Setup program that installs the driver software automatically, or in a largely automatic

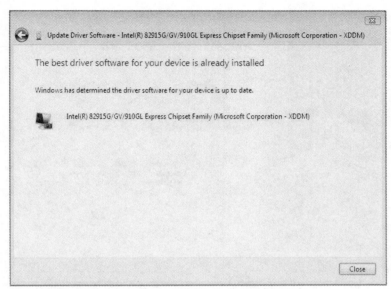

Fig.5.46 In this case no more recent driver was found

fashion. It is then just a matter of restarting the computer to make the changes take effect, and the hardware is then ready for use.

Updating

It is advisable to check that the video driver software you are using is the latest version, and one way of doing this is to go to the manufacturer's web site yourself to check for updates. The alternative is to let Windows do the searching for you. This is done by going into Device Manager and finding the entry for the piece of hardware that you would like to update. Double-click the entry to launch its properties window, or right-click its entry and choose Properties from the pop-up menu. Select the driver section of the properties window (Figure 5.43) and then operate the Update Driver button.

A new window will then appear on the screen (Figure 5.44), and this offers the choice of having Windows search the computer and the Internet for a newer driver, or just the computer. In this case it is the Internet that we wish to search for a new driver, so it is the upper link that is activated.

Fig.5.47 The first window of the Add Hardware wizard

The window then changes to the one shown in Figure 5.45, where three options are offered. These are to always search online, to only search online on this occasion, or to not search online at all. Either of the first two options will suffice in this case.

There will then be a delay while the search is made. You will be asked if you wish to go ahead and install the newer driver if something suitable is found. It is then just a matter of going ahead with the usual installation process, which is unlikely to require any input from the user. In this example a more up-to-date driver was not available, as explained by the information window of Figure 5.46.

Correct channels

The installation CDs supplied with most hardware includes a Setup program. However, in some cases the disc contains device drivers but it does not include a program to install the drivers. The same is true of driver software obtained via the Internet. Where the instruction manual gives installation instructions, or the installation method is described in a

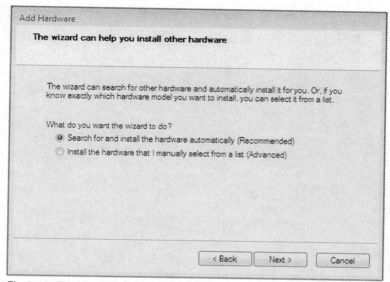

Fig.5.48 The driver can be installed manually or automatically

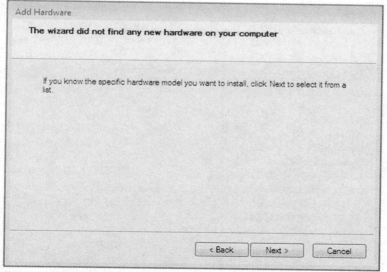

Fig.5.49 Automatic detection was not successful this time

5   The Operating System

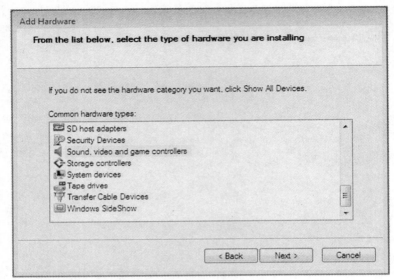

Fig.5.50 Choose the appropriate type of hardware

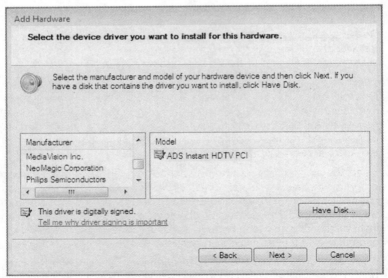

Fig.5.51 If it is listed, choose the device you are trying to install

The Operating System 5

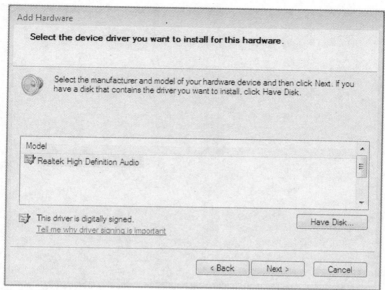

Fig.5.52 Operate the Have Disk button and locate the driver files

Read.me file, always follow the supplied instructions. Using the wrong installation method could result in serious damage to the operating system, making it impossible to boot into Windows.

With some low-cost hardware you are simply left to your own devices. One way of tackling the installation of hardware of this type is to launch Vista's version of the Add Hardware Wizard. Go to the Control Panel, if necessary set the Control Panel to the Classic View, and then double-click the Add Hardware Wizard icon. This launches the first window of the Add Hardware Wizard (Figure 5.47).

Heed the warning notice about using the manufacturer's installation program wherever possible. Check the installation CD to ensure that it does not contain an Install or Setup program. Where the driver software was downloaded from a web site, check the site carefully for installation instructions, and also look through the downloaded files for a Read.me or other text file that might contain installation advice, or a Setup program.

If you are sure that there is no installation program, operate the Next button to move the wizard on to the next stage Figure 5.48. The Add Hardware Wizard uses the normal technique of providing information

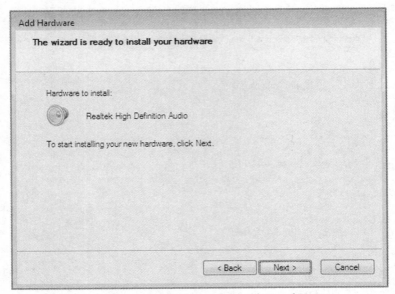

Fig.5.53 Confirm that you wish to install the driver software

screens and offering various options. This window gives the option of installing the device manually or having Windows try to detect it. There is no harm in trying the detection method, but it is likely Windows is incapable of detecting the hardware if it has not done so already. If you opt for automatic detection it is likely that you will still end up taking the manual route. Anyway, for this example I tried automatic detection, which, as expected, failed to find the new hardware (Figure 5.49).

Operate the Next button in order to proceed with manual installation. This produces a window like the one of Figure 5.50. This gives a list of hardware types, and you must select the correct category for the device you are trying to install. Moving on to the next window (Figure 5.51) gives a list of manufacturers in the left-hand section, and devices for the selected manufacturer in the right-hand section. Obviously you should select the appropriate entry for your device if it is listed, but this is unlikely.

It is normally necessary to operate the Have Disk button, which brings up a window like the one of Figure 5.52. Either type the path to the disc and folder containing the device drivers, or use the Browse option to

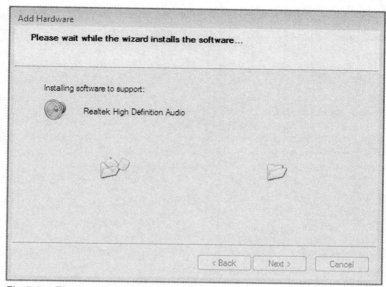

Fig.5.54 The installation is under way

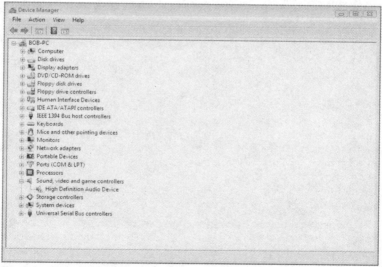

Fig.5.55 There is a problem with the soundcard

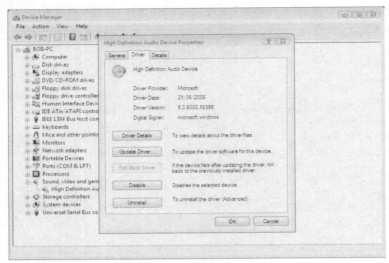

Fig.5.56 Operate the Update Driver button

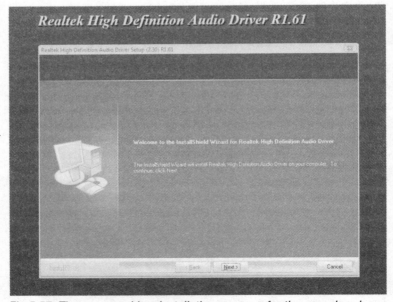

Fig.5.57 There was a driver installation program for the soundcard

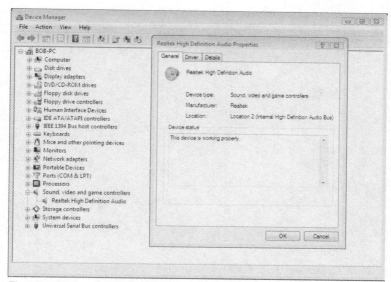

Fig.5.58 The soundcard driver software has been installed

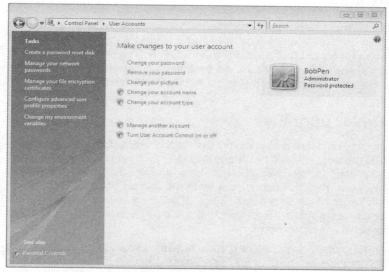

Fig.5.59 The User Accounts window

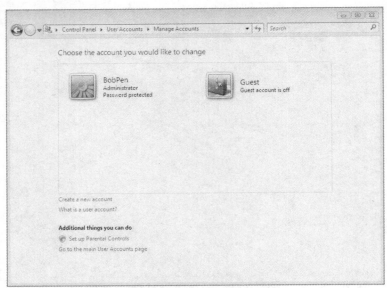

Fig.5.60 Left-click the "Create new account" link

locate the drivers. Having pointed Windows to the drivers, operate the Next button. You are then asked to confirm that the specified driver software should be installed (Figure 5.53), and the installation will then go ahead (Figure 5.54). It will probably be necessary to restart the computer in order to complete the installation of the new driver software.

Driver upgrade?

In many cases the problem is not that Vista has failed to find the hardware. The problem is that it has found and identified the hardware, but it can not find a suitable driver. There will be an entry for the hardware in Device Manager when this occurs, but there will also be a yellow exclamation mark against the entry (Figure 5.55). The General section of the device's properties window will explain that the driver software is not installed and that it is not working.

Although there is no matching driver software installed, the Update Driver button in the Driver section of the properties window will be active (Figure 5.56). It is therefore possible to update the non-existent driver using the

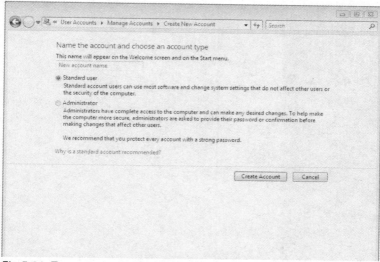

Fig.5.61 Type a name for the account into the textbox

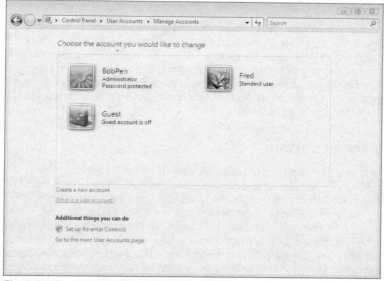

Fig.5.62 The new account has been created

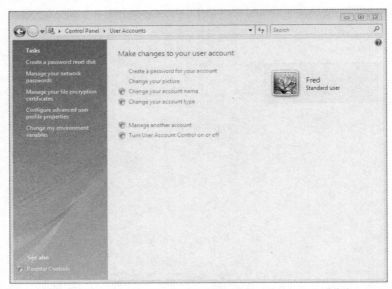

Fig.5.63 Left-click the "Create a password for your account" link

normal procedure. Make sure that the driver software is available on one of the computer's drives so that the update facility can find it when it goes through its search routine. The device in this example is a soundcard which came complete with a driver installation program. Running this program (Figure 5.57) and restarting the computer removed the exclamation mark in Device Manager and put the soundcard into full working order (Figure 5.58).

User accounts

One user account is produced as part of the installation process, but any further accounts have to be added once Vista has been installed and is working properly. The first step in adding a new account is to go to the Control Panel and double-click the User Accounts icon. This launches a window like the one in Figure 5.59. Then left-click the "Manage another account" link, and in the new version of the window (Figure 5.60) left-click the "Create a new account" link. This switches the window to the one shown in Figure 5.61. Type a suitable name for the account into the textbox.

Fig.5.64 Enter the new password twice. The password hint is optional

The type of account is selected using the two radio buttons. An administrator account provides freedom to make changes to the system, but these abilities are not needed for day to day use of the computer. A standard user account, or limited account as it used to be termed, is generally considered to be the better choice for normal use, since its restrictions reduce the risk of the system being accidentally damaged. Note that you might not be able to install programs when using a limited account. Also, some programs produced prior to Windows 2000 and XP might not be usable with a limited account. Consequently, there is no alternative to an administrator account if maximum flexibility is required.

Having selected the type of account using the radio buttons, operate the Create Account button. The original User Accounts window then returns, but it should now contain the newly created account (Figure 5.62). There are other facilities in the User Accounts window that enable the log-on and log-off settings to be altered. By default, the Welcome screen is shown at startup, and you simply have to left-click the entry for the new account in order to use that account. Note that the new account will start with a largely blank desktop. Each account has its own desktop and other settings, so each account can be customised with the best

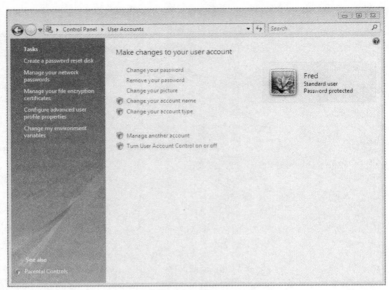

Fig.5.65 The account is now password protected

settings for its particular user. Of course, if software is installed using an option that makes it available to all users, then it will be available via all newly created accounts.

Accounts are not password protected by default. To add a password, log on to the relevant account, and then go to the User Accounts window (Figure 5.63). Next, left-click the "Create password for your account" link. At the next window (Figure 5.64) the password is typed into the top two textboxes, and a hint is entered into the other textbox. The hint is something that will jog your memory if you should happen to forget the password. Next operate the Create Password button, which takes things back to the User Accounts window (Figure 5.65), which should now show that the account is password protected. This completes the process, and the password will be needed the next time you login to that account.

Antivirus software

Windows XP and Vista have some built-in security measures such as a basic firewall program and a phishing filter in Windows Explorer, but there is no proper built-in anti-virus software. When you buy a new PC it almost invariably comes complete with a pre-installed anti-virus program. This usually has a major limitation in that the virus database can only be updated free of charge for a month ot two. The program will usually go on working once the initial free period has expired, but without an update subscription its virus database will soon start to become out of date, and the effectiveness of the software will be compromised. Even so, it does mean that your computer is protected right from the start, which is important if it will be connected to the Internet. It is particularly important if it will be connected to the Internet by way of a broadband connection of some sort.

The situation is clearly very different when you build your own PC, since it will have no pre-installed software. It might actually come complete with a time-limited trial version of an antivirus program, since these are often supplied as part of the software bundled with the motherboard. This type of software is sometimes supplied with other major items of hardware, such as graphics and sound cards. Most of the major antivirus software producers seem to have free trial versions of their products available as free downloads or available on the discs supplied with computer magazines. Consequently, there should be no difficulty in getting your newly built PC properly protected even if there is no bundled antivirus software and you do not already have something suitable.

An alternative approach is to use one of the totally free antivirus programs that are available via the Internet. Probably the best known of these is Grisoft's AVG Antivirus Free, which usually compares very well when tested against full commercial antivirus products. Importantly, it is not just the software that is free. Daily updates for the virus database are also available free of charge, and with no time limits. The Grisoft site is at:

www.grisoft.com

On the home page there might be a link to the free version of the program, but it does not seem to feature quite as prominently in the home page as it did in the past. At the time of writing this, the web address for Grisoft's free software is:

http://free.grisoft.com/doc/1/lng/us/tpl/v5

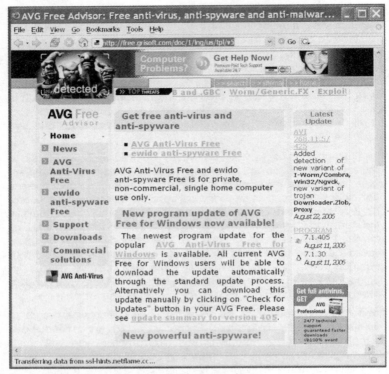

Fig.5.66 The home page for AVG's free software

If there is any difficulty in finding the home page for the free edition, try using "AVG", "free", and "edition" in any good search engine. Having found the right page, it will look something like the web page of Figure 5.66. This gives some information about the free software available from Grisoft, including their antivirus program. Operating the AVG Anti-Virus Free link in the left-hand column brings up the page that deals specifically with this software (Figure 5.67). This page includes a link that enables the program file to be downloaded. In fact there are a number of links, but it is the one for the Windows installation files that is needed in this case. It is actually just a single file that is downloaded, but this is an archive that contains all the installation files.

The Operating System 5

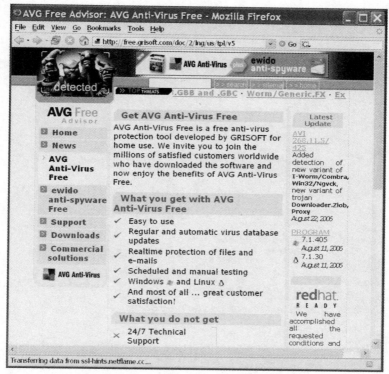

Fig.5.67 This is the page that deals specifically with AVG Free

There are also some documentation files available, and it is possible to read these online (Figure 5.68) provided your PC has the Adobe Acrobat Reader program installed. However, it is definitely a good idea to download them and store them on the hard disc drive in case they are needed for future reference. It is a good idea to at least take a quick look through the Reference Guide which, amongst other things, provides installation instructions.

Daily updates to AVG are available free of charge, and will download automatically when the PC is booted into Windows. Although the program is free, it should always be as up-to-date as possible. This program has a reputation for being very efficient, and it did once detect a couple of backdoor Trojan programs on my system that a certain well known

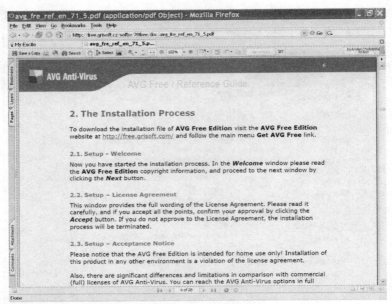

Fig.5.68 The documentation can be read online

commercial program had failed to detect. It is certainly one of the best freebies on the Internet, and it generally performs very well in comparison to commercial equivalents.

Earlier versions of the free AVG program had one major limitation, which was the lack of a rescue mode of the type provided by Norton Antivirus and some other programs. In the current version there is a basic facility that enables a rescue disc to be produced. This can be used to backup important system files so that they can be restored if the originals become damaged by a virus. There is still no facility to boot from a floppy disc or a CD-ROM drive and then run virus checks. Anyway, the program works effectively in the background detecting the vast majority of viruses, Trojans, etc., so there is little likelihood of a rescue mode being required.

Points to remember

If you are scapping an old PC, it might not be possible to use its operating system on your new PC. Some bundled versions of Windows are tied to a particular computer and will not boot if they are transferred to a different PC. It is unlikely that it will be possible to use an obsolete version of Windows with a new PC due to a lack of suitable driver software for the hardware.

Installing Windows Vista on top of an existing version might cure problems with the operating system, but it is not guaranteed to do so. Installing Windows Vista "from scratch", with all the previous files removed from the hard disc should effect a cure to any Windows problems. If it does not, the computer probably has a hardware fault.

When reinstalling Windows Vista from scratch it is necessary to reformat the hard disc, which can be done as part of the reinstallation process. This clears away any trace of the original installation, but all data will also be removed from the partition. Therefore, make sure that any important data is reliably backed up prior to installing Windows Vista from scratch. Data should not be lost when reinstalling Windows XP on top of the existing version, but it is a good idea to back up any important data in case there are problems.

The reinstallation process is largely automatic, but the user has to provide some basic information. The Setup program installs the Windows files and sets up the essential hardware.

Once Windows Vista has been reinstalled, some further work is usually required in order to get all the hardware properly installed. The screen resolution and colour depth might need adjustment. Some hardware has its own installation routines and does not go through the normal Windows routes. In fact, most hardware is now installed in this way. Always install hardware in accordance with the manufacturer's instructions.

Install the device drivers for system hardware on the motherboard first, followed by the video drivers, and then any other drivers that are needed. Do not install applications software until all the hardware is installed and working properly.

Any user accounts and passwords are lost when Windows Vista is installed from scratch. These can be rebuilt by going to the User Accounts window, which is accessed via the Control Panel.

It is possible to reinstall Vista over an existing installation, provided the existing installation is not too seriously damaged. This will leave your original data, settings, and programs fully operational, and much as they were before the problem was encountered. This type of reinstallation is achieved by "upgrading" the existing installation.

6

Troubleshooting

Prevention

Provided you proceed carefully, checking and double-checking everything as you go, and observing the basic anti-static handling precautions, you will be very unlucky indeed if the finished computer fails to start up correctly. However meticulous you are though, there is still an outside chance that things will not go perfectly, and if you take an "it will be all right on the night" approach to things it is likely that things will be far from all right when the new PC is switched on.

This is definitely something where the old adage that "prevention is better than cure" applies. Most computer components are reasonably idiot-proof, and if an error should be made it is unlikely that any damage will occur. This possibility can not be totally ruled out though, and there is a small but real risk of mistakes proving to be quite costly. Check everything as you go along, and then carefully recheck the finished PC before switching it on.

If possible, get someone to check everything for you. Having fooled yourself into making a mistake it is easy to make the same mistake when you check the finished unit. The mistake will probably be glaringly obvious to a fresh pair of eyes.

Blank expression

A faulty PC may start to go through the initial start-up routine and then fail at some stage, usually after the initial BIOS checks as the computer goes into the boot-up phase. Alternatively it may simply refuse to do anything, or sit there on the desk producing "beeping" noises with a blank screen. We will start by considering likely causes if the computer does very little, or even nothing at all.

If switching on the PC results in nothing happening at all, with no sign of cooling fans operating or front panel lights switching on, the obvious first step is to check that power is getting to the computer. Is the power lead plugged in properly at both the computer and the mains outlet, and is the mains supply switched on at the outlet? It is a silly mistake to forget to plug the computer into the mains supply or to switch on the supply, but it is easily done in your haste to try out the new PC. Also check that the fuse in the mains plug is present and correct.

A PC power supply is a fairly sophisticated piece of electronics that contains numerous protection circuits. The fact that it fails to operate even though it is receiving power does not necessarily mean that it is faulty. It could simply be that a protection circuit is detecting a problem somewhere and is shutting down the supply circuit. An overload on one of the supply lines could cause this, but is not a likely cause of the problem with a new PC. However, you can not totally rule out the possibility that the cause of the problem is a fault in one of the components that the supply is powering.

Leads

A more likely cause is that the leads carrying the output of the supply are not connected properly. With the old AT power supplies it is possible to get the two supply connectors swapped at the motherboard, but this is not possible with modern PC supply units due to their single main power connector. In theory, with a single connector it is impossible to get things wrong, but in practice this type of power connector can be difficult to get properly into place. In fact this applies to most types of power connector, and I suppose it is a byproduct of making the connectors fit very firmly together so that good connections are produced.

It is worth removing and refitting the power connector to the motherboard to make quite sure that it is fully pressed down and into place. These connectors lock into place, a connector is not fitted properly if you can free it without releasing the locking mechanism. In normal use an ATX power supply is switched on and off via a simple pushbutton switch on the front of the case, and not by way of a conventional on/off switch in the mains supply. Check that the on/off switch is connected to the motherboard correctly. Fitting the leads that connect vaious items on the case to the motherboard tends to be rather fiddly, and mistakes are easily made when installing these leads.

If the PC uses a motherboard that requires one or two supplementary power leads, make sure that these are both connected to the motherboard correctly. The larger of the two additional connectors is normally left unused with modern Pentium 4 motherboards, but it is advisable to check this point and not make assumptions. An ordinary 20-pin power connector can only be used with a 24-pin connector on the motherboard if the instruction manual states that this is acceptable, or the appropriate adaptor is used.

AMD approved

Occasionally there is a problem with a PC that seems to power-up correctly, but does not go into the POST routine. In fact the PC will usually start correctly on some occasions, but not on others, with the fault occurring randomly. This seems to occur more with PCs based on AMD processors than those having Intel chips. It seems to stem from a problem with the power supply, which is probably failing to establish the main supplies with suitable rapidity, or perhaps there is some initial noise on the supply lines that is causing problems.

Anyway, whatever the cause, you either have to learn to live with the problem or try fitting a new supply. When building a PC based on an AMD processor it is advisable to obtain a power supply that is AMD approved. This should avoid these start-up problems. Also, if the supply should fail to work properly with a motherboard fitted with an AMD processor, you then have good grounds for complaint.

If the mains supply seems to be getting through to the power supply unit all right, and the on/off switch and motherboard are connected to the power supply correctly, it is time to look further afield for the problem. It is unlikely that a faulty drive is causing an overload, but it is as well to check this by disconnecting the drive power leads.

It is worth making the point that you should not disconnect and reconnect any leads with the computer switched on. Doing so with power or data leads could result in costly damage, with you creating more faults than you fix! If any changes to the cabling are required, switch off the computer, make the changes, and then switch on again. Ideally the drive data cables should also be disconnected when making this test. With no power supplied to the drives they could provide abnormal loading on the data cables and could conceivable cause damage to the motherboard, although the chances of this occurring are admittedly quite remote.

It is possible that the problem is simply that the power supply is overloaded. This is very unlikely to happen provided you use a supply having a rating of at least 350 watts. Bargain PC cases having supplies rated at 300 watts or less are fine for rejuvenating an ageing PC, but are not well suited for use as the basis of a new computer. A rating of 350 watts is usually adequate, but a supply rated at 400 watts or more is better if the PC has a lot of drives, expansion cards, or a fast processor with lots of memory.

An overloaded power supply may not simply result in the PC refusing to start. In my experience it is more likely that the PC will start up all right but it will tend to sporadically reset or switch off for no apparent reason. The power drain varies from one instant to another depending on what the PC is actually doing. Presumably one of the supply rails drops to an inadequate level during peaks of power consumption, causing the PC's monitoring circuits to reset or switch off the computer.

On the cards

If removing power from the drives does not effect a cure it is time to restore power to the drives and move on to the expansion cards. Switch off the computer, remove all the expansion cards, and then switch on again. In my experience the expansion cards are often the cause of problems, and removing them will often result in an otherwise "dead" PC bursting into life. If the cause of the problem is a faulty card, reinserting the cards one by one will soon reveal which card is at fault. When the computer ceases to start up again, the last card restored is the faulty one. Of course, the computer must be switched off before each card is installed. Adding or removing a card with the computer switched on does not guarantee that something will be damaged, but it nearly does.

Do not be surprised if having restored all the cards in the computer it still starts up properly. This will not be due to the faulty card having been miraculously cured, but is simply due to the fact that it was not originally installed correctly. If a card is not slotted into the motherboard correctly it can cause short circuits that will prevent the power supply from operating. The expansion card system used in PCs is a decided asset, which makes it easy to produce custom PCs that exactly suit given requirements. It also makes it easy to change the configuration of a PC to suit changing circumstances.

The drawback of this system is that there are numerous contacts on the expansion card connectors, and the card and motherboard connectors must be accurately aligned if everything is to work properly. Some PCs fit together better than others, but it can sometimes be difficult to get the cards into place, and nothing seems to fit correctly. When this happens the usual cause is the motherboard being slightly out of position on the base panel of the case.

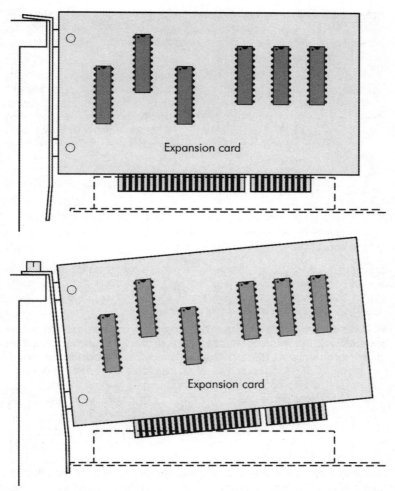

Fig.6.1 A mounting bracket can cause problems if it does not have the correct right-angled bend

On the level

Do not simple wrestle with the expansion cards until they are eventually forced into place. Apart from the very real risk of damaging the cards and the motherboard, boards forced into place in this fashion are unlikely

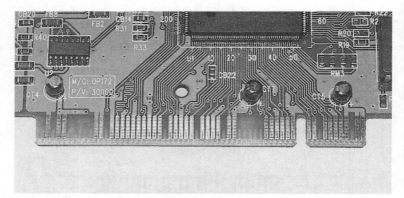

Fig.6.2   The gap between adjacent contacts on an expansion card is very small, making accurate alignment of the card and slot absolutely essential

to stay in place very long. If expansion cards are proving troublesome it is usually possible to sort things out by slightly loosening the screws that hold the motherboard in place. Fit the expansion cards and then tighten the motherboard's mounting bolts again.

You may occasionally find that an expansion card plugs into place perfectly well, but when its retaining bolt is tightened it tends to lift up out of its expansion slot. In most cases it is only the front end of the card that shifts out of position. The usual cause of this is the metal mounting bracket on the card not having a proper 90-degree bend at the top where it bolts to the rear of the case. This results in the card tending to lift out of the expansion slot at one end when the fixing bolt it tightened. This is shown in somewhat exaggerated form in Figure 6.1. The cure is to carefully bend the bracket to the correct angle with the aid of a small vice or some sturdy pliers.

Note that it only needs the card to lift slightly at one end or the other to totally "gum up" the computer. There are only minute gaps between the metal contacts on the connector of an expansion card (Figure 6.2). If the connector fits into the expansion slot at a slight angle this produces short-circuits along the rows of terminals. This in turn produces short-circuits on the supply lines, causing the power supply to shut down. With luck this should prevent any damage from occurring, but it is much better if you can spot a badly fitting card before you switch on the PC.

Another occasional cause of problems is a mounting bracket that is too high or too low on the expansion card. If it is mounted too low down on the card it will prevent the card from going down into the slot correctly. When this occurs it is usually possible to loosen the screws that fix the bracket to the card, pull the bracket into the correct position, and then retighten the screws.

Another problem with the expansion card system is that it only needs one bad connection to prevent the entire computer from working properly. This is something that tends to be more of a problem after a computer has been in use for some time and the connectors start to corrode slightly. Nevertheless, even with new equipment it is possible that the metal terminals on one or other of the connectors could be slightly dirty or corroded, and that bad connections could cause problems. This is a very real possibility if you build a "bargain" PC using components that have been in storage for some time prior to you purchasing them. There are special cleaning fluids, etc., for use with connectors, but simply inserting and removing an expansion card a few times should do the trick.

The problem could be due to a faulty memory module short-circuiting the supply, and removing the module or modules from the motherboard might bring results. It could also be that the processor is faulty and is overloading the supply, but this is not very likely. It is not a good idea to power up the motherboard without a processor installed, so unless you have another processor that can be tried on the motherboard it is difficult to test for this.

Substitution

If none of this gets the power supply operating it is likely that either the motherboard or the power supply itself is faulty. Do not be tempted to open up the power supply unit and prod around inside to see if you can see what is wrong. A modern PC power supply is a complex piece of equipment that uses a lot of specialised components and quite advanced techniques. Many electronics engineers are not qualified to sort out this type of equipment and it is certainly well beyond the scope of an electronics handyman. Also, it is potentially lethal to dabble with any equipment that connects direct to the mains supply, and it is certainly not something that should be undertaken by anyone who is not properly qualified.

So how can you determine whether it is the supply or the motherboard that is at fault? Sorting out problematic PCs is much easier if you have

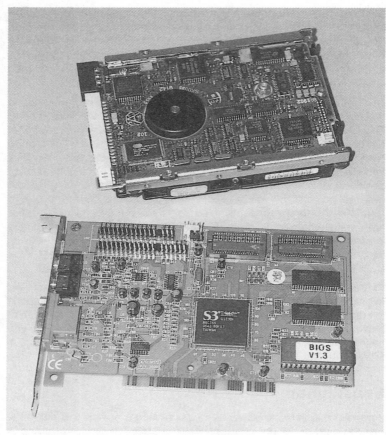

Fig.6.3 Keep old hard disc drives, video cards, etc. They can be invaluable when things go wrong

some old parts that can be used as an aid to fault finding. This is one reason for me not recommending do-it-yourself PC building to people who have little or no previous experience with PCs. Most long-standing PC users have a collection of old components that have been replaced by more up-to-date components. These days they often have one or two complete but ageing PCs.

I would certainly recommend that you hold on to any PCs or PC components that are working and not totally obsolete, as these can often be useful when sorting out a troublesome PC. Items such as old PCI audio cards, AGP or PCI video cards, and low-capacity IDE hard disc drives (Figure 6.3) can be invaluable when trying to sort out a faulty PC. Old but working floppy or CD-ROM drives are also valuable for fault finding and are well worth keeping for this purpose.

In this case an old motherboard could be temporarily installed in the case to see if the power supply can be persuaded to burst into action. Alternatively, the new motherboard could be installed in an old case to see if it functions correctly. In either example there could be problems if the new case and motherboard are of the ATX variety, and the old equipment has AT connectors. For some years now it has been standard practice for AT motherboards to be ATX compatible, so unless the "spare" motherboard is really old it should be compatible with a new case. The old power supply might have a low power rating by current standards, but it should be sufficient to power a basic PC having a minimal set of drives and expansion cards.

If the new motherboard works in an old case, then clearly the new motherboard is not faulty. Presumably it is the new power supply that has the problem. If the old motherboard works properly in the new case, then the new power supply is functioning correctly and it is almost certainly the new motherboard that is faulty. This method of substituting a component that is known to work for one that is thought to be faulty is the basis for much PC faultfinding. Without specialised and expensive pieces of test equipment to check individual components it is the only practical method of determining which parts of a faulty PC work properly, and which do not.

Incidentally, if you return a component that is suspected of being faulty, it is unlikely to be tested on a special test bed or using some advanced piece of test equipment. It is much more likely that it will be installed in a working PC to see what happens. In other words, professional testers make great use of the substitution method, which is the quickest, easiest, and most reliable method of testing practically any computer component.

Partial failure

It is unusual for a faulty PC to simply "play dead" at switch-on, and the more usual problem is the computer starting up but reporting an error and failing to boot-up. Sometimes it fails to boot because the error brings things to a halt before the boot-up phase is reached. In other cases the error message will include a phrase like "boot failure", which means that the BIOS has tried to boot the PC but has failed to find a valid operating system. We will consider pre-boot failures first.

If the computer seems to be starting up normally, but there is no video signal, the obvious initial check is to see whether or not the video card is installed correctly. In the past it was the video card that was most likely to give problems if there was a problem with physical alignment of the cards. These days the video card will presumably be an AGP type or one of the PCI Express variety, complete with a locking mechanism to prevent any lifting at the front of the card. It is still worth checking that the card is properly in place, and that the locking lever has properly hooked into the card's cut-out and locked into place.

Also check that the signal lead for the monitor is connected properly to the video card and at the monitor if it is detachable at this end as well. If none of the monitor's indicator lights switch on it is likely that the problem is a complete lack of power to the monitor rather than an absence of video output from the computer. There is normally an indicator light switched on even if a modern monitor is receiving no video signal. Either another light switches on or the light changes colour when a video signal is received. If the monitor is completely "dead", it is not receiving power and the power lead and plug must be checked. In the unlikely event that the monitor is powered via the power supply unit, try powering it directly from the mains supply. This will require a different power lead, but monitors can normally use a standard mains lead of the type used with many modern electrical and electronic gadgets.

If necessary, borrow the computer's power lead and try using the monitor on its own. Obviously you will not get any response from the screen, but an indicator light should switch on if power is getting through to the monitor. If this results in it working, either the original power lead is faulty or the power supply unit is faulty and is not providing any power on the mains output socket.

If the monitor itself appears to be faulty, do not be tempted to open the case and start delving around inside. There are very high voltages present inside a conventional (CRT) monitor, and these voltages can remain for some time after the unit is switched off. The interior of a monitor is potentially lethal and only trained engineers should attempt repairs to this type of equipment.

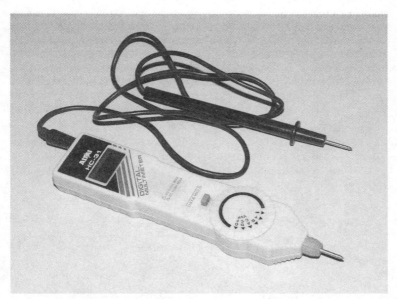

Fig.6.4 A digital test meter having a continuity tester function

Lead checking

When faultfinding on PCs you will soon need to check leads for broken wires. There are inexpensive test meters available that have a continuity tester setting that is ideal for this sort of thing. In addition to any visual indication, the unit normally produces a "beep" if a short-circuit is detected across the test prods. A miniature digital instrument (Figure 6.4) is well suited to this type of testing, but is somewhat over-specified. A basic analogue multimeter (Figure 6.5) will do the job well, but these days it is unlikely to cost much less than one of the more basic digital units.

Something much more basic than a test meter is adequate for testing leads, and even an old torch bulb and battery style continuity checker (Figure 6.6) will do the job perfectly well. The test prods and leads can be the genuine article, but they need consist of nothing more than two pieces of single-strand insulated wire with a few millimetres of the insulation stripped away to produce the prods. This is admittedly a bit crude, but when testing computer leads it is often necessary to get the prods into tiny holes in the connectors. With the improvised prods there

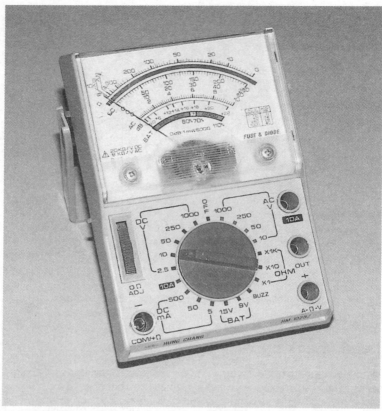

Fig.6.5 A cheap analogue multimeter is useful for checking leads

is no difficulty in doing so because they are so narrow, but with proper prods they are often too thick to fit into the connectors.

Testing cables is often rather awkward because you need four hands! You require one hand per test prod and another hand per connector. The easy way to tackle the problem is to fix both connectors to the workbench using clamps, or something like Bostik Blu-Tack or Plasticine will often do the job quite well (Figure 6.7).

With heavier cables such as printer types it is better to clamp the connectors in place, because Blu-Tack and the like may not have sufficient

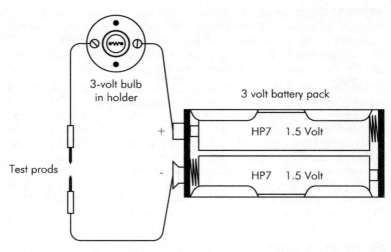

Fig.6.6 A simple continuity checker for testing leads

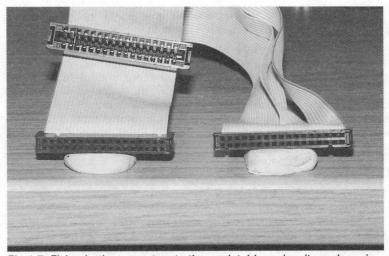

Fig.6.7 Fixing both connectors to the work table makes it much easier to test leads

275

sticking power to keep everything in place. With the connectors fixed to the bench and the metal terminals facing towards you it is easy to check for continuity because you then have both hands free to hold the test prods. Provided the workbench is well lit you can also see exactly what you are doing, which should help to avoid errors.

Incidentally, if you use a test meter for cable testing, on the face of it the meter is also suitable for checking the supply levels on the motherboard and other simple voltage checks. I would definitely advise against prodding around on the motherboard or an expansion card using a test meter. With the intricacy of modern boards it is quite tricky to do this, and there is a high risk of the test prods causing accidental short circuits. These could in turn ruin expensive items of hardware. The meter can be used to check for the correct voltages on a disc drive power cable and for simple continuity tests on cables that have been totally removed from the PC, but it is advisable to go no further with it than that.

Error messages

Returning to the subject of problems during the initial testing by the BIOS, it is possible for things to simply grind to a halt, but a more likely cause of the problem is that the BIOS has detected a problem and brought things to a halt. The screen may display a message along the lines "Press F1 to continue", but there is probably no point in trying to continue with the boot process if there is a major fault present in the system.

The error message may be rather cryptic, giving nothing more than a number for the error. The computer may also do a certain number of "beeps" from the internal loudspeaker over and over again, which is another way of indicating the nature of the fault. Unfortunately, motherboard instruction manuals do not usually give any information about the exact meaning of the error messages, but this information might be available at the web site of the BIOS manufacturer. It is worthwhile looking in the manual to see if it gives any guidance. Some instruction manuals are much more comprehensive than others.

These days the error message usually gives some indication of what is causing the problem, with an error message along the lines "keyboard error or no keyboard present". With the BIOS telling you the cause of the problem you can obviously go straight to the component that has failed to work properly. It is then a matter of checking that the keyboard is connected correctly, the memory modules are seated correctly in their holders, or whatever.

Once again, the substitution method can be used to nail down the exact nature of the fault. It the BIOS reports something like a memory or keyboard problem and everything seems to be plugged in correctly, there is a tendency to jump to the conclusion that the keyboard or a memory module is faulty. This could well be the case, but it is also possible that the problem is due to a fault in the motherboard.

If the keyboard is not functioning, try swapping over the keyboard with that of another PC. If the new PC fails to work with the replacement keyboard, but the other PC works perfectly well with the keyboard from the newly constructed PC, it is clearly the motherboard that is faulty. On the other hand, if the new PC works with the replacement keyboard and the other PC fails to work with the keyboard from the new PC, it is clearly the keyboard that is faulty.

Anomalies

Things in the computing world are not always as clear-cut as they should be, and if you are very unlucky you may be faced with an anomaly. For example, in our keyboard substitution example you might find that on swapping the keyboards both computers work fine, but on swapping them back again the new PC fails to work again. I can not say that I have ever experienced this problem with keyboards, but I have certainly encountered one or two memory modules and expansion cards that are rather selective about the computers they will work in. I have also heard of others having similar problems with mice and CD-ROM drives.

It is difficult to explain this sort of thing, and there is probably more than one cause. In days gone by there were certainly problems with expansion slots and cards that were not engineered with adequate accuracy. Some combinations of motherboard and expansion card would just about fit together well enough to work while others would not. Obviously there should never have been any problems of this type, but a lot of PC components were in the "cheap and cheerful" category, and were simply not up to the task.

This sort of thing seems to be extremely rare these days, and the more likely cause of problems is some slight electrical incompatibility, or two components in the system refusing to peacefully coexist for some obscure reason. Some makes of hard disc drive do not get on well together for example, particularly when trying to use an old drive alongside a new one. Some CD-ROM drives and hard drives seem to suffer from a lack of compatibility, although it is not advisable to use this combination on the same IDE interface for performance reasons.

If you are unlucky enough to find yourself saddled with one of these incompatibility problems you may be entitled to return the item that is causing the trouble. The difficulty is in determining which component is the cause of the problem, and it is understandable if suppliers are reluctant to take back items that work fine when they try them in their test PCs. If you persist with your complaint most suppliers will reluctantly do so, but you may prefer to be pragmatic about this sort of thing and rearrange the PCs slightly so that they all work, and the incompatibilities are avoided.

It is probably not worthwhile spending large amounts of time trying to get incompatible components to function together. Bitter experience suggests that in most instances they will never do so. Fortunately, this type of thing is relatively rare these days, so you would be very unlucky to encounter a serious problem of this type. Problems with device drivers rather than with genuinely incompatible hardware are another matter. If you have a PC that almost works but there are a few obscure problems it is odds on that the trouble is due to a faulty device driver. As pointed out previously, a visit to the relevant manufacturer's web site will usually produce a fully working device driver that cures the problem. Failing that, the manufacturer's product support team might have a solution or a way of working around the problem.

Memory

In some cases the BIOS will detect and report a memory problem, but if there is a total failure of the memory circuits or a problem with the processor the BIOS start-up routine may grind to a halt or never get started properly in the first place. Often the PC will slowly beep away without entering the POST, rather than doing the usual one or two beeps and then starting the POST routine. There are other problems that can cause this, but in my experience it usually indicates a memory problem.

When a memory fault is suspected, carefully check again the section of the motherboard's manual that deals with memory matters. Make sure that you are using an acceptable memory arrangement, and that the motherboard is not fitted with an unacceptable mixture of memory types. Unlike SIMMs, DIMMs can usually be used in multiples of one. Also, it does not usually matter which DIMM holders are used and which are left empty.

However, check the motherboard's instruction manual to make sure that there are no restrictions on the way that the memory modules are used. It might be necessary to fit the modules in the correct bank of sockets for the memory to work correctly. There are usually a few restrictions when

Fig.6.8 A close-up showing the locking arm of a holder within the notch of a DIMM

using DDR2 memory modules, such as having to use memory modules of the same size in each bank. In practice it is advisable to always use identical memory modules, and I do not just mean modules of the same capacity. Experience suggests that the best reliability is obtained by using memory modules from the same manufacturer, and having identical ratings for CAS latency, etc.

DIMM capacities

When the memory is in the form of DIMMs, the motherboard will probably not accept DIMMs of all capacities. Are you using memory modules that are supported by the motherboard? Where the motherboard has provision for both standard DIMMs and the DDR variety it will probably not be possible to use all the memory sockets. In most cases a mixture of normal DIMMs and the DDR type is not allowed at all, and you can therefore only use one or the other.

Modern motherboards are generally more accommodating than those of a few years ago, but when choosing the memory for a modern PC it is still essential to read the "small print" in the relevant section of the motherboard's manual. Also be very careful to avoid expensive mistakes and obtain the right type of memory first time.

A problem with the memory is most likely to be caused by one of the memory modules not fitting into its holder correctly. The quality of holders for memory modules is often quite poor even on some of the more up-market motherboards. This tends to make it quite difficult to fit the modules into the holders, and in some cases they can be difficult to remove as well. When in place correctly the modules should lock into position, so try giving the modules a gentle tug to see if they pull free from the holders. If a module pulls away from its holder, even at just one end, it is not fitted in the holder correctly, and is unlikely to work reliably.

Although polarised, it was often possible to fit SIMMs the wrong way round. DIMMs are less problematic than SIMMs, and I have not experienced a similar problem with them. Nevertheless, perform a visual check to ascertain that the DIMMs are fitted the right way round, fully pushed down into their sockets, and fully locked in place. If a DIMM is fully pushed down into its holder the locking arms on the holder should fit into the cutouts at the ends of the module. One end of a properly locked DIMM is shown in the close-up shot of Figure 6.8.

With two polarising keys, one of which is well off-centre, there is no excuse for trying to fit a DIMM the wrong way around, and in theory anyway, it should not even start to fit into the holder. Whenever problems with the memory are suspected it is a good idea to remove the memory modules and refit them. This often seems to cure the problem.

Processor

The chance of a problem occurring with the microprocessor are very low, because the processor will only fit onto the motherboard the right way round, and very high quality ZIF sockets are used on even the cheapest of motherboards. If the processor fails to function properly the most likely cause is the motherboard being configured incorrectly. If the motherboard has some form of automatic processor detection facility, check that the right processor is specified on the initial start-up screen. If the wrong processor is identified it will be necessary to go into the appropriate section of the BIOS Setup program and set the processor parameters manually.

Note that if you are using a processor that has a clock frequency that is actually lower than its "equivalent" speed rating, it may well be the true clock frequency that the BIOS will use on the initial start-up screen. This depends on whether or not the BIOS specifically supports the processor you are using, and in most cases it will. Usually the name of the processor and its actual clock frequency will be displayed by the POST routine. Obviously there is a problem if the reported speed does not match up with the nominal or actual clock frequency of the processor.

If the motherboard is configured via jumpers or DIP switches, check the motherboard's instruction manual carefully again to ensure that you are using precisely the required settings. Sometimes there is a problem with the reported speed of the processor being about 25 percent slower than the correct figure. This usually means that the motherboard's bus frequency is too low, and that it is running at 100MHz instead of 133MHz for example.

Setting the correct bus frequency via the BIOS or a jumper on the motherboard, as appropriate, will take the processor's clock frequency to the correct figure and take the PC up to full speed. An error in the opposite direction is rarer, since the BIOS will usually default to the lower setting. Similarly, where the bus frequency is set via a jumper, the default setting will usually be the lower operating frequency. Erroneously setting the bus frequency to the higher frequency would probably result in the PC grinding to a halt soon after switch-on, so it is worth checking the relevant jumper if the PC exhibits this problem.

It might also be worthwhile clearing the CMOS memory in case this has become scrambled and is causing start-up problems. This is achieved by removing the relevant jumper from the motherboard, waiting about half a minute or so, and then replacing it. Most manufacturers recommend that the power supply should be disconnected from the motherboard while the CMOS memory is cleared. Presumably there is otherwise a slight risk of a residual charge in the power supply keeping the memory operational.

Discs

Discs and the BIOS were covered in chapter 4, and this topic will not be covered in detail again here. With the automatic detection systems of the average BIOS, the discs may all function perfectly well without the user altering any settings. Even so, it is advisable to carefully check the relevant BIOS settings if any drive problems are experienced. It is definitely a good idea to go into the BIOS Setup program to check the main settings when a new PC is first switched on.

As pointed out previously, there can be rare problems with incompatibility between certain IDE devices. This mainly occurs when using an old hard disc drive and a new one, and it can also occur when using some hard drive and CD-ROM combinations. This seems to be an innate problem with the drives, but it can often be resolved by shifting one of the drives from one IDE interface to another. In most cases this means having the problem devices on separate IDE interfaces, but apparently in some cases it can be necessary to move them from separate interfaces to the same IDE channel.

Note that if you are using a UDMA33 or later disc drive, special drivers will be needed in order to get maximum performance from these. These days any new hard disc drive will be UDMA100 or later, and some CD-ROMs, etc., have UDMA33 or faster interfaces. The motherboard and (or) drive should be supplied with any necessary Windows drivers and full installation instructions. However, these drivers will not always be required, since many of them are included as part of a modern version of Windows. Remember that UDMA66 and later hard disc drives require a cable specifically for this type of drive and not an ordinary IDE cable. In the interest of performance, try to avoid having fast and slow devices on the same IDE interface. This is not a problem with most modern PCs, which have the slower drives on the IDE interface and the faster drives on serial ATA types. In fact serial ATA interfaces avoid many of the problems of the past.

Floppy problems

The most common mistake with floppy disc drives is to get one of the connectors on the data cable fitted the wrong way round. If you try to boot from the floppy drive it is inevitably unsuccessful, but it can also result in the data on the disc being corrupted. Having cleared the fault you try to boot from the disc, but this again proves to be unsuccessful. This gives the impression that the floppy disc drive is faulty or still installed incorrectly, but it is actually the corrupted disc that is causing the problem. It is advisable to have one or two spare boot discs handy so that you can try an alternative disc if the computer refuses to boot from the floppy disc for no apparent reason.

If there is a problem with a floppy connector fitted the wrong way round, or with the wrong ends of the cable connected to the drive and the

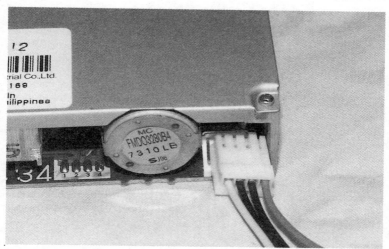

Fig.6.9 The power connector is erroneously fitted one set of terminals to the right

motherboard, this should be immediately obvious. During the initial BIOS checks and the boot-up sequence the drive light of the floppy disc drive will usually switch on and off a few times, but with the cable connected wrongly the light usually stays on continuously. If the drive light comes on at switch-on and stays on, switch off and check the data cable. Of course, these days it is quite common for the floppy drive to be omitted. Make sure that the BIOS is set up correctly if the floppy drive is omitted, as it might otherwise produce an error when it fails to find the nonexistent drive.

The 5.25-inch power connectors are reasonably foolproof, but they are often a very tight fit. If a drive that uses one of these power connectors fails to do anything at all, make sure that the connector is fully pushed into the drive. The smaller power connectors used on 3.5-inch floppy discs are a different matter. Some drives have properly polarised connectors that only permit the power lead to be fitted correctly. Unfortunately, most 3.5-inch drives seem to have very "cheap and cheerful" power connectors that do permit errors to occur. Mistakes here can result in damage to the drive and (or) the power supply unit, so it is definitely a good idea to get it right first time.

The most common mistake is for the power connector to be shifted one terminal out of alignment. In Figure 6.9 the connector is fitted one terminal

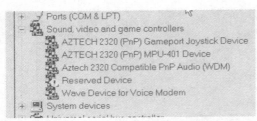

Fig.6.10 The exclamation mark indicates a problem with one of the soundcard's device drivers

too far to the right, and it is not difficult to see that there is something wrong. Apart from the fact that the connector is too far to the right, it is also at a slight angle to the drive's connector. It is easy to spot the mistake with the drive outside the case, but it can be more difficult to see this problem in a real-world situation with the drive installed in the case. Often you will be able to feel that the connector has not fitted into place properly, because it will not fully push into place. The mistake should be obvious if you take the time to look carefully at the connector.

Late problems

Problems do not always come to light when a PC is going through its initial testing or booting into Windows. Everything might seem to be all right until the operating system has been installed, after which some of the hardware may fail to work properly. Having installed Windows on a new PC it is always a good idea to go into the Windows Device Manager to check for any problems.

To do this with Windows Vista, operate the Start button and then select Control Panel, the Classic View link near the top left-hand corner of the screen, and then operate the Device Manager icon. Operate the Continue button if a warning message appears. You can then look down the list of devices in search of the dreaded yellow exclamation marks that indicate a problem (Figure 6.10). With Windows XP it is a matter of first selecting Control Panel from the Start menu and then double-clicking the System icon. Then operate the Hardware tab and finally operate the Device Manager button.

Initially there will usually be a few problems reported by the Device Manager, and this is simply because some of the drivers for the motherboard's built-in hardware have not been installed. These days motherboards are invariably supplied with a disc and (or) CD-ROM with various driver programs that have to be installed before everything will operate to perfection. The motherboard's instruction manual should give full details of the drivers provided, and how to install them. With the particular configuration you are using you may not need all the drivers supplied, so read the manual carefully to determine which software must be installed.

The ports can often be switched on and off via the BIOS Setup program, so if there is a problem with a port it is as well to go into the BIOS and check that any absent port is actually turned on. If a port is active, but is not detected by the operating system or an error is reported, it is likely that the port hardware is faulty. Unfortunately, since the standard ports are integrated with the motherboard these days, this means that the motherboard is faulty and must be replaced.

One possible exception is if you are having problems with the USB ports under an old operating system such as Windows 95. Most versions of Windows 95 do not have proper USB support, and it is advisable to upgrade to Windows XP or Vista if you intend to use the USB ports. Note that it can be impossible to run an old operating system on a modern PC due to a lack of suitable drivers. Users of an old version of Windows can be left with no option other than an upgrade to a modern version of Windows. Unfortunately, it is likely that some of your old software will not run properly using a modern version of Windows.

Some soundcards have a game port that can also act as a MIDI port, although this is becoming something of a rare feature. Integrated audio systems sometimes have the same facility. These days it seems to be the convention to have the MIDI port switched off by default, so it is usually necessary to enable this port before it can be used. Where appropriate, the manual for the soundcard or motherboard should explain how the port is switched on and off. In the case of an integrated audio system, the MIDI port is usually controlled via the BIOS Setup program. Note that this form of MIDI port is not a standard type and that it can not be used with standard MIDI data cables. Special PC MIDI cables are required, and these include a small amount of interface electronics.

I have very occasionally had Device Manager show a problem with a piece of hardware that actually performs flawlessly. This was not exactly a rarity with Windows 95, but it seems to be much less common with later versions of Windows. I am far from certain about the cause of this problem, but there is presumably a minor flaw in the device drivers that "fools" Windows into thinking that there is a problem. In this situation it is best to take a pragmatic approach and not waste time trying to cure a nonexistent problem.

The opposite problem can also occur, with Device Manager reporting that everything is all right when there is clearly a problem. This is rare,

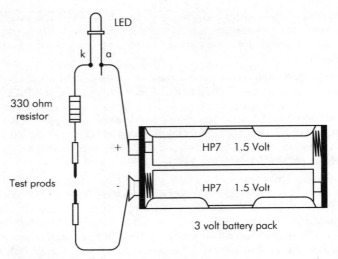

Fig.6.11 A low-current continuity tester using a LED

but it can happen from time to time. One possibility is that the device drivers for the hardware are faulty or that the wrong ones have been installed. Try going into Device Manager, uninstalling the drivers, and then reinstalling them again. If that fails to cure the problem, visit the hardware manufacturer's web site and look for updated device drivers. It is likely that there is a hardware fault if loading the correct drivers fails to cure the problem. Windows will detect some hardware faults, but by no means all of them. The "all clear" in Device Manager is not a reliable indicator that the hardware is functioning perfectly. It just means that the hardware is present and connected to the rest of the PC correctly, and does not guarantee that it is fuly operational.

Right leads

When you have been building PCs for some time you inevitably end up with a lot of leads and other odds and ends. When building a PC based on an AT motherboard it is tempting to simply grab the first serial or parallel port lead and blanking plate that comes to hand. This is not really a good idea though, since leads that look much the same may actually be wired up very differently. The serial, parallel, USB, and Firewire port leads supplied with motherboards are not all the same, and you

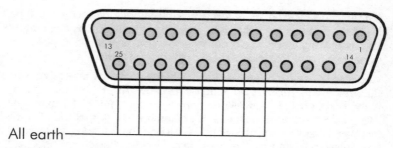

All earth

Fig.6.12 The earthed pins on a parallel port connector

could certainly end up with a non-operating port by using the lead from one motherboard with a different motherboard.

When dealing with apparently faulty serial and parallel ports that connect to the motherboard via a lead, it can be helpful to use a continuity check to determine whether or not the port is connected properly to the

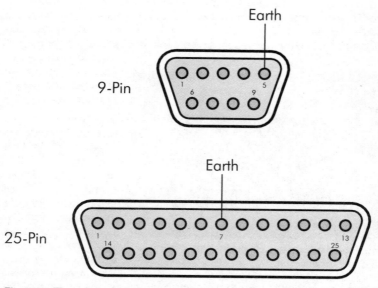

Earth

9-Pin

Earth

25-Pin

Fig.6.13 The earthed pins of 9 and 25-pin serial port connectors

motherboard.   However, a torch bulb continuity tester of the type described earlier is not suitable for this type of testing. The test current used is too high, and could damage the port hardware. Only use a proper test meter that is designed for this sort of testing.

Alternatively, use a modernised version of the continuity tester that uses a LED rather than a torch bulb. Figure 6.11 shows a suitable arrangement. All the parts should be available from a shop or mail order company selling electronic components and equipment. Note that the LED will only work if it is connected the right way round. The cathode ("k") terminal is normally indicated by that lead being shorter than the anode ("a") lead and the cathode side of the body is usually (but not always) flattened slightly. Do not omit the resistor. Without this component a high current will flow, resulting in almost instant destruction of the LED.

Down to earth

The quick and easy way of checking that the leads are connected properly is to check for continuity between the chassis of the computer and whichever terminal or terminals of the port connector should be earthed. For a parallel port it is pins 18 to 25 that should be earthed (Figure 6.12). For 25 and nine pin serial ports it is respectively pins seven and five that should be earthed (Figure 6.13). If the right pins are not earthed and some of the other pins are, either the cable is connected incorrectly at the motherboard or you are using an unsuitable cable and bracket assembly.

Fig.6.14 The power LED connector is out of position

The port connectors on motherboards are often simplified versions of IDE connectors. Unless some form of polarizing key is incorporated into the design, it is possible to connect the leads either way round. With a motherboard of this type you must refer to the manual to find pin one on each of the connectors, and then make sure that the red lead of the cable connects

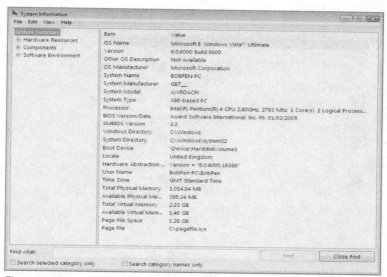

Fig.6.15 Some basic information about the finished PC can be obtained from the built-in facilities of Windows

to this pin. It is also possible to fit many of these connectors one row of pins out of alignment. Fortunately, these cut-down connectors are now relatively rare, but due care needs to be taken if you should encounter a motherboard that uses them.

Of course, these days the vast majority of motherboards are of the ATX variety, with the main ports fitted direct on the motherboard. On the face of it, this largely avoids problems with leads to off-board port connectors. However, ATX boards usually have a number of optional ports that are implemented by way of a lead and back-plate assembly. This method is used to implement additional USB ports, front-panel mounted audio connectors, and this sort of thing. Note that the leads and back-plate assemblies are often optional extras and not supplied as standard with the motherboard. With this type of thing always be careful to obtain the correct items for the make of motherboard and to fit them correctly.

Minor problems

Most problems with a newly constructed PC are actually quite minor. Probably the most common of these is one of the front panel lights failing

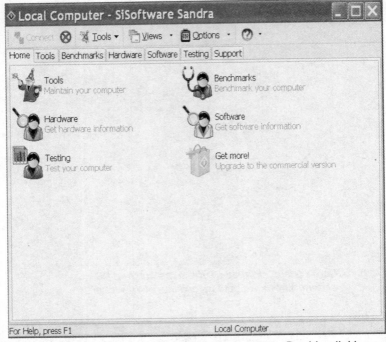

Fig.6.16 The opening screen of Sisoft Sanda 2003. Double-clicking an icon runs the appropriate utility program

to operate. As pointed out in chapter three, these lights are light emitting diodes (LEDs) and not miniature light bulbs. Consequently they will only operate properly if they are fed with a supply of the correct polarity. If a light fails to operate, try reversing the connector to see if that cures the problem.

If the integral loudspeaker or any of the LEDs and switches that connect to the motherboard fail to work, carefully check the connections to the connector block on the motherboard. Getting these items plugged into the motherboard tends to be a bit fiddly, and it is often difficult to see what you are doing. Unless you have small fingers it will probably be easier using a pair of long-nose pliers or tweezers to manoeuvre the connectors into position. Incidentally, these tools are also useful for setting jumpers on the motherboard.

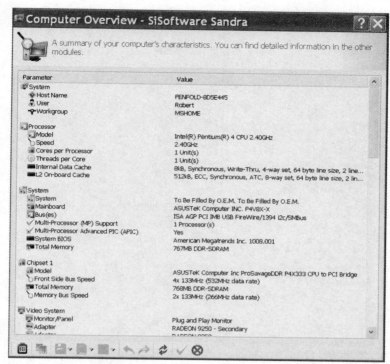

Fig.6.17 This screen provides some general information about the PC

It can be helpful to shine a torch on the connector block so that you can see exactly what connects to where. Better still, get a helper to hold the torch so that you are free to concentrate on the connections. It is easy to get a plug shifted along the block by one set of pins so that one pin is unconnected, or it connects to the wrong pins. In the example of Figure 6.14 the power LED connector is shifted one row of pins to the left. A close visual inspection should soon reveal any problem of this type.

Be meticulous

Obscure problems can occur with a new PC, but they are relatively rare with modern PCs. In the vast majority of cases the computer will boot-up properly and work well if you are careful to get everything connected

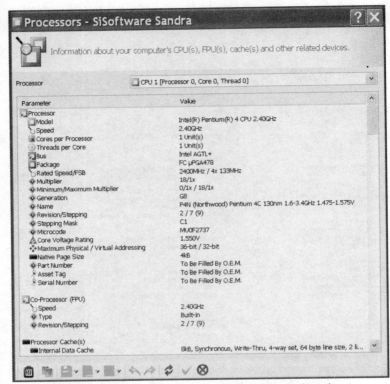

Fig.6.18 This window provides some detailed information about the processor

properly. When a newly assembled PC fails to work properly it is hardly ever due to a faulty component, and is usually due to something very fundamental like a connector that has come adrift or is fitted the wrong way around.

When something goes wrong we would all rather blame someone else, but if you check through a troublesome PC and fix any mistakes it will almost certainly work flawlessly when you try it out again. Always resist the temptation to rush at things. Trying to put a PC together in the shortest possible time more or less guarantees that mistakes will be made. Concentrate on getting everything right and give each part of construction as much time as it requires. The newly completed PC should then work first time.

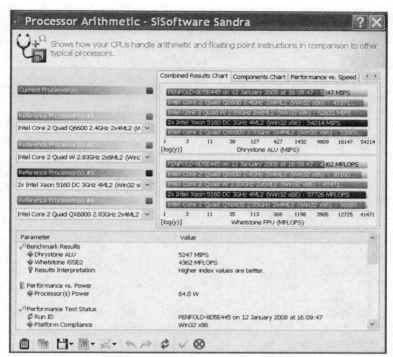

Fig.6.19 This test of the maths co-processor shows that it is operating at an appropriate speed

Check-up

Having completed the PC and installed the operating system, many users like to check that the computer is running reliably and that the amount of memory, processor speed, etc., is all correct. Windows can provide some basic information about the processor and the amount of memory installed. With Windows XP or Vista, go to the Start menu and then select Accessories, System Tools, and System Information. The System Information will take a few seconds to probe the system and then a Window like the one in Figure 6.15 will appear. This indicates the type of processor, its clock speed, and the amount of memory fitted (Total Physical Memory).

There are numerous diagnostic and testing programs that can provide further information and test the reliability of various parts of the PC. The

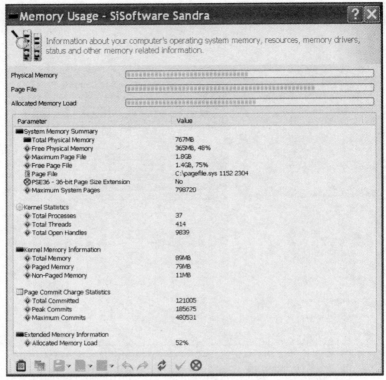

*Fig.6.20 Information about the memory and its use is provided here.
In diagnostics and testing programs the RAM is usually
referred to as "physical memory"*

basic version of Sisoftware's Sandra is a very useful program that can
be downloaded free of charge. A more advanced version is available as
a commercial product. This is the web address to visit:

www.sisoftware.co.uk/sandra

The opening screen (Figure 6.16) has tabs that are used to select the
required section of the program, and icons that are used to access the
various test and information screens. The two screens of Figures 6.17
and 6.18 respectively show some general information about the PC and

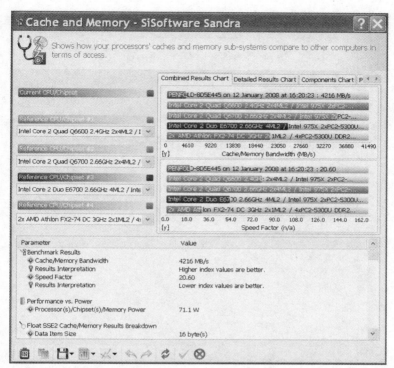

Fig.6.21 The memory seems slow in comparison to the reference figures, but this is simply due to the test PC being fitted with relatively slow memory

some detailed information about the processor. Figure 6.19 shows the result of testing the maths co-processor of a 2.4GHz Pentium 4 PC. Typical test results for a range of processors are provided in addition to the results from the PC being checked. This makes it easy to assess the results, and in this case the test figures seem to be in line with the typical results for a 2.4GHz Pentium 4 PC.

Memory testing

Detailed memory information is available (Figure 6.20) and the speed of the memory can also be tested (Figure 6.21). In this example the memory seems to be rather slow compared to the reference memory figures, but

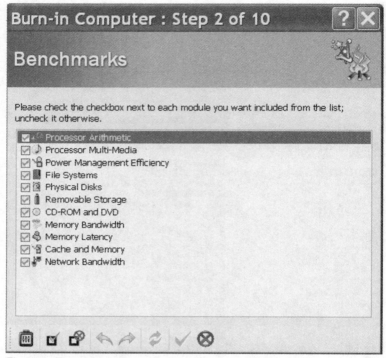

*Fig.6.22 The selected tests can be run a specified number of times,
         or run indefinitely if preferred*

the memory in the test PC is slower than the memory types supplied for
comparison purposes. The memory of the test PC is actually performing
quite well for its type.

Various tests and information are available from the other modules, and
one of these provides benchmark speeds tests (Figure 6.22). Another
produces a test report that points out possible problems and includes
suggestions for improving the computer's perrformance (Figure 6.23).
In order to make the most of this type of thing it is necessary to have a
certain amount of technical knowledge, and in some cases some in-
depth technical know-how is needed. However, some useful pointers
can sometimes be gleaned from one of these test and analysis reports.
Be warned though, that this type of thing is a bit like reading a medical
book. You can find that your PC has practically every known computer

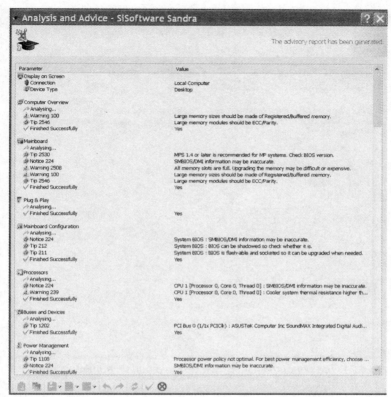

Fig.6.23 The analysis section of the program has produced a long list of test results, with advice included where appropriate

ill, plus a few that were previously unheard of! Many of the possible problems pointed out by this type of report are not really problems at all. In some cases it is simply that for some reason the analysis program has not been able to properly analyse that part of the computer. With removeable disc drives for example, there are often problems reported by analysis programs simply because there are no discs in the drives being tested. It helps you read the documentation for that part of the program, and make sure that you are using the correct test conditions. Another cause of reported problems is that the hardware in your PC does not do things "by the book", but it is quite likely that most other PC hardware uses the same shortcut, and that it is of no real consequence.

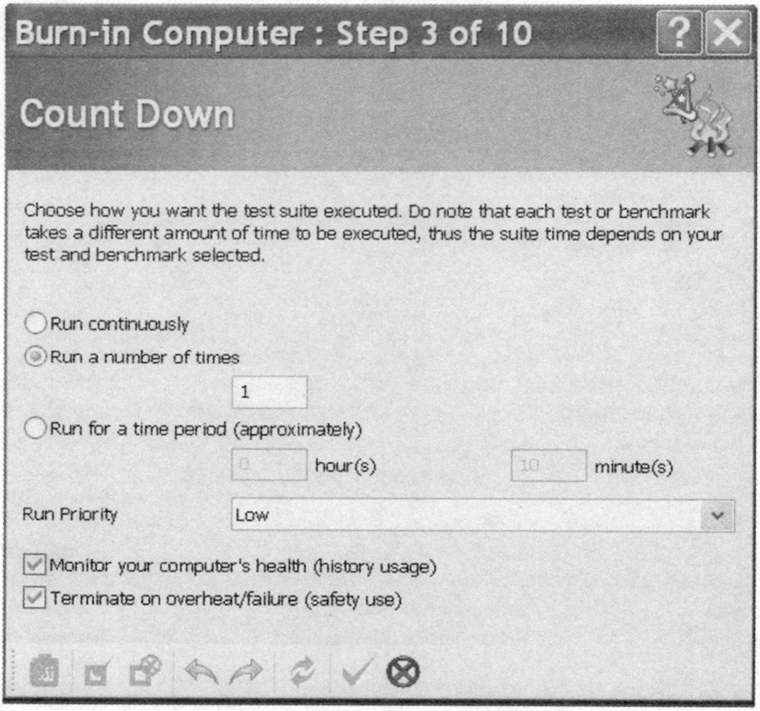

Fig.6.24 The benchmark tests can be run a certain number of times or indefinitely

In a few cases it is possible that something is genuinely not quite right, and that some simple corrective measures can be taken. However, do not be tempted to tinker with the BIOS, hardware, or the operating system unless your are sure that you know exxactly what you are doing. It is probably easier to make things worse than it is to make a worthwhile improvement.

Like most programs of this type, with Sisoft Sandra you can select a set of tests that are then carried out a large number of times so that the computer's reliability can be checked. The selected benchmark tests (see Figure 6.22) can be run a specified number of times or indefinitely (Figure 6.24). It is certainly a good idea to give a new PC the "once over" with some test and diagnostics software. Some of these programs can also be used as an aid to diagnosing faults.

Points to remember

Prevention is better than cure, so always give the finished PC at least a cursory check before switching on and testing it. Ideally you should check that all the cables are present and correct.

Again, prevention is better than cure, so do not be tempted to ignore anti-static handling precautions. It will be time consuming and costly to replace components that were unnecessarily "zapped" by a static charge.

Check for the obvious, such as a lead that has become disconnected at one end, or drive power cable you have forgotten to plug in. In the vast majority of cases where a newly constructed PC fails to work it is something as simple as this.

If the motherboard uses configuration jumpers or switches, check that it is configured properly for the processor you are using. The configuration charts in motherboard instruction manuals are sometimes a bit ambiguous, so check them with a "fine-tooth comb" to ensure you are interpreting them correctly.

Check that the expansion cards are all properly seated in their holders. It only needs one of the cards to be slightly out of position to render the PC completely inoperative.

Try reducing the computer to one that is as basic as possible. Disconnect the hard disc drive, CD-ROM drive, and any non-essential expansion cards so that the PC is just a basic single floppy machine. If this works, reinstate the drives, etc., one by one until the PC fails to work. The last device added is then the one that is causing the problem.

Never open up a faulty monitor as there is little chance of fixing it and a good chance of killing yourself. Monitors operate at very high and extremely dangerous voltages, and these voltages can remain present even after the monitor has been unplugged from the mains supply and switched off.

Check that the memory modules are fitted into their holders properly. DIMMs are reasonably foolproof, and are certainly much better than SIMMs in this respect. However, DIMMs can still give problems unless you are very careful when fitting them.

Never connect or disconnect anything while the PC is switched on. Altering the cabling while a PC is switched on could easily cause costly damage. Definitely do not add or remove an expansion card or a memory module while the PC is switched on. This virtually guarantees that something will be damaged.

If an expansion card is suspected of being faulty, the easiest way to test it is to use it in another PC. Alternatively, try another expansion card in the PC that is giving problems. Keep old video cards, hard disc drives, etc. They are useful for substituting in a faulty PC to help track down the duff component. It is obviously not worthwhile keeping anything that is totally obsolete and not usable in a modern PC, but anything else is potentially useful.

Faulty components in new PCs are actually quite rare. If you get everything put together properly it is highly unlikely that your new PC will fail to work.

Never be tempted to open up the power supply unit. It is not the sort of thing that can be sorted by the average handyman, or even those with some knowledge of electronics. The power supply connects to the mains supply and is potentially lethal. If a power supply unit is found to be faulty, either the power supply or the complete case and power supply should be replaced.

There are plenty of programs available that can be used to check the speed and reliability of the finished PC, and some will help to diagnose faults. It is a good idea to give a newly completed PC a check with one of these programs in order to determine whether everything is functioning as it should.

Index

Symbols

A

B

Index

Index

Index

Index